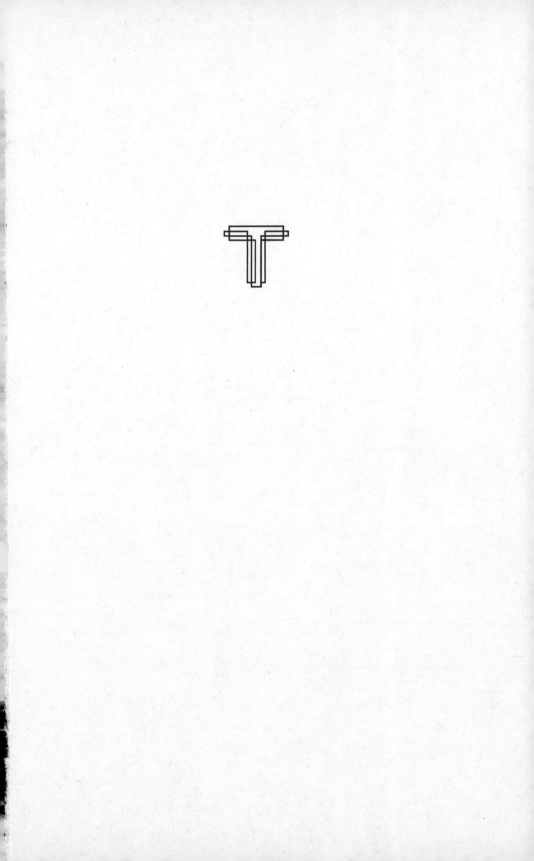

CRACKING THE CUBE

Going Slow to Go Fast and Other Unexpected Turns
in the World of Competitive Rubik's Cube Solving

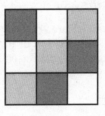

IAN SCHEFFLER

TOUCHSTONE
New York   London   Toronto   Sydney   New Delhi

Touchstone
An Imprint of Simon & Schuster, Inc.
1230 Avenue of the Americas
New York, NY 10020

First Touchstone hardcover edition October 2016

TOUCHSTONE and colophon are registered trademarks
of Simon & Schuster, Inc.

For information about special discounts for bulk purchases,
please contact Simon & Schuster Special Sales at 1-866-506-1949
or business@simonandschuster.com.

The Simon & Schuster Speakers Bureau can bring authors
to your live event. For more information or to book an event,
contact the Simon & Schuster Speakers Bureau at 866-248-3049
or visit our website at www.simonspeakers.com.

Interior design by Kyle Kabel

Manufactured in the United States of America

10   9   8   7   6   5   4   3   2   1

Library of Congress Cataloging-in-Publication Data
Names: Scheffler, Ian.
Title: Cracking the cube : going slow to go fast and other unexpected
turns in the world of competitive Rubik's Cube solving / by Ian Scheffler.
Description: New York : Touchstone, 2016.
Identifiers: LCCN 2016016374 (print) | LCCN 2016019512 (ebook) |
ISBN 9781501121920 (hardcover) | ISBN 9781501121937 (pbk.) |
ISBN 9781501121944 (Ebook)
Subjects: LCSH: Rubik's Cube. | Mathematical recreations.
Classification: LCC QA491 .S325 2016 (print) |
LCC QA491 (ebook) | DDC 793.74—dc23
LC record available at https://lccn.loc.gov/2016016374

ISBN 978-1-5011-2192-0
ISBN 978-1-5011-2194-4 (ebook)

To my parents

We turn the Cube and it twists us.

—Professor Ernő Rubik

CONTENTS

TO GO FAST, YOU HAVE TO GO SLOW

I put the petals on the daisy, solve the cross, insert the corners, then the edges. Veer right at the Jesus Fish and finish with an algorithm that makes it look like I'm trying to disarm a bomb, fingers flying every which way in a desperate attempt to stop the clock.

44.82 seconds.

Not bad—the first time I've broken a minute in competition—but not nearly good enough. The barrier I'm trying to cross is twenty seconds, the equivalent, in this world, of the four-minute mile: go sub-20 and you join an elite club. Once, the barrier was all but impassable. Now it's the standard by which all comers are judged.

Most people will likely never solve Rubik's Cube, so going under twenty seconds may not mean much if you haven't cubed, but in competition, a few seconds can make all the difference.

There are nearly six hundred cubers in this cavernous ballroom. All here at the Riviera Hotel and Casino in Las Vegas for the 2013 Rubik's Cube World Championship. Some, like me, are novices.

This is only my second competition. Others have attended dozens, or even upward of one hundred tournaments. We will be ranked by the average of five solves, with the best and worst removed. This is to prevent a lucky (or unlucky) solve from skewing the results. The top two hundred will qualify for the second round.

Each of us will start our solves from the same randomized positions. The scrambles, as they're called, are generated by TNoodle, a computer program. The scrambles are interpreted by the scramblers. And they need interpretation. To an outsider, they look like complete gibberish: R' F2 R2 D2 L U2 R U2 R2 U2 B2 U L' F U2 F L U B' L' F', for instance.

The finals are a moon shot for me, so like many here, I'm playing for a personal best, or PB. Everyone knows who stands a chance of winning the competition: Feliks, Mats, Cornelius. They are the professional athletes—they go by one name only, like Messi and Ronaldo—and have the sponsorships and devoted fan bases to prove it.

My second solve is slower, much slower than my first.

54.01 seconds.

It's hard to know what, if anything, I did wrong. Each solve is different, not by choice, but by necessity. Rubik's Cube can be arranged more than forty-three quintillion ways. One quintillion is one billion squared. One followed by eighteen zeroes. If you stacked forty-three quintillion Rubik's Cubes end to end, they would reach 261 light-years into space. That many Rubik's Cubes would cover the earth 273 times over, to the height of a five-story building.

I'm solving Rubik's Cube like most of the competitors, one layer at a time. This is known as CFOP, an acronym for the steps involved—Cross, First Two Layers, Orientation, and Permutation of the last layer—as well as the Fridrich method, after Jessica Fridrich, the Czech woman who helped invent it and first put it online. The method resembles the assembly of a layer cake: you start on the bottom, by making the cross. The cross sets up the first two layers, after which you tackle the last layer.

My third solve starts off well. I'm cruising past the first two layers—the pieces are favorably set up—when I throw a glance at the timer. It still reads below thirty seconds. My heart starts to race. I could wind up with a solve in the thirty-second range, a massive PB.

Only my Cube refuses to cooperate. The last layer starts to fissure. I can see the innards of the puzzle, glistening and black. If your Cube "pops," that is to say, if it explodes, during competition, you are allowed to pick up the pieces, but there's almost no point.

Technically, I'm not solving the Cube invented by Ernő Rubik, the Hungarian professor and architect who brought Rubik's Cube to life in 1974. Instead, I'm using one of the latest speedcubes, the DaYan ZhanChi, designed by Daqing Bao, a Chinese puzzle maker. From the outside, the ZhanChi resembles Rubik's Cube: six sides, with nine stickers each, divided among six colors: red, green, yellow, blue, orange, and white. But inside, the ZhanChi is entirely different.

If you were to disassemble Rubik's Cube, you would find that the pieces are as blocky inside as they are outside. There are axles hidden inside the puzzle, which hold the centers in place; the other twenty pieces are designed to support one another. The rear ends of the corners and edges interlock, allowing you to rotate the puzzle while maintaining its shape.

From the right angle, hidden inside the puzzle, you will see the pieces connect to create a sphere. In a way, this makes sense. The sphere is the only shape whose every point is equidistant from the center. Just like continents migrating around the globe, each sticker of Rubik's Cube has to slide around the puzzle. But the original evinces only a rough semblance of a sphere, with the effect that the pieces are difficult to turn.

The ZhanChi, by contrast, is all curves below the surface. The pieces are carefully machined to glide past one another with a minimum of resistance. Like a ball bearing set loose on a freshly waxed floor, it will keep spinning even after you let it go. The puzzle is to Rubik's Cube what speed skates are to regular ice skates, hence the term *speedcube*. But the speed comes with a catch: if you're not careful, you can turn the ZhanChi *too* fast, and threaten its integrity.

The World Championship is sponsored by Seven Towns, Ltd., the British firm that owns the rights to Rubik's Cube. They know we're not using their puzzles, but they don't try to stop us: to anyone watching, we appear to be solving Rubik's Cubes. Even cubers refer to puzzles by that name, the way everyone refers to facial tissues as Kleenex. In the end, it's great publicity for the official brand.

When I slam the timer to a halt, I hesitate to look at the clock. 40.13 seconds. If I had only turned the puzzle a little more carefully, I wouldn't have had to pause so often and would have ended up with a better time.

After my fourth solve—an uninspired 50.75—one of the scramblers catches my attention.

He gives me a strange bit of advice. Go slower, he says. Like, 80 percent. The adrenaline, he explains, will push me to go faster without my realizing it. I'm reminded of a quote from one of the fastest cubers in the world, a seventeen-year-old Australian named Feliks Zemdegs, who's solved Rubik's Cube in 5.66 seconds: "You don't really think. You just do it."

For my last solve I pick up my Rubik's Cube as if in slow motion. The first turns feel almost painfully lethargic, like I'm churning a barrel of molasses with a shovel. I'm going so slow I'm even having thoughts beyond the Cube in my hand. The solve appears to be proceeding automatically. For fear of throwing myself off course, like I did earlier, I don't dare to look at the clock. Still, it's hard to imagine this will be anything but my slowest attempt.

When I stop the timer, I do so carefully, as if I were trying to touch the keys of a piano as softly as possible. It reads 33.24 seconds, or nearly seven seconds faster than my previous personal best. It's one of the fastest solves I've ever recorded, in competition or at home.

CHAPTER 02

NERD CAMP

When I first encountered Rubik's Cube, the puzzle was all but dead. I was born in 1990, the year the Berlin Wall was officially demolished. The eighties were on the way out. This meant the end of Gorbachev, *Magnum, P.I.*, and big hair. I would hear about the decade as if it were ancient history.

Rubik's Cube, of course, is an icon of the 1980s. That's when it was first released to the general public. The puzzle debuted internationally in 1980. Before long, it was everywhere. Literally. By 1982, more than one hundred million Rubik's Cubes had been sold, making it not only the most successful puzzle, but one of the most successful toys, of all time.

In the early 1980s, *National Geographic* sent a correspondent deep into the Amazon. She returned with an image of two boys playing in front of a thatched hut. The caption grumbled about the invasion of "machine-age products" into the land occupied by the Wayana, a people that had spent centuries isolated from Western society.

The two boys, of course, were playing with Rubik's Cube. Clad in red loincloths, the boys wore expressions of utter befuddlement. Their eyes were fixed on the puzzle. How it got there, and whether or not the kids ever figured it out, was never explained.

But their bewildered looks would have been familiar to millions of people around the world.

What had begun in Communist Hungary was now a worldwide phenomenon. Indeed, it was almost entirely divorced from its origins. President Ronald Reagan once held up the invention of Rubik's Cube as a sign of America's entrepreneurial greatness. Evidently, it was not apparent to Reagan that Rubik's Cube had come from behind the Iron Curtain.

The peak in retrospect was likely the first Rubik's Cube World Championship held in Hungary in 1982 and presided over by the great Cube inventor himself. The competition was organized by Brian Cartmell, a legendary British PR executive. A former journalist, Cartmell, who passed away some years ago, once staged the UK Monopoly Championship inside actual public utilities, including a nuclear power plant. "My father had a reputation for trying to make national news out of, you know, very thin amounts of material," his son, Gary, told me. The World Championship attracted headlines all over the world.

Of course, like any product that goes viral—and Rubik's Cube might be said to be one of the first, at least in the modern sense, appearing in all manner of mass media, and cutting across national borders—the puzzle had an expiration date.

Within a few years, the market was flooded with copycats, there was a distracting and costly infringement suit, and people simply got tired of not being able to solve it. You can't fault them. In those pre-Internet days, there were only a couple of ways to untangle Rubik's Cube: figure it out on your own, which virtually no one did; take it apart and put it back together; peel off the stickers; or purchase a strategy book. These sold millions of copies, but evidently served little use, or at least failed to support the patience of their readers. Once the puzzle had saturated the market, the backlash began.

In Palo Alto, California, a pair of brothers patented "The Cube Smasher." According to the instructional booklet attached to the yellow mallet, the goal was to club, whale, hit, torture, trap, smash, punch, swat, flatten, and possibly flog Rubik's Cube into forty-three quintillion pieces.

By the time I discovered the puzzle, Rubik's Cube was, to quote one executive, "in the closeout bin." What had once been the most famous toy in the world now found itself in the same position as He-Man and Reebok Pumps: as a relic of a bygone era. Rubik, despite his socialist beginnings, had become very rich, but his successive efforts to recapture the magic of his Cube came up short. There was Rubik's Magic—a mechanical puzzle whose goal was to untangle a set of rings printed on plastic squares attached by pieces of string—not to mention Rubik's Snake, a twisty set of triangular prisms. Neither of these had anything like the success of Rubik's Cube; Rubik made the headlines from time to time, including in the late 1980s, when two young men burgled his villa in Budapest. The government daily reported that the burglars may have been searching for new puzzle ideas.

In the late 1990s, when I discovered the Cube for myself, I didn't have a clue about its backstory. In fact, I had no idea it was even called Rubik's Cube. I saw a small cube hanging on a key chain in the gift shop of the California Science Center, in Los Angeles, where I grew up. In retrospect, it probably wasn't a licensed product. One side was metallic purple.

When I took it home, I immediately discovered its purpose. Or, rather, I happened upon it by accident. Like any kid—I was eight or nine years old, a pudgy collector of Pokémon cards, reader of comic books, proud owner of a squadron of GI Joes—I wanted to explore the puzzle's possibilities. So I turned it, first slowly, and then faster, as the sides got more and more mixed up.

I was mesmerized by the patterns that appeared and disappeared as I turned the Cube. Years later, when I learned more about Professor Ernő Rubik, the puzzle's inventor, I would read that he was similarly delighted. In fact, it was what first captivated his attention. He never set out to make a puzzle, but an impossible object, one you could turn and turn and turn without ever changing its shape.

Of course, as anyone who has ever played with Rubik's Cube knows, the challenge comes next. In an unpublished manuscript, Rubik once compared the experience of trying to untangle his puzzle to attempting to return home after a long walk. "It was at that moment," he wrote, "that I came face-to-face with the Big Challenge: What is the way home?"

Try as I might, I couldn't find the way home either. It seemed like it should have been easy—after all, it had started out solved. I should be able to return there, I thought. Only, every twist seemed to make the puzzle more messed up.

When I was fourteen years old, in the summer of 2005, I attended the Center for Talented Youth, a program at college campuses around the country run by Johns Hopkins University. CTY is basically voluntary summer school: you attend class from morning until evening, learning the equivalent of a college semester in three weeks. The course I signed up for was called Crafting the Essay.

One of the first lessons concerned icebergs. In *Death in the Afternoon*, Ernest Hemingway wrote that, if a writer knew something and the reader knew it, too, it functioned like the mass of an iceberg, concealed beneath the surface. You could omit whatever that thing was and the story would not only remain intact, but be stronger for it. What stayed under the water supported what you could see, giving it a certain dignity.

This lesson was put into practice in meeting my fellow students. They hailed from all over the world—Ireland, the Philippines, Alaska. It was dangerous to assume anything about them. I had never been around so many precocious people before. CTY selects students according to aptitude: as reported by the *New*

Yorker, which wrote a piece about the camp, "The center accepts only the top one percent of all students—those who score as well on the SAT in junior high as the average student does as a high school senior."

On the surface, we all looked like we belonged at Nerd Camp, the epithet the *New Yorker* used to title the piece. We were, most of us, in the throes of puberty, the specter of acne hovering over our faces, our fashion sense defined by the number of pockets on our cargo shorts. But, like a lot of people who started out with goofy grins and even goofier ideas, who knew where we might end up? As I later learned, CTY's list of alumni includes Facebook's Mark Zuckerberg; Google's Sergey Brin; and Stefani Joanne Angelina Germanotta, better known as Lady Gaga.

Take, for instance, Toby Mao. He had signed up for the same class as me, I later found out, because his mother wanted him to write better college essays. He played the cello—indeed, he would initially major in music in college, with the hope of playing professionally—but he also lifted weights in the basement of his high school with the janitor. We found this out when he read one of his first essays.

In detail, he laid out his after-school routine at a prestigious prep school in the San Francisco Bay Area. After introducing the janitor, he described how the two of them would pump iron, lifting weights after everyone else had gone home. Mao wasn't bulky—he wore a blue Gap hoodie that was a few sizes too big—but he had a grip like steel. I found this out by accident, when I offered to shake his hand.

But his strength wasn't the only thing his placid surface concealed. One day—in my memory, it was the first day of camp—he sat next to me. I didn't know his name yet. I didn't know anything about him. All I knew was that he seemed unusually preoccupied while our teacher, Cory, a recent MFA grad with long legs and honey-blond hair, was diagramming Hemingway's iceberg theory on the whiteboard. At that moment, I heard a strange clicking noise that seemed to be coming from Mao, who had thrust his hands deep in the front pocket of his sweatshirt and was moving them rapidly up and down.

When the clicking became too much, Cory looked around, as if searching for a stray insect. Not seeing anything, she returned to the whiteboard. A few moments later, I glanced over and saw that Mao's frantic motions had ceased. His hands were no longer hidden in his pocket. They held to the light a Rubik's Cube. It wasn't scrambled, like mine still was, buried deep in my closet, but completely solved, every side neatly aligned, a solid block of color.

I had never seen anyone solve Rubik's Cube before. Evidently, it was no big deal to Mao. He put the puzzle back in his pocket and started twisting it again. It seemed beyond belief—could he not only solve Rubik's Cube, but solve it without even looking at it? The teacher homed in on the sound and eventually took the Cube away before I could ask Toby how he had completed it.

Of course, the fastest way to render something popular is to make it illicit. Before long, everyone had a Rubik's Cube. At lunchtime, we brought them out, struggling to align the pieces. Mao served as our guru, showing us the way.

The first lesson was obvious and yet hardly obvious at all. The center of each face, Mao explained, never changed. That is, it could only rotate, not change its relative position. This had to do with the puzzle's construction, he said. Because of the axles hidden inside Rubik's Cube, the centers were effectively fixed in place, relative to one another. At first, I had no idea what this really meant. What were the implications of the centers never changing? The rest of the puzzle seemed to do nothing *but* change, like the colors of a kaleidoscope.

Fortunately, Mao was a patient, if occasionally stern, teacher. He wandered among us like Socrates in the agora, showing us how we had erred, and correcting us on the path to the solution. The importance of the centers, he explained, was that each color belonged to a certain side. If you knew to which side each color belonged, you could develop a strategy. Simply look at the center, in other words, and you knew which color that face had to be.

This was a revelation. No longer was Rubik's Cube just a mass of colors, a bog without a map. I could look at the white side, for instance, and know that every white sticker belonged there. The same went for yellow, and so on and so forth. What's more, the relationship between the sides came into focus. If the centers were always fixed, then certain colors always belonged adjacent to one another, or opposite one another. White, for example, sat across from yellow. (At least in the most popular configuration of Rubik's Cube—the one in which Cubes sold everywhere except Japan are routinely stickered.)

With this map in hand—white opposite yellow, blue opposite green, and red opposite orange—I could begin to find my way forward. I could see where each sticker was supposed to go. Only, as I soon learned, *sticker* was something of a dirty word, at least for Mao. It was a rookie mistake to focus on the stickers. Elementary. If that's all you did, you were doomed. Even if you managed to line up all the stickers on one side, what then?

In fact, you could have one face entirely matching but the rest of Rubik's Cube in utter chaos. This led to the second lesson: solve pieces, not stickers, Mao said. At first, I had no idea what he meant. Weren't the stickers the functional unit of Rubik's Cube? In fact, this was but an illusion. Mao took apart his Cube to explain.

The corners were units in and of themselves, he showed us, pulling them out, one by one. There were eight of them. And while you could move them around—changing their orientation or swapping them with other corners—for all intents and purposes, the three stickers they presented were fixed in relation to one another.

This is what Mao meant by solving pieces. If you wanted to put a white corner into place, for instance, you needed not only to align it with the white center, but also make sure its other two stickers aligned with the appropriate sides. In other words, each corner was distinct, even those that belonged on the same side.

Putting these pieces in the right place proved challenging. What if a piece that was already in place was blocking the piece you were about to insert? And how did you deal with pieces that were in the correct position, but incorrectly oriented, like a book that's been shelved in the right place but turned upside down? There was never one right answer to any of these questions—you could align the pieces any way that worked, and there was typically more than one means of accomplishing the task.

I would later learn that these are called algorithms. At the time, all I knew was that Mao would tell me to take the pieces where they wanted to go. In addition to the eight corners, there were twelve edges, nestled in between the corners, each of which had two stickers, bound together like peanut butter and jelly. Of the white edges, for instance, which might have otherwise looked alike to me, one was adjacent to red, another to blue, another to orange, and another to green—four different pieces. To solve each piece, Mao seemed to say, you had only to follow it like a dowser with his rod, letting it pull you along until you hit water, so to speak, and the piece fell into place.

Two weeks later, all of us could solve Rubik's Cube. That left us one week to compete. To see how fast we could go. Even though it was 2005, well before the advent of smartphones, I was nearly unique in having a wristwatch. Like a sailor wandering about a foreign wharf, I was press-ganged into service: my job was to offi-ciate the duels between Mao and Mateus Moitinho de Almeida, a Filipino with a floppy bowl cut and braces. Moitinho de Almeida, who knew Mao from previous summers, was the only classmate who knew in advance how to solve Rubik's Cube.

I had gotten my Rubik's Cube at Aahs, a novelty store with

branches across Los Angeles. This version was official—speed-cubes didn't appear until some years later, when it became apparent there was a market for them—and yet distinctive: it had been designed to commemorate the twenty-fifth anniversary of the release of Rubik's Cube. Rather than the traditional white, my Cube had one silver face, which shone like a mirror when solved.

As we all soon learned, the stickers included with store-bought Rubik's Cubes peeled once you solved them enough. Moitinho de Almeida bragged about his stickers. By contrast, those on his Cube were specially made, ordered by his father, who owned a restaurant and did work with specialty vendors. Made of vinyl rather than thin sheets of translucent plastic over white backgrounds, they chipped rather than peeled.

Watching Mao and Moitinho de Almeida duel up close was like having front-row tickets to a prizefight. They would exchange Rubik's Cubes, scramble them, and then hand them back. Sometimes, even from a short glance, they could tell whether a given scramble would lead to a good start. They would look at me, at which point I would count them off. The moment I activated the timer on my watch, they began to furiously twist and turn their puzzles. Their fingers were a blur, moving too fast for me—for any of us, who had gathered around them, as if to watch a school-yard fight—to understand. They seemed to inhabit a different universe, one in which time operated on a scale we couldn't comprehend. Like sumo wrestlers, they grunted, their feet squared to one another, their knees slightly bent.

The moment I saw the movement cease—more often than not, it happened wherever Mao was standing—I stopped the timer. Typically, the time registered fell below twenty seconds. The rest of us could only gape in wonder. Then the two of them exchanged puzzles once more. The whole cycle began again. It repeated over and over and over. The race was never really won. Mao was insanely competitive. It was hardly enough just to win. There was always the next contest. Once, he cornered me when I was on the way to lunch. I was wearing a T-shirt intended to be a game, the purpose of which was to read the colors in which the words on the shirt were printed. The challenge was that the words were the names of colors themselves—only the two rarely matched up. Blue, for instance, was written in green. (The trick color was white, printed in white.) Mao wanted me to time him reading the shirt. He had to find out how fast he was.

When he finished—it took him about half a minute—he had all his friends go, too. He had to learn who was the fastest. If it wasn't him, he vowed to practice until he beat everyone.

No one was into solving Rubik's Cubes at my high school. When I broke mine out, I became something of an eccentric. It actually got me in trouble once, just as it'd gotten Mao in trouble at Nerd Camp. One of my seatmates in French asked if I would teach him. We finished our work early and I began to impart exactly what Mao had taught me. The room was hardly silent—there were students muttering phrases in French—but still, the clicking of our Rubik's Cubes carried. The teacher was having none of it. She forbade us to ever solve in class again, and recommended we read the magazines tucked away in the corner.

This was an odd form of punishment, as we soon learned. The standards of mainstream publications in l'Hexagone were wildly more permissive than those of their American counterparts. I recall, in particular, a profile of the billionaire Richard Branson. If it had appeared in Forbes, the piece would no doubt have featured a portrait of Branson wearing a power suit. This publication, by contrast, had a double-page spread of him riding a Jet Ski off his private island with a nude model in tow.

Figuring that this was hardly the worst thing in the world—although only in French class would looking at images of nude women be more appropriate than solving Rubik's Cubes—my classmate and I called it quits. I taught him bit by bit, in other classes, but that was the end of my career with Rubik's Cube. Or so I thought.

Shortly after I graduated college, the Cube twisted back into my life. And it did not let go so easily this time. In search of topics to write about that might interest magazine editors, I stumbled on an article online mentioning the upcoming 2012 U.S. National Rubik's Cube Championship. It was to take place at the Riviera Hotel and Casino, where Liberace once held court, in Las Vegas. Were my playground rumbles really slated for a major competition in Sin City? In my mind's eye, I saw show girls wandering in a sea of people solving Rubik's Cubes, so obsessed with the puzzle that they didn't even look up.

The website created for the competition itself was sparse, mostly white, with a little colored type. It was maintained by a group billing itself as the World Cube Association. There was no qualification to enter. You simply paid the registration fee and showed up. I was considering doing just that when I noticed something even more unusual—to my mind, anyway—on the list of those registered to compete.

On the phone, Toby Mao sounded just the same. He was going to help organize the competition, he said, as if it were the most normal thing in the world, like assisting a neighbor with a Sunday cookout. Apparently, he had competed many times before, even set the world record for a single solve in 2006. I had had no idea there *were* world records in cubing or that solving Rubik's Cube as a sport even existed.

Mao laughed at my ignorance. There were competitions all over the world, he said. In fact, his older brother, Tyson, helped to set them up. Tyson had cofounded the World Cube Association with

Ron van Bruchem, a middle-aged Dutch banking IT consultant, while he was in college.

How had I not heard of this before? I was taking notes on a piece of paper with a dull pencil; I asked if Toby wouldn't mind repeating himself. He proceeded to outline the extent of this hobby: cubing was everywhere, from Europe to Australia. He didn't practice much anymore, he added—he was too busy, working in health-care consulting in the San Francisco Bay Area—but he could arrive in almost any foreign city and feel assured he would have a place to crash. The WCA operated in upward of sixty countries.

I was even more surprised when Toby told me that he and Tyson had been responsible for teaching Will Smith to solve Rubik's Cube for the 2006 film *The Pursuit of Happyness*, in which Smith, playing Chris Gardner, a homeless single father turned millionaire stockbroker, solves Rubik's Cube to win over the man who ultimately hires him at a brokerage firm. They'd been flown to Los Angeles, Toby said, and spent a week or so on set.

So Smith really could solve Rubik's Cube? I asked. Sure, Toby said. He'd learned just the way I had. One layer at a time.

When I asked Toby if I could come and write about the upcoming competition, he sounded almost outraged. "What do you mean?" he asked. "You're not going to compete?"

If I'd only known how deeply the Cube would entangle itself in my life, I might have proceeded with more caution. In just a few years, I would be literally cubing myself to sleep.

THAT'S GOOD COMPETITION!

I stood outside the room and listened. The carpeting at the Riviera Hotel and Casino is dense.* Thick burgundy pile interwoven with gold and green threads, a garish pattern repeating ad infinitum. It was made to absorb most sounds—footfalls, trundling carts, luggage—but whatever was on the other side of the door was too much. The beat emanating from within was percussive, incessant, like the collision of rain with a tin roof.

Inside, dozens upon dozens of people had gathered at tables, spread around a giant ballroom. They were hunched in concentration, all their attention focused on their hands. In their twisting fingers lay brightly colored shapes: cubes, pyramids, irregular prisms. The shapes were themselves changing shape. The colors cycled from one permutation to another with all the rapidity of traffic lights gone haywire.

The sign in the lobby had warned me what to expect, scrolling by like the ticker on CNN: WELCOME TO THE 2012 U.S. NATIONAL RUBIK'S CUBE CHAMPIONSHIP. Still, to see it all in person was a bit of a shock. One of the volunteers running the

---

* Or rather *was* dense. In 2015, the Riviera closed.

competition had checked my name off the list and given me a lanyard with an ID number: 2012SCHE01. This number would track my progress as a cuber. I was now officially a member of the World Cube Association.

The first thing I saw when I walked through the doors was a mosaic. Several cubers had assembled about a hundred Rubik's Cubes into a rectangular configuration that resembled Pikachu, the small, yellow, rodentlike Pokémon. The image was like a pointillist canvas: the individual Rubik's Cubes appeared scrambled at random, a mess of yellow, white, red, and orange, but the dots added up to a recognizable shape: *pika pika!*

A woman with a blond bouffant was grading the mosaic, going over a checklist on a clipboard in her hand. There were several others nearby, laid out on easels, including a slot machine and the King himself: Elvis, reborn not as a tubby impersonator, although one was doubtless not far away, but as a pixelated version of himself, in the bright hues of Rubik's Cube. The woman introduced herself as Lynn Brown. She lived in Southern California. Her son, Cameron, she told me, had gotten into cubing, and she'd come along for the ride.

When I remarked that I'd never seen anything quite like this—I noticed a number of cubers wandering around with the sort of bulky earmuffs favored by airport employees who work on the tarmac, to quell the noise—she told me that she hadn't either. "Yeah, they do take it pretty seriously," she said, "and it's funny, because even Cameron, he's just like 'No, just don't talk to me right now.' And I understand. You have to focus! It's like any sport, I would imagine: 'Get your head in the game!' "

The night before, I sat in on the staff competition. When I arrived, Toby was serving as one of the judges in 4x4, an event that is like driving off-road in one pertinent quality: the 4x4, essentially a Rubik's Cube that's been enlarged, with four squares per edge, instead of the traditional three, is far more forbidding and wild than the original puzzle.

The 4x4 encapsulates many more permutations than the 3x3 Rubik's Cube. In the United States, it would be 7.4 quattuordecillion. In much of Europe, 7,400 septillion—because hardly anyone uses numbers this large, different countries have different names for them. Originally, the 4x4 was marketed as "Rubik's Revenge."

"I don't really know what my time was," Toby said. "But it wasn't good." The cutoff for solving the puzzle—the point at which, in the interest of time, the cuber would be prevented from finishing the attempt—was one minute and thirty seconds. In other words, faster than I could yet solve the original Rubik's Cube. (At the time, the world record for the 4x4 stood at 26.77 seconds for a single solve; 30.81 seconds for an average of five solves.)

To Toby, however, speed wasn't the issue. He just hadn't practiced enough. This wasn't by choice. He simply didn't have time. "I forgot a lot of moves I was supposed to do," he said. Still, even though he didn't really cube anymore, the competition presented a chance to see old friends. As they appeared, one by one, at his judging station, he introduced me to them. The first to arrive was Vincent Sheu, whom I later learned chaired the WCA Regulations Committee, and was the outgoing president of the Rubik's Cube Club at the University of California at Berkeley, where he was currently in graduate school.

Sheu, a tall, handsome young man with thick dark hair, approached the 4x4 musically, humming along to each twist like a metronome keeping the beat. "Oh, shit," he pronounced, at one point, while Toby calmly told me about the strategy for attacking the puzzle: "With any Big Cube you turn it into a 3x3," he said.

Further curses notwithstanding, Sheu made the cutoff: one minute 21.22 seconds. Next up was Tim Reynolds, a recent MIT grad proudly sporting his class ring. "He's a cool guy," Toby said. Apparently, Reynolds was able not only to solve the 4x4, but to keep up a conversation at the same time. When I asked Toby if anyone was sponsoring the competition, it was Reynolds who replied that both Seven Towns, Ltd., and Winning Moves, the license holder and one of the distributors of Rubik's Cube, respectively, had chipped in.

"Not as much as the Europeans, though," Toby added, a little disdainfully. "If you go to European competitions, they blow money on, like, break-dancers."

"That's only Worlds," Reynolds replied, referring to the World Championship. When I asked Toby if Worlds—which was slated to take place in Las Vegas, at the Riviera, the following year— would have break-dancers, he guffawed. "This is America," he said.

Chris Krueger came to the judging station. He was a soon-to-be graduate student in biology, who once held the blindfold world record.

In the taxonomy of organizing competitions, Krueger occupied an unheralded but crucial role, that of the runner: he was ferrying puzzles to and from the scrambling table. "It's more efficient this way," Toby said. The 4x4 Krueger had just deposited belonged to one of the few females on staff. "This is Jaclyn," Toby said. A petite young woman with brown hair took her seat at the table. "You ready to go?" Toby asked.

"This is going to take forever," she said.

I asked Toby if I'd have the chance to meet his brother. I was starting to get the impression that Tyson, who was in his late twenties, a couple of years older than Toby and me, was something of a titanic figure in the world of cubing, if such a small world can be said to contain titans. One of the staffers, a recent physics grad from Brown named Arthur Adams, said, "Tyson is like the Steve Jobs of cubing." Adams explained, "Sometimes he's hard to get along with, but he gets things done." The comparison went even further: Tyson wore similar glasses and was also known for occasionally wearing a turtleneck, and worked in Silicon Valley.

Toby wasn't sure. His brother, he thought, was probably doing a supply run to Target. "We need some stuff," he said. Every timer required batteries, for instance, and that amounted to a significant number of batteries, since there were so many timers. Part of the reason the staff had arrived a day early was to set everything up: in the ballroom, there were rows of folding tables, each with two timers and two displays, one placed at either end.

The timers, Toby explained, were borrowed from speedstacking, the quirky pastime of stacking and unstacking plastic cups as fast as possible. Known as StackMats, the timers were interesting to look at: oblong plastic touchpads, connected to digital readouts that faced the audience. The competitor touched his or her hands to each end of the pad until a small blinking light went from red to green. At this point, he or she lifted his or her hands, and the clock began to tick upward, red numerals rapidly replacing one another.

Tyson was so busy that I didn't so much as glimpse him until that evening, when the staff, or at least a good part of it, made an excursion to the Bellagio, just down the road.

The line to the dinner buffet crawled along, in a warren of brass piping, amid a rocky outcropping that appeared to have once belonged to Disneyland's Pirates of the Caribbean ride. Tyson was restless. Waiting in line, he jimmied his feet and paced back and forth. His bias, it appeared, was for action—for setting up competitions, which was, after all, why he had come here—and there was now nothing to do but wait. He spoke at a rapid clip, as if he had not only practiced what he was going to say, but had said it many times before.

In fact, he probably had. This Mao had been making media

appearances for years. Once, he solved Rubik's Cube blindfolded on CNN. Anderson Cooper, who has reported from some of the most dangerous war zones on the planet, looked completely baffled. "I don't understand a word you just said," Cooper told Mao when he tried to explain his technique. Despite Mao making a slight error—a few pieces wound up out of place—Anderson was nonetheless bowled over. "Frankly, I believe you can do it," he said.

Mao had also appeared as a contestant on *Beauty and the Geek*, the reality show that was a bit like *Survivor*, only all the women were beauties and all the guys nerds. At the time, Mao was still a student, at the California Institute of Technology, pursuing a degree in astrophysics. He didn't win, but according to his old roommate, dozens of their classmates staged viewing parties. Since he was contractually prohibited from telling them what happened, they were devastated when Tyson and his partner had to drop out. His efforts were not entirely unrewarded: he was once recognized at the mall by a horde of teenage girls. As Anderson Cooper said, "God knows the ladies love a Rubik's Cube master."

Every activity has its Svengali—the person who brought it out of obscurity and into the mainstream. Or, rather, Svengalis, since rarely does something become a success without the input of multiple people. The actual Svengali, of course, was hardly benign—the novelist who created him once illustrated him as a spider at the center of its web.

Tyson never had nefarious plans for cubing, but he had plans for it, which is more than most others can say. In the early 2000s, it was a pastime that existed mostly on the Internet. The 2003 World Championship, the first since 1982, was put together by a Canadian software engineer named Dan Gosbee. It was a success—nearly one hundred people, representing more than a dozen countries, competed, drawing media coverage from across the globe—but it was not well managed, and the fallout was such that there threatened never to be a World Championship again.

The 2003 World Championship ended in acrimony. The reasons for this were, admittedly, rather piddling: as might be expected, there were problems that no one, including Gosbee, had anticipated. There was a shortage of timers, for instance. There was also no official rulebook, which led to a number of unfortunate mishaps.

One competitor had no idea how to solve Rubik's Cube. He tried and he tried and he tried. Half an hour later, he was still trying. There were nearly one hundred contestants, but only four timers. "We said, 'You have to stop now,'" Ron van Bruchem, the WCA cofounder, later recalled. "He said, 'No. There's no rule to stop me. I can go on forever if I want to.'"

On a popular message board, a handful of cubers voiced their displeasure. Gosbee, who had gone to great lengths to make the competition happen, took it personally. He felt his efforts weren't being properly appreciated and soon decided to leave the nascent community.

Tyson watched all of this from a distance. He had read about the World Championship in the *San Francisco Chronicle*, his hometown paper. Neither he nor Toby felt ready to compete; they'd only learned to solve Rubik's Cube a few weeks before. Tyson wasn't happy to learn about the falling-out. "Like, we're going to wait another twenty-one years for another World Championships?" he recalls wondering. "How can we make this a regular thing?"

While Tyson was learning to solve Rubik's Cube, he came across a video posted online. It featured Shotaro Makisumi, aka "Macky," a Japanese cuber. He was demonstrating his other talent, juggling, tossing so many balls into the air it was difficult to count their number. What struck Tyson wasn't the act of juggling itself—although that was no doubt impressive—but the background against which it was filmed.

Tyson had never met Makisumi. But in the insular world of cubing, he had heard of him. The official world record was still that set in 1982, at the first World Championship: 22.95 seconds. In the intervening years, Chris Hardwick, a teenager in North Carolina, created a place online for the next generation to post their best times. (It was later taken over by van Bruchem, on his website.) Hardwick called it the list of Unofficial World Records.

In the fall of 2003, many of the records were held by Makisumi. Tyson had always assumed he lived in Japan, because his nationality was listed as Japanese. Only there he was, in the video, juggling inside the 24 Hour Fitness in downtown Pasadena, just a few minutes away from Tyson's dormitory at Caltech. "I went to go find this kid," Tyson recalled, "because, like, I'd never seen anyone solve a Rubik's Cube in seventeen seconds."

That fall, Makisumi, who lived in Arcadia, a well-to-do suburb north of Los Angeles, had a strange encounter. He was just thirteen years old but already taking classes at the local high school. This is where Tyson, accompanied by Mark Polinkovsky, his roommate, a Moldovan-born physics student from upstate New York, found him.

The two of them asked Makisumi if he wouldn't mind solving Rubik's Cube. "It was ludicrous, right?" Polinkovsky later said. "Macky just looks at it and starts twisting, and, you know, twenty seconds later, or even less, maybe it was like fifteen seconds," the Cube was solved. "The thing was just *done*," he said. "It was phenomenal."

With Makisumi as the centerpiece, Tyson put together a local competition in the student lounge at Caltech. "It didn't strike me until later that it seemed weird," Makisumi told me of Tyson approaching him. He was just excited to solve Rubik's Cube. Across the Atlantic, in the Netherlands, van Bruchem kept tabs on the proceedings. The following summer, he and Tyson founded the World Cube Association.

More than one person told me that Tyson is someone who gets things done. He is a doer; he wants to build things, as they say in Silicon Valley. Not long after graduating Caltech in 2006, he worked as a consultant, but quit after a few months. He then took several jobs as a high-frequency trader, jumping from Beverly Hills to New York to San Francisco.

By the time I met him, he was working as a product manager at Zynga, the mobile gaming company. His job was to help oversee the poker game. "I'm trying to make it not a job," he said, of his work organizing cubing competitions. In the past, he had traveled as far as Peru to help run tournaments. "I'm trying to make it take less time."

The goal of the World Cube Association is, to quote the charter, "to have more competitions in more countries with more people and more fun, under fair and equal conditions." When Tyson started organizing competitions, in 2004, only a handful of countries had ever hosted tournaments that would later be deemed official: the United States, Hungary, and Canada. Now the list includes dozens of nations on six continents, from Iran to Malaysia.

Each of these competitions, by rule, had to have a delegate present, a member of the WCA familiar with the regulations. The WCA is run a bit like the American government. There's the executive branch—the board—which directs the organization. Then there are the delegates, the legislature, who take care of actually running the thing. Like the Senate, the delegates break off into different committees, one of which deals with regulations. None of these positions are paid, which is perhaps the WCA's greatest strength and most potent weakness. It attracts only the most committed cubers, but has trouble retaining them.

Until recently, all decisions were made by the board, but the organization got too big—there were simply too many things to handle. It was a bit like trying to expand a religion: in regions where there were no delegates, the organization had to send them to spread the gospel of cubing. Which is why Tyson found himself, a few years ago, schlepping a suitcase full of Rubik's Cubes to Lima.

He had received a message from a Peruvian man who wanted to host a Rubik's Cube competition. The stars aligned—Tyson had vacation time—and he found himself helping to establish speed-cubing in Peru. "There's more than just, like, getting up to code," he said. Natán Riggenbach, who would later serve as my judge at the World Championship, was the beneficiary of the voyage: "There are cubers in many parts of the country," Riggenbach said. Riggenbach is tall and lean, with a deeply tanned face. Trained as an engineer, he runs a zip-lining business with his sister in the Colca Canyon. Before Tyson's visit, his daughters got into cubing. The younger one, Jael, solved Rubik's Cube in fifteen seconds only five months into her life as a cuber. Riggenbach laughed. "I've taught them all I can, you know?"

His next task was to spread the word himself. Ordained by Tyson, so to speak, he could host competitions. In relation to the countries in which cubing sprouted, Peru is very poor. "They cannot all go to Lima," Riggenbach told me, of the cubers in Peru. "If I can travel to different parts, then we can have competitions in Arequipa and Trujillo and so on."

Country by country, the organization expanded, until it was—well, I wasn't sure what it was going to become, so I asked Tyson. Did he think speedcubing would turn into something like the National Spelling Bee, televised on ESPN?

He wasn't sure. "It depends on the circumstances," he said. Spelling, he pointed out, was a generic good—there was no trademark on words. ESPN was free to televise the competition, without fear of the lexicographical society sending lawsuits their way. Rubik's Cube, by contrast, was privately held. He didn't have anything against Seven Towns, Ltd., the company that had made Rubik's Cube what it was. After all, if the company hadn't brought Rubik's Cube to the world, there would be no speedcubing at all. Seven Towns would likely have to be involved if cubing wound up on national TV.

Still, if Seven Towns were running the show, Tyson figured there would probably be less choice about whose puzzles got to make it onto the stage. "Imagine that, like, fine, you have it on TV, you have a competition," he said, "but you have to use their Cube." In fact, at the 2005 World Championship, Tyson said, the WCA acceded to their demands, and allowed only Rubik's brand Cubes, which were, admittedly, then the best on the market. But there was a problem, he told me: not every country had access to the same puzzles. (In Japan, the 2x2 Rubik's Cube was larger, which made it easier to solve, since you had more leverage.)

"There's a reason why it's called the World Cube Association," Tyson later told me. "And not the World Rubik's Cube Association." He and Ron wanted to make it a sport, not a commercial. "If we're going to make this a sport," he added, "it doesn't make sense that I demand that you use a certain brand of shoe, or a certain brand of, like, pole-vaulting pole."

To Riggenbach, who was standing in line with us, his daughters back at the Riviera, the whole idea of cubing ever turning into something people would pay money to watch or that advertisers would covet was kind of absurd. "We have them at public places," he said of competitions in Peru. "And only a few people go and take a look for a few minutes and then just walk away. They find it impressive, but they get bored pretty quickly."

When I pointed out that millions of people watched the National Spelling Bee, thrilling to words like *logorrhea* and *cymotrichous*, he shook his head in amazement. "I think it's really boring!" he said.

The competition was slated to last three days. On the first day, the most out-of-the-way events were held. If this were the Olympics, it would be the day of the fifty-kilometer race walk. Something no one really wants to see—or, at least, that no one has learned to love yet. In the world of cubing, these are often, oddly enough, the most challenging endeavors.

Wandering around the venue, observing one event after another, I recognized the pinched and strained expression of children preparing for a particularly interminable exam. This was the multiblind competition. It's hard enough to solve Rubik's Cube with your eyes open. Harder still to solve it blindfolded. Multiblind is to solving Rubik's Cube blindfolded what ultramarathons are to regular marathons. Only the strong survive, and by strong I mean mentally fortified beyond mortal means. You don't just solve Rubik's Cube once, but many times, one after the other, without stopping, all the while completely blindfolded.

"It's a very, very painful process that I would not wish upon anyone," said Chester Lian, a college student from Malaysia. Lian deposited fifteen Rubik's Cubes at the table helmed by the scramblers for the event, in a chamber down the hall from the main ballroom at the Riviera. Like the rest of the entrants, Lian would have one hour.

During that time, he would be allowed to inspect his puzzles. He was not allowed to make any moves until the blindfold was in place, but he could murmur, chant, tap his feet—anything to aid in his attempt to memorize the configuration of every Rubik's Cube. Then, once he made himself devoid of sight, the attempt would begin. "I hate doing this," he said.

* * *

Even a newbie like me could appreciate the tension in the multi-blind room. Spectators whispered to one another as if watching a surgery in an old-timey surgical theater, afraid to derange the surgeon. There were lots of shuffling feet, jiggling fingers, twitching joints. Most of the entrants, I noticed, were wearing the enormous, industrial-grade earmuffs I'd seen dotting the main room.

They also had sleep masks hanging around their necks. The sort of thing you wear to block the light streaming in the windows on a plane. Only these sleep masks were chosen to showcase the personalities of each cuber. Lian's was bright yellow, just like the Pikachu doll he placed on the table. That of another cuber was bright green and gave the impression that the cuber had a second face—that of a frog.

Sitting in front of most of the contestants was a music stand bearing a piece of cardboard. The moment the contestant donned his or her mask, one of the judges pushed the music stand closer, in between his or her hands, so it stood between the blindfold and the Cube.

The purpose of this became apparent when you looked at Lian's setup: he wore his cardboard around the neck, supported by a piece of wire, instead of using the music stand. Someone had written on the cardboard, in black marker, DON'T CHEAT. If this extra deterrent seemed excessive, I later learned it was actually the rule, and for good reason.

Mátyás Kuti was cubing's golden boy. He was Hungarian, and in 2008 he owned more world records in more disciplines than anyone else. "I KNOW he can do it," one of his fellow Hungarian cubers, Milán Baticz, wrote online. "But he cheated his WRs ☹."

What Kuti had done was, in retrospect, quite obvious: he simply peeked under the blindfold. One of the greatest cubers in the world had been caught cheating in multiblindfold, and it remains one of the great scandals of cubing. Now it was impossible to see Rubik's Cube even if you were looking right at it: the cardboard stood in the way.

It didn't really matter to Lian. After inspecting his Rubik's Cubes for the better part of the hour, frowning at some configurations, smiling at others, he pulled on the blindfold and began unscrambling them. Lian later told me that his method relies on transforming the stickers of Rubik's Cube into a memorable pattern. Each sticker is assigned a letter, with the result that each Cube becomes a string of twenty to twenty-five letters.

Lian didn't set out to solve multiple Rubik's Cube blindfolded. He discovered he was good at it by accident. At his second competition, he decided to give it a shot. He had never practiced the event. He had never even attempted solving more than one Rubik's Cube blindfolded. "I got three out of three," he said.

As I watched him in Las Vegas, it was hard to believe he couldn't see. His fingers moved as nimbly as if the blindfold were not there. In multiblind, the score is recorded as the number of Cubes solved correctly minus the number of Cubes solved incorrectly. Lian had gotten up to seventeen out of seventeen using the full hour the previous year, which was good enough for the world record. Despite his prowess, he takes a self-deprecating view of his accomplishments. "I've never improved," he told me, with a snort.

Not all competitors use the same technique. Mike Hughey, one of Lian's opponents, a middle-aged computer programmer from Indianapolis, who arrived with his wife and two daughters, favors a more colorful method. Rather than translate each sticker into a letter, he turns it into an image, which becomes part of a fictional narrative playing out in his head. (The same technique is popular in competitions devoted to the art of memory, as the journalist Joshua Foer details in his book *Moonwalking with Einstein*. The technique is known as the Memory Palace, and dates back to ancient Greece.)

Evidently, neither method is foolproof. Lian solved twelve of his fifteen Rubik's Cubes; Hughey, nine of thirteen. When the first attempt ended—there would be another one Sunday, and the best score would count for the final tally—I asked Hughey what some of the stories were he had used. "So, I had, um . . . Underdog," he told me, "leaned over a rail and put down his iPod, looked through a telescope to see Donkey Kong riding on the USS *Enterprise*, and he was examining a big wall of owls out in space."

My own solves were distinctly less challenging. I had never solved Rubik's Cube on record. Searching the WCA database, I found there was one other Scheffler: Didac Ponseti Scheffler, a Spaniard, who, at the Spanish National Championship, in 2007, had registered an average of one minute 23.91 seconds; a best solve of one minute 16.41 seconds.

With any luck, I hoped I might beat those numbers. Unfortunately, I knew so little about the competition procedures that I threatened to miss my opportunity entirely: the WCA recommends reading the rulebook first, which extends to some thirty pages, and includes lines like "Regulations 5b5c and 5b5d supersede 5b5a and 5b5b." Having only skimmed it, I had no idea you were supposed to bring your puzzle to the scrambling table solved. It makes sense, of course—why should the scramblers have to solve your Rubik's Cube?

As a result, I wound up having to stand there while the round got under way, solving my puzzle—the DaYan ZhanChi, which I had purchased online, at Toby's behest—while the scramblers looked on, waiting for me to hand it to them.

It's one thing to tackle Rubik's Cube at home. You can listen to music. You can pause if something goes wrong and decide to scrap the solve, to start over. And nobody is watching. In competition, what happens happens. If the puzzle pops, you have to pick it up, put it back together, and keep going. If you make a mistake—insert the right piece in the wrong place, say—the time will reflect your error, and there's nothing you can do about it. The clock is merciless, ticking ever upward.

I was too green to know yet that each solve is essentially like a play in football: it happens so fast that you can't expect to know what you did wrong. The only way to analyze your failure is to have some objective measurement, which you can consult after the fact, to determine the source of your error.

In football, of course, the answer is game tape. Teams employ people whose only job is to film each play. The following week, the coaches go over the tape, dissecting the plays, to determine if a play succeeded, and if so, by accident or design. If it failed, the tapes provide clues as to how to correct the mistake next time. As the saying goes, tape never lies.

In cubing, the answer is the same. I learned that lots of cubers record their solves. This is for two purposes: one, to reconstruct them, in the case of a record, so everyone else can follow along. And, two, if the solve was subpar, how to avoid such errors in the future.

Unfortunately, I hadn't prepared for this. All that remains of those first five solves is my memory: I felt anxious. There was no explaining this. Growing up, I played clarinet in some of the world's most famous concert halls. Yet here I was, in a decaying casino, sweating profusely, worried the Cube might slip right out of my hands.

The first solve was a struggle. I barely broke two minutes. One minute 57.94 seconds. I had no idea what I was doing. I was just trying, blindly, to follow what Toby had taught me. I had barely practiced, since I knew I wouldn't be competitive, a decision for which I was now kicking myself. It was embarrassing to show up and not be able to really play the game. I didn't have the proper conditioning.

The second solve was even worse. Two minutes and change. Any chance of beating Didac Ponseti Scheffler was quickly vanishing. Now I could only hope that I wouldn't finish last. My third solve headed in the right direction: one minute 27.04 seconds. The fourth solve was a bit slower, but hardly as slow as the first two: one minute 41.55 seconds. And my fifth and final solve was my fastest yet: one minute 26.52 seconds.

It felt good to go fast. Even if fast, for me, was slow in comparison to anyone else. (The judge, in my memory, looked almost bored, eyeing the clock like a schoolchild waiting for class to let out.)

Not long after the round finished, the results were posted by the door. The cutoff was the top one hundred. The time to beat was an average of 16.02 seconds. I came in not quite last. My average was one minute 42.18 seconds. Good enough for 243rd place.

"We call it competition, but that's not what it is," said Chris Krueger. "It's about improving your own previous times." Krueger has a scholarly affect: round glasses and brown hair in a bowl cut. He didn't make the cut for the second round either, even though his average—19.52 seconds—was close to a personal best.

Krueger wasn't the only veteran to miss the cut. "There are generations of cubers, right?" Tyson had said, the previous night. Those who learned in the 1980s, those who brought about the rebirth of Rubik's Cube in the early 2000s, and those who caught on later, the next generation, the hordes of teenagers and tweens and even children who were sharing their times on YouTube.

One of the earliest cubers, Lars Petrus, a computer programmer in his fifties, was in attendance, and made something of an entrance. Sitting onstage, Tyson announced that if Petrus, who had a personal best average of 20.48 seconds, broke twenty seconds, everyone in the audience would get a free plush Rubik's Cube. "Fourth solve, we're looking for seventeen seconds or less," Tyson said.

The proof was on the scoreboard. Hardly any of the veterans I spoke to—neither Toby, who once held the world record for a single solve; nor Tyson, who held the world record for solving blindfolded; nor Petrus, who represented his native Sweden at the first World Championship, in 1982, and clocked an average of 22.67—made the second round.

"There are only a couple of people who actually have a chance of winning this competition," Krueger told me. He put air quotes around the word *winning*. To him, evidently—and to the other veterans—cubing wasn't just about cubing. It was about something else.

In a sense, cubing competitions are like conventions. Since so much of cubing life takes place online, it's one of the few chances to meet people you've only ever seen on YouTube. One cuber lots of people seemed to be gravitating toward was Cameron Brown, a skinny teenager from California. He had a swoop of sandy-blond hair, which immediately called to mind Justin Bieber. Only whereas the pop star is of average height, Brown was built like Gumby: as lanky as a beanpole, his limbs draped in the sort of clothes that make teenagers everywhere look almost indistinguishable.

Brown is something of an entrepreneur. He was seventeen years old, on the verge of his senior year in high school, but had already been running his own Cube-related business since middle school. His mother, Lynn, whom I had met earlier as she graded the mosaics, handed me one of his business cards. It had blue-and-black graphics fronted by white type. The font looked like the typeface used in the posters for *Batman Forever*, the ill-fated reboot starring Val Kilmer:

SPEEDCUBESHOP.COM

THE ONE-STOP SHOP FOR ALL YOUR CUBING NEEDS!

When Brown was in the sixth grade, he went to the movie theater for his birthday. The film he wanted to see was sold out, so he wound up watching *The Pursuit of Happyness*. "And I saw him solve it, of course," Brown said. His mother soon bought him a Rubik's Cube from Toys "R" Us.

One weekend, not long after seeing the movie, at his dad's house—his parents are divorced—he solved Rubik's Cube for the first time. "I was, like, 'Whoa! I want to do that again,'" Brown told me.

For an entire year, he practiced and practiced and practiced. At that point, he discovered he wasn't the only one: not only were there competitions, there were more advanced methods. "Once I found out about, like, Fridrich," he said, "I just kept improving on what I had."

In the 1980s, Brown's father, Layne, a gregarious fellow in a polo shirt and baseball cap, learned to solve Rubik's Cube when he was working at Baskin-Robbins; one of his coworkers taught him. "I still come across people," Layne said, "whenever people see Cameron do it, or they hear about it, they say, 'That would take me, you know, a month.' And I'm like, 'No, actually, you would never be able to do it. You don't understand.'"

Layne, who had also accompanied his son to the competition, works in the export-import business. Specifically, he deals in shoes. One day, as he recalls, Cameron approached him. "I always used to order Cubes from China," Cameron told me, "like every other kid." Only he was getting tired of waiting weeks for packages that sometimes never came.

His father had an office in Hong Kong to which he traveled

frequently. Cameron asked if he wouldn't mind carrying the puzzles back in his suitcase. "I said, 'It's going to be your money, and if you fail, I'm not going to bail you out,'" Layne recalls saying.

"It was supposed to be just those fifty and done," Cameron said. "But people kept wanting more and more." His father had warned him, "This is a risk. This is what business is." But he surprised even Layne. "He sold 'em in, like, a *week*," Layne said.

According to Cameron, his business was the first online store based in the United States to specialize in speedcubing. "If I hadn't had this job," Cameron told me, "I would be working as soon as I could, like age fifteen or sixteen, at Target or McDonald's, but it's at the point where I'm saving up for college and stuff."

In recent years, his customer base had expanded. "I pretty much haven't found a country I haven't gotten an order from," he said. He's shipped products to Japan, Belgium, Greece. When I asked if he was known at his high school as the Cube guy, he said he tries to keep it low-key. "I don't like to brag about things I own," he said. "But I saved up and I was able to buy my own car."

Every week, he said, he gets e-mails from cubers asking for advice. "It's a bunch of kids who think it's an easy income," he said. "But it's actually a real business. Like, you can't treat it as a child's game. Because it's real customers and real money being exchanged. And, like, even doing taxes and things."

His father, Layne, beamed. "I was a big athlete," he said. "But this is its own sport. And I'm just as proud to see him come here and, you know, I remember the first competition we went to, when a little boy came up and asked him for his autograph."

He assumed a squeaky voice. "Are you CamCuber?" he asked, referring to Cameron's YouTube handle. "Will you sign my Cube?" In his normal voice, Layne resumed, "I was like, 'Oh, my God!'" He burst out laughing. "He's like a celebrity!"

* * *

The night before the final day of competition, Tim Reynolds threw a party. It took place at the Riviera, in the room of Bob Burton, a math teacher from New Jersey and Jaclyn Sawler's boyfriend. Presumably because the competition had brought so much business to the hotel, Burton had been furnished with an enormous suite overlooking the Las Vegas Strip. The initial purpose of the party was to enter all of the data from the competition.

We sat for some time, all of us, quietly checking the hundreds and hundreds of score sheets accumulated from the competition so far. Of all the tasks required to run a competition, data entry is the least sexy. There is no twisting of puzzles. No opportunity to witness world records. There is, frankly, nothing exciting about it, but it is nonetheless absolutely essential. Until they are entered online, the data from the competition are just marks on scraps of paper. Oftentimes, the scrawl of one judge or another was difficult to read, which led to a belabored discussion of the difference between the numerals five and six. In most cases, the difference would have hardly affected the final outcome, but in others it would have drastically changed the resulting average.

Around midnight, in Burton's suite, a very unique race began. It involved three components: a red Solo Cup of beer, a Rubik's Cube, and a timer. The goal of the race was to finish the beer and solve Rubik's Cube in fewer than twenty seconds.

The first two contestants were veterans of the cubing scene: Jeremy Fleischman, a computer programmer from the Bay Area. Wearing thick glasses, his orange beard scruffily trimmed, Fleischman looked every bit like he'd wandered off the set of a Seth Rogen flick. Only his brainpower, evidently, even under the influence of alcohol, was hardly impaired. The other contestant was Legolas. Not the elfin warrior portrayed by Orlando Bloom in the *Lord of the Rings* trilogy, but David Gomes, a young man with long, flowing hair. Gomes, who was working in construction at the time, had put his hair up in a bun.

The two activated their timers. The question was which to do first—drink the beer or solve the Cube? Both elected to raise the cups, which they downed with great gulps. Then they set to work on the Cubes. Whatever heady mix of alcohol and adrenaline was pumping through their veins appeared not to slow them down. When they slammed the timers to a halt, the result was impossible to call. The timers told the story: Fleischman, 21.78; Legolas, 21.74 seconds.

The crowd roared. "Damn!" shouted Chester Lian. "That's good competition!"

The following day, I had a chance to see what real competition looked like. Out of 250 contestants, the field in the main event had been winnowed first to 100, then 32, then 16. The finalists hailed from half a dozen countries: the United States, with ten contestants, was the most widely represented. There were also two finalists each from Canada and South Korea. One finalist was from Thailand.

They were all male. "It's actually really fun," said Sarah Strong, a Canadian cuber. She meant that, because there were so few women present, they generally got more attention from the press. Strong, one of the few veteran female cubers, also said that since the community was so friendly, everyone got along, regardless of gender. "Everyone wants to get faster," she said. "It's not really competitive where, 'I want to win, I don't care about everyone else.'"

Still, as I would later learn, in discussions with other female cubers, the issue is hardly so pat. It's one of the lamentable features of cubing that its gender ratio is so skewed. Some female cubers may be too young to realize it, but it seems to be part of the larger problem in STEM fields of women being underrepresented. Of course, there's no reason it should be this way: anyone, of any gender, can excel at solving Rubik's Cube.

The stage was cleared of all but two tables, side by side. Each one had one timer and one display. The finalists were sequestered in a room down the hall, to prevent those who had yet to solve from learning anything about the times they had to beat.

For the first time all weekend, the sound of cubing was rendered inaudible. It was drowned out by the noise of the crowd. "The defending American champion from 2011"—a burly musicology student named Dan Cohen—"isn't here," said Tyson, holding the microphone like the emcee at a prizefight, "so it's really anyone's game."

The finalists came out two at a time, in reverse order, starting with the slowest pair. Tyson introduced them and then off they went. You could hear the puzzle tinkling, like a small glass ornament breaking over and over again. It sounded eerie in the cavernous ballroom. The finalists solved one after the other. Each solve was followed by a round of applause. In a lot of ways, it wasn't unlike a round of golf: the audience politely clapped for every solve, but certain performances got a much louder response than others.

Each of the finalists came out to entrance music. Some elected to play classic pump-up songs. The theme from *Rocky*. "The Final Countdown." Others were less orthodox. The theme from Super Mario Bros., for instance, in all its eight-bit glory. One of the contestants dropped to the stage for a bit of impromptu break dancing. But what got the most attention was speed.

Thompson Clarke, the Canadian teenager responsible for the break dancing, was the first onstage to break eight seconds, with a 7.65-second solve. It probably wouldn't save his average—he had a counting 12.25—but he jumped out of his seat nonetheless.

It wasn't easy to tell who was in the lead. Still, even I could pick up that something pivotal had occurred when Andrew Ricci, a floppy-haired teenager from Massachusetts wearing a hoodie and flip-flops, completed his fourth solve and jumped out of his chair as if he had been struck by lightning. The timer said it all: 6.15 seconds.

"I've been telling him he's gonna be champ," said Rob Stuart, a towering Australian. I had tried to get to Ricci but was foiled by the crowd that collected around him once the results were announced. "He's been getting faster and faster and faster," Stuart said.

The results were so close it was no wonder I couldn't call it, even though I'd sat in the front row. The second-place finisher, Phillip Espinoza, a college student from near San Diego, clocked an average of 9.64 seconds. The third-place finisher, Kevin Hays, a soon-to-be college student from the state of Washington, averaged 9.82 seconds. Both results would have captured the national title the year before.

After I spoke with Ricci, who averaged 9.55 seconds—a little off his personal best—I talked to his father, a balding man with a cell phone attached to his belt who worked in quality control for a multinational electric company. To him, winning was beside the point. There was a camaraderie to cubing he hadn't found elsewhere.

Still, as I was beginning to learn, the camaraderie of cubing was strangely competitive. You wanted to push yourself where you had never gone before, which meant you had to throw yourself against your friends. This attitude was hard to shake. I noticed Ricci arm-wrestle one of the cubers who had just congratulated him. They had to see who was stronger.

NOW, THIS IS A PRECIOUS THING

J essica Fridrich is a professor of engineering at Binghamton University in upstate New York. She studies the concealment and recovery of information in digital images. If you give her ten digital cameras and one digital photograph, she can tell you which camera took it. If you were to alter a photograph, using, say Photoshop, she could determine that, too.

As academics go, Fridrich is not especially famous. She doesn't produce TV shows, like Henry Louis Gates Jr., or write bestselling books, like Brian Greene, although her work did appear some years ago in a movie starring Michael Douglas. (In it, Douglas, a corrupt district attorney, is found to have tampered with photographic evidence.) Fridrich lives in a modest city and teaches at a modest institution. For decades, Binghamton thrived on the success of IBM, headquartered just down the road, in Endicott. The company moved on. The city did not. "Binghamton hasn't changed a bit," the writer David Sedaris, who was born there, once told a reporter. "I mean, they've built maybe one new house since I lived there."

In many ways, Fridrich is one of those academics you have never heard of, but whose work is nonetheless critical. She writes papers with titles like "Estimation of Primary Quantization Matrix in Double Compressed JPEG Images," which seem completely obscure, designed to baffle all but the specialist. But her work is significant enough to have been funded by the United States Air Force. To what end, she cannot say, because she does not know. "They could solve a lot of their problems, I guess," she says, with a wave of her hand.

I have never studied steganography—the technical term for concealing information in text or data—or steganalysis—the process of uncovering said hidden information. My experience with codes extends no further than I expect that of most people does—I once attempted to decipher the message included in a box of Cracker Jack. Steganalysis and steganography are both literally Greek—they derive from *steganos*, which means "covered, concealed, or protected," and *graphein*, "to write," and *analos*, "to investigate"—and, metaphorically speaking, Greek to me.

Fridrich is a celebrity of sorts, though, just not for her academic work. Before she immigrated to the United States and obtained her PhD, Fridrich was like any teenager in Eastern Europe, or anywhere else for that matter, in the early 1980s: obsessed with Rubik's Cube. Only, unlike virtually every other teenager, she made inroads in solving the puzzle. In 1982, she won the first Czech National Championship and represented her country at the inaugural World Championship. In the late 1990s, she uploaded her system to the Internet, where it was later found by Tyson and Toby, who taught a watered-down version to me.

The yearbook from CTY that I keep in my closet is by now a little dog-eared. But the signatures at the back are still clear: On the penultimate page, in orange marker, Toby scrawled, "hit Sub-20 Ian." He didn't even sign the message, or offer anything in the way of assistance. Mateus Moitinho de Almeida, on the other hand, was more specific: "Go to speedcubing.com, memorize the

Fridrich algorithms and hit sub-20!" The degree to which cub-ing dominated our thoughts is apparent in the other signatures. Siobhán, a camp mate from Ireland, appended the following postscript: "P.S. Put the Rubix [sic] Cube DOWN!"

This was the first time I heard of Fridrich. When I revis-ited the yearbook, after reconnecting with Toby, it struck me that I had never followed up on any of it. In fact, I had no idea who—or what—Fridrich was. The name of a computer? It had seemed like such a long shot that I would ever solve Rubik's Cube in under twenty seconds that I had never bothered to visit the website Mateus mentioned. It had the algorithms, explaining how to solve Rubik's Cube one layer at a time, but no mention of Fridrich.

I later learned that this is because Fridrich's method was in-dependently developed by a number of people in Europe. Ron van Bruchem, who created speedcubing.com in 2000, prefers the term CFOP—not out of any animosity toward Fridrich, but be-cause he feels it proper to recognize that the method had multiple contributors. Fridrich, for her part, doesn't dispute this. In fact, she has been open about the fact that she learned many things from other cubers, including the first Dutch champion, Guus Razoux Schultz.

Fortunately, Fridrich had a website of her own, hosted by the University of Binghamton. Visiting it felt like stepping into the past—the 1990s, to be exact, which is when Fridrich built it. In fact, it's one of the oldest sites devoted to Rubik's Cube on the Internet; one of the few entities that predates it is cubelovers, one of the earliest mailing lists, maintained by the Massachusetts Institute of Technology, which dates to 1980.

The site is fronted by a home page that's really a page—like a collage with different titles pasted on, images bumping up against one another in the clunky style of early HTML. It estab-lishes right away who Fridrich is—a distinguished professor in the school's department of electrical and computer engineering.

There is a picture of her in the upper-right-hand corner: a woman with cornflower-blue eyes and chestnut hair.

At the bottom of the web page is a GIF of an electric-blue mouse, its eyes bugging out and tongue contorting in horror at the sight to its left: Rubik's Cube. Like Jerry, fleeing Tom Cat, the mouse begins to run to its right, its legs churning as if wheels stuck in the mud. But, of course, it's a GIF: the mouse never gets away. "If you want to learn how to solve Rubik's Cube in 17 seconds," the caption reads, "click it!"

In person, Fridrich is tall, with slightly accented English. She laughs often, and enjoys telling stories. Her office, on the top floor of Binghamton's engineering school, a slate glass building overlooking the Susquehanna River, has one square window, which faces west. She chose the office, she told me, because the sunset reminds her of the Southwest—her favorite place in the United States. On her desk, next to her computer, a small clay model of a Jeep runs over a hunk of rocky terrain—a sculpture made by her daughter.

Even though Fridrich has left the Cube behind—she no longer participates in competitions, or updates her website—it has followed her to Binghamton. Across the hall, one of her former rivals, Miroslav Goljan, another Czech expat, works in her research group. On her bookshelf, a friend spelled out Fridrich's name in Rubik's Cubes, the white and blue sides arranged to make the outlines of the letters. She normally keeps most of her Cube memorabilia at home, but when I visited her in 2013, she brought a selection to show me.

"Now, this is a precious thing," she said. Fridrich withdrew a careworn notebook from her bag. It appeared once to have been olive green but had since faded to a dull gray. On the cover, where she might have signed her name, Fridrich had instead long ago doodled the outline of a Rubik's Cube in red ink. She riffled through the pages with a smile on her face. Inside, the notebook contained leaves of graph paper, covered with spidery diagrams in blue ink. "I should digitize it," she said.

The notebook contained the sum total of Fridrich's knowledge about Rubik's Cube. On her desk, Fridrich had arrayed many things—the medal she was awarded at the first World Championship, a weighty pendant in the shape of a Cube; a photograph of Ernő Rubik, signed in blue ink by the man himself; her trophy from the first revival of the World Championship, in 2003, where she took second place; newspaper clippings, in Czech and English, testifying to her accomplishments, including a write-up in the *New York Times*; not to mention a letter from Thomas Libous, a local state senator, who was later found guilty of lying to the FBI in a corruption probe—but Fridrich held the notebook in highest esteem.

Growing up in Czechoslovakia, like so many youths in Eastern Europe, Fridrich tried her hand at chess. She had no interest in it. If she made a move, she was immediately criticized. She lacked formal knowledge and had no way to discover it for herself. "I don't think I would be cubing, really, if there was already a system in place and everything lined up for me," she said. "There was no one who would say, 'Hey, I have the best system. Why don't you learn this?' . . . Because there was this unknown element. That's for me."

Fridrich was first exposed to Rubik's Cube thanks to her precocity for mathematics. In 1981, she attended a symposium for young mathematicians from across Czechoslovakia. She was sixteen years old. The brightest star was not any one of the professors who'd come for the occasion, but Rubik's Cube, which one fellow attendee had brought along. "I got my share, you know, like, for a couple of minutes," Fridrich recalled. "And I . . . I loved it.

"I mean, it's just so simple, you know," she added. "It doesn't need any manual or explanation, you just bring the Cube, turn the face, and everybody knows what the task is, and you kind of immediately realize how difficult it is to put it back together." For

Fridrich, it was nearly as difficult to get ahold of Rubik's Cube herself. "Even though you could get it in Austria, Germany—West Germany, I should say," she said, it was impossible to purchase in the Eastern Bloc. "The way people would get Cubes, in 1981, in the spring, they would go to Hungary, and buy it in Hungary."

Fridrich purchased her first Rubik's Cube from a vendor on the street, in Budapest, as if it were a form of contraband. The puzzle came in a little brown lunch bag, like a bottle of alcohol. The price, in her memory, was not a princely sum, but, for Fridrich, hardly insignificant. "I was willing to pay just about anything," she said.

In those days, Fridrich lived in Ostrava, a large industrial city about 250 miles by train from Prague. It lies in the northeast of the country, by the Polish border. When she was young, she showed promise as a long jumper. She toyed with the idea of pursuing it professionally, but her health was poor; she often suffered from strep throat. Then she dreamed of becoming an astronomer, an avocation her father deemed too impractical. "We have two observatories," she recalls him saying. "How many astronomers do we need?"

But astronomy led her to math. "I had to learn how to use math," she said, "and it showed me how powerful it is." When she wanted to see Venus in the daylight, for instance, she had to compute when the planet would travel through the local meridian. Once, she decided to calculate how faint a star her telescope could detect. The formula required a mathematical operation that she didn't yet understand. When she asked her teacher at school to explain it to her, Fridrich came away marveling that pushing numbers around could explain the universe. "Math is power," her teacher said.

To solve Rubik's Cube, you could twist it at random until all of the pieces fell into place. Unfortunately, there is not enough time for such a strategy to succeed. Performing one twist every second, it would take more than one trillion years to cycle through every permutation of Rubik's Cube—much longer than the universe is thought to have existed, which is about fourteen billion years. (This assumes, of course, that it would take the entire time to arrive at the solution.)

Fortunately, mathematics has a solution. Or, rather, a set of tools with which to create one: group theory. Whether or not you've ever heard the term before, there's a good chance you've encountered and perhaps even benefited from it. If you've ever used public key cryptography, the form of secure communication made famous in the wake of leaks by Edward Snowden, the former National Security Agency contractor, you've leveraged the ability of group theory to cut through massive chunks of data. The same goes for ordering packages online; it's trivial, as far as group theory goes, but identification numbers are often checked using simple group operations.

The first solution to Rubik's Cube of which Fridrich learned was based on group theory. This was before she had a Rubik's Cube of her own; she read about the solution in *Kvant*, or *Quantum*, a Russian magazine. The system used algorithms based on commutators, one of the key operations of group theory. Not to get too technical, but a commutator takes the form of the product of two operations and their inverses—in mathematical terms, where a is the first operation and b the second, $aba'b'$. Unless the operations are commutative—that is, unless they can be switched without changing the result, just as one times three can be rewritten as three times one—the commutator will reorder the group, but only slightly.

When it comes to Rubik's Cube, this means that commutators will gradually transform the puzzle, like a tractor tilling a field, slowly turning over the soil. By the time she actually had Rubik's Cube, Fridrich knew the solution backward and forward. She had been practicing it on bits of paper, drawing out the algorithms by hand.

Later that summer, she came across another solution in a different magazine, this one far more advanced. It divided Rubik's Cube into three layers, which were solved sequentially. The last layer was partitioned into four phases: orienting the edges, so the last layer assumed a cross shape, then repositioning the edges, so they matched the other sides of the Cube; and finally doing the same operations—orientation and permutation—to the four corners.

Fridrich started timing herself. Every so often, she would read items in the newspaper about people who had solved it faster than she had. She would see a note, for example, that someone in Canada had solved Rubik's Cube in thirty-eight seconds, when it still took her fifty. Finally, when she got down to thirty-eight seconds, she would read another notice, sharing that someone else had solved it in thirty-one seconds. "I was kind of trying to catch up with the world," Fridrich told me. She wasn't doing it alone: a friend of hers from high school, Luděk Marek, had joined her on the journey, and was just as obsessed with Rubik's Cube as she was.

In order to shave off extra seconds, they started to modify the system in the magazine. "Both of us noticed that it might be advantageous to exchange these four phases," Fridrich said. "And instead, first orient everything—make the layer yellow—and then permute everything. Because that was easy to recognize." Fridrich pulled out Rubik's Cube to demonstrate. The air filled with clicking as she twisted it until the top layer resembled the letter *T*, two bars of yellow squares intersecting one another. "We would flip these two edges," she said, and with a long, manicured finger, she indicated the negative space under the arms of the *T*, where the edges were stashed. At the moment, they were incorrectly oriented, their yellow faces pointing in the wrong direction. "Not only would these two edges get fixed," Fridrich said, "but the whole face would be solved." To demonstrate, she applied a sequence of twists to the puzzle. The yellow side gleamed like a fresh daisy.

What Fridrich had discovered was that certain moves could slice through the group of possible arrangements of Rubik's Cube like Alexander's sword through the Gordian knot. Each of these algorithms had the potential to reduce the moves for the last layer using the method in the magazine by 25 percent. "I said, 'Well, you know, what if we developed an algorithm for every one of those positions?'" Fridrich told me. The number of algorithms required was surprisingly few. "I calculated there were forty positions only," she said. "And I put them in my notebook."

The pages of Fridrich's notebook are yellowed, the thin blue lines faint, but the diagrams are no less clear. She showed me the pages she used to enumerate all the forty orientation cases. (Fridrich didn't count mirrors; some cases were essentially flipped across the middle of Rubik's Cube; for those cases, Fridrich simply flipped the algorithm.) "If you look at the top layer," she said, pointing to the diagrams, "you can easily recognize, like, this pattern, this pattern." Indeed, Fridrich noted several that resembled letters of the alphabet. Some also resembled shapes. Numbers thirty-eight and thirty-nine, for instance, had been described to me by Toby as "The Jesus Fish" and "The Manta Ray."

As far as I know, Fridrich hadn't heard these names. But the point was the same. After you solved the first two layers of Rubik's Cube, what remained fell into one of a relatively small number of easily identifiable patterns. If you could develop an algorithm to orient all of the remaining pieces at once, then you could drastically reduce the time it took to solve them.

Fridrich developed her algorithms by hand, along with her friend Marek. They removed pieces from the first layer and then put them back in using different moves. In essence, they were performing another operation from group theory: conjugation. In mathematical terms, conjugates take the form of an operation, a, followed by another, distinct operation, b, and close with the inverse of the first operation, a'. This sounds complicated but is actually quite simple. Every time you take something out of the fridge, you are performing conjugation writ large. The setup, a, is opening the door of the refrigerator. The second operation, b, is removing whatever it is you want, say, a sandwich. The closing move, a', is the reversal of the first operation, when you close the fridge door.

The purpose of conjugation is to alter something in a group while leaving the surrounding elements intact. In the metaphor of the fridge, conjugation allows you to remove what you want without destroying the fridge itself. Opening and closing the door is much safer to the integrity of the fridge than, say, going after it with a pickax. The same principle applies to Rubik's Cube. If you perform an operation, say, by twisting the right-hand face ninety degrees clockwise, and then twisting the upper face ninety degrees clockwise, but then reverse the first operation, by twisting the right-hand face ninety degrees counterclockwise, you will have affected only a limited portion of Rubik's Cube. Indeed, it will look as if you have removed two pieces from their normal resting place, not unlike having removed that sandwich.

In this way, by trial and error, Fridrich deduced algorithms to all of the cases in question. She wrote them in her notebook in a language she devised, in which different letters stood in for the faces of the Cube. It looked only slightly less foreboding, to me, than the notes she had written in Czech: $R^2\ L^2\ H^2\ \underline{L^2}\ \underline{R^2}\ P^2Z^2\ D^2$ $\underline{P^2}\ \underline{Z^2}\ R$, for example.

In part, this was because I was accustomed to the notation devised by David Singmaster, a mathematics professor in Britain, which is the standard for cubers worldwide. Singmaster used letters to symbolize each face. These letters apply with respect to the solver. R is the right-hand face, L the left-hand face, F the front face, B the back face, U the upper face, and D the down face. Each letter denotes one ninety-degree turn. The addition of the prime symbol (') reverses the turn. The number two doubles a turn. There are a handful of other symbols—x, y, and z for rotations; lowercase letters, for double-wide turns—but those are the basics.

That left only permutation, which involved rearranging the pieces of the last layer.

Otherwise, the last layer would have been one color on top—in this case, yellow, since Fridrich always started on its opposite, white—but variegated on the sides. There is a small chance, of course, that by orienting the last layer you will also permute it. But the odds of this happening are less than 2 percent—one in seventy-two. Fortunately, the last layer, once oriented, takes only twenty different forms, not including the solved state.

Fridrich devised an algorithm for each of these, as well. Then she started to practice them. One day, at the end of the summer, her aunt saw her twiddling with her Rubik's Cube. Why was she playing with it so much? her aunt wanted to know. Well, Fridrich said, she was sure there would be a championship at some point. "Everybody was laughing," Fridrich told me. "But I just knew, you know, that this was my destiny somehow."

In the spring of 1982, there was an announcement in *Mladý Svět*, a Czech publication: anyone wishing to enter the Czech National Championship had to submit his or her times solving all six sides of Rubik's Cube to qualify for the finals, to be held in Prague. This peculiar wording led to a man arriving who could solve only one side of Rubik's Cube at any given time. "The time he submitted was for that one layer!" Fridrich recalled.

Unsurprisingly, armed with their new system, she and Marek were both invited to Prague. The competition took place inside a TV studio. In Fridrich's memory, the contestants took the stage and placed their Cubes on light-sensitive diodes. When they lifted the puzzles, at the signal of the announcers, the timers began to tick. The timers stopped only when Rubik's Cube was laid precisely over the diode, preventing light from activating it.

Before the competition, her father had vowed that he would quit smoking if she won. The contestants were ranked by the best of three solves. In the second round, Fridrich notched a 23.55-second solve. After the competition ended, Fridrich, who had traveled by train and was staying with her aunt, asked if the producers would allow her to make a phone call. She got her father on the line. "You are stopping smoking!" she said.

"You really won?" he said. "I can't believe it." He started to cry.

In the weeks and months that followed, Fridrich became something of a local celebrity. Not long after the special aired, the letters started pouring in. They weren't even addressed right. Some had her name and that of the city, Ostrava. Others were simply addressed to "The Winner of the Rubik's Cube Championship." Somehow, the post office figured out where to send them. Most of the letters asked her to explain her system. "How come you're so fast?" Fridrich remembers them saying. That fall, *Mladý Svět* published the diagrams from her notebook. One day, on the train to her university—she commuted from Ostrava to Prague—she saw a young man attempting to solve Rubik's Cube. Fridrich asked him what method he used. The Fridrich method, he said. You know, the one from the magazine. Do you know all of the algorithms? she asked. He conceded that he did not. When she admonished him, saying he would never reach his full potential, he asked how she solved it. "I solve it the same way," she told him. "I'm Fridrich."

The World Championship took place in the summer of 1982, in Budapest. The venue was the Pesti Vigadó, a soaring, antique concert hall on the shore of the Danube. Fridrich arrived at the event with one of the fastest qualifying times. Only, as she tells it, the conditions were less than ideal. "I don't know of any other championship that was run officially where people would not be allowed to bring their own Cubes," she said. In those days, cubers lubricated their Cubes with anything they had at hand—some even went so far as to sand down the interior parts. In Budapest, however, the cubers would only be allowed to compete with out-of-the-box Cubes provided by the organizers. According to Fridrich, the puzzles had not been broken in.

"I have to say," she told me, "that the first World Championship was extremely unfair to many people." In addition to the stiff Cubes, some, she claims, were improperly stickered. "One had white against yellow, which is what I was used to. And the other standard was white against blue." Some competitors, she says, received Cubes to whose coloration they were unaccustomed. "It slows you down tremendously," she said.

In the event, Fridrich came in tenth, out of nineteen competitors. They were ranked by the best of three solves. Her mark, 29.11 seconds, was 6.16 seconds off that of the winner, Minh Thai, a Vietnamese refugee to the United States, who clocked a 22.95-second solve. Still, the competition was hardly a disappointing experience. Fridrich's travel to Budapest had been paid for by the organizers. It was the first time she had ever flown on a plane. Along with the other competitors, she was put up in the Budapest Hilton. It was a far cry from the *paneláks*, the concrete panel apartments that dotted Ostrava, in which she grew up. "I remember being, like, 'Wow!' You know. What a hotel, and so insanely expensive!"

When she returned home, Fridrich was a conquering hero. To finish high school, she had to take a state exam. At one point, when she was replying to a physics question, the examiners asked her to stop talking. They wanted to see her solve Rubik's Cube. "There are definite moments," Fridrich said, "in your life that you can point to and say, '*That* changed my life.'" For her, one of those moments is winning the National Rubik's Cube Championship.

The other came in 1995, when she was introduced to the man who advised the Air Force Laboratory in Rome, New York. Before the dissolution of the Soviet Union, Fridrich had worked for a mining institute in Ostrava, helping to model the effects of boring holes in rocks. The year of the Velvet Revolution, in 1989, when Czechoslovakia peacefully became the Czech Republic, many of her friends went into business. Fridrich wanted to remain in science. She immigrated to the United States, where she obtained her PhD at Binghamton University. But she had no idea how to get a job. Fortunately, the air force was looking for someone with a specialty in chaos theory and nonlinear dynamics.

In principle, any system could have taken root when Rubik's Cube began to revive. But—and it's debatable whether this is due to chance, or Fridrich's method being objectively better than any alternative—today you can go to any Rubik's Cube competition in the world, and virtually everyone will be using her techniques, even if they do not know her name. "I would compare it to a house," Fridrich told me, "where, you know, you lay out where the bedroom will be, where the garage will be, and the living room will be," but then the people who take up occupancy in the house move around the furniture.

In the years since she first put her system online—a development she expected would be of so little consequence that she did not include a hit counter to track visitors to the site—new algorithms have been developed. "They were no longer hand-designed," Fridrich said, "but computer-generated." This allowed them to be optimized for certain turning styles. "You know, I'm one of the old-schoolers," she told me. "I turn the cube by grabbing, by grabbing the sides. But the modern way of twisting is really finger pushing, by pushing the sides with your finger."

Fridrich laments that what began as a means to solve Rubik's Cube efficiently has become the only means of solving it. "Nowadays, there is *the* system." Fridrich wrinkled her nose. "They all look the same now. You no longer have the diversity that you saw in the first World Championship." She pointed out that only one of the top three finishers—Guus Razoux Schultz, of the Netherlands—solved Rubik's Cube layer by layer. The other two, including the winner, Minh Thai, unscrambled Rubik's Cube by solving all of the corners first, then turning their attention to the edges.

Still, Fridrich was impressed that her method had been taken so far. "I quickly realized that, you know, the youngsters are going to just run us over, you know, in a completely unbelievable way," she told me, with a grin. "I always thought that the limits of speedcubing were, like, at thirteen seconds." She pointed to Feliks Zemdegs, at the time the world record holder for an average of five solves, with a mark of 7.53 seconds. "That is absolutely amazing," Fridrich said. "I would never think that this is possible."

Earlier, I demonstrated a solve for Fridrich, showing her what I knew of her system. I still solved using the beginner's method—the watered-down version that I had learned at summer camp. (Toby and Tyson had developed the method together, the better to instruct novices.) Instead of solving the first two layers in two stages—the cross, and then pairing the corners and edges—I used three. First, I solved the cross, then I inserted the corners and edges—the rest of the first two layers—individually. My version of the last layer was a hodgepodge of algorithms, designed less to be efficient than to be memorable. Whereas Fridrich, sitting across her desk from me, could unscramble and solve the last layer with ease, I fumbled my way through only after many trials. For each phase—orientation and then permutation—I typically needed to repeat my simple algorithms several times to have the desired effect. "You are probably too old," Fridrich told me.

She stopped going to competitions when she realized that she didn't have a chance. "I may attend one of the World Championships just to spectate," she said. "I would be, what, hundredth in the world?" Actually—and I didn't tell her this—she would have barely cracked the top five thousand, which admittedly would still have placed her in the top quartile of cubers worldwide. "Who cares who is the hundredth in the world?" she said. Zemdegs, she pointed out, set his first records when he was just a teenager. "It's quite possible that the best age for cubing is shifting down now," she said. "Feliks is probably still lightning fast, even though he is now, what, seventeen, or something like that?"

YOU DESERVE TO WIN

You could hear the air conditioning, spilling from the vents. In a long room at the Riviera Hotel and Casino, in Las Vegas, littered with empty tables, Feliks Zemdegs and Mats Valk sat across from one another. "Do you want to race?" Valk asked.

"We'll race out there," Zemdegs said.

Zemdegs, a seventeen-year-old from Melbourne, had taken off his headphones to respond. Now he returned his attention to Rubik's Cube, which sat on the table in front of him. Like Valk, a seventeen-year-old from Amsterdam, he was waiting for his name to be called. The two of them had reached the finals of the 2013 World Rubik's Cube Championship and been sequestered in what passed for the greenroom. Most of the sixteen finalists had left already, in twos, to the stage, where they completed their solves like professional golfers teeing off, one after the other, alternating until their five solves had been attempted.

None of the cubers in the greenroom—Valk and Zemdegs were accompanied by Philipp Weyer, a baby-faced teenager from Germany, and Drew Brads, a precociously adult-looking thirteen-year-old from Ohio—had any idea how fast the cubers onstage had gone. This was by design. There was no scoreboard to check, no way to tell who was in the lead. "I think that guy's going to win," Valk said, pointing at Brads. The rest of them nervously laughed.

In any other sport, of course, winning would be everything. If you follow golf, you know exactly who is leading at all times. Every stroke, every shank, is tracked in real time. Every golfer knows where he or she stands, with the effect that every attempt becomes pregnant with meaning. The difference of one stroke can be the difference between first and second place.

While winning isn't everything in cubing, some competitiveness unavoidably enters the equation at the World Championship. "I got the last one," Zemdegs told me, before the finals of the 3x3 began. "So at least I won something." He had just captured the title in the 4x4, vanquishing Sebastian Weyer, Philipp's twin, and Valk, who came in second and third, respectively. He looked palpably relieved. Despite having entered the finals of the 5x5, a cubic puzzle with five cubies per edge, as the favorite—he held the world record—he had ceded his title to Kevin Hays, a towering American college student whom I'd met at the U.S. Nationals the year before. Hays had also won the 6x6 and 7x7, cementing his reputation as the master of the so-called "Big Cubes."

Now, Zemdegs, who had taken time off from high school to attend the competition, along with his mother, Rita, a dentist, looked demonstrably less relaxed. Wearing an orange hoodie and shorts, he tapped his feet, clad in flip-flops, on the floor. Valk, for his part, was almost goofy. Earlier, he had asked Zemdegs what he was listening to. "'Billie Jean,'" Zemdegs said, upon which Valk broke into a hoarse falsetto.

"'Billie Jean is not my lover!'"

Presently, seeing me watching him, Valk, who had a striped polo shirt with yellow sunglasses hanging from the collar, held out his arm, to see if his hand was shaking. When it appeared steady, he gave me a wink. He asked Zemdegs how he felt.

"Nervous," Zemdegs said.

"Really?" Valk replied.

Valk shrugged. "I feel pretty relaxed," he said, and returned to cubing.

Zemdegs and Valk had been left alone because they were the highest seeds. In competition, the highest-ranked cuber generally solves last, for the same reason that, in baseball, the home team bats second. It's not possible to know, unless you're calculating your average in your head, what times you need to defeat your opponent, but if you solve last, and get the times you want, you don't have to worry about anyone else following you.

Tyson Mao, who was organizing the World Championship— his last competition before, at the age of thirty, he would retire from cubing, to spend more time with his job and fiancée—had arranged the finals like a cage match. Each contestant entered to music of his choice. Breandan Vallance, the 2009 world champion, a young man from Scotland, strutted across the stage to the bombastic saxophone solo from "Thrift Shop," the hit by Macklemore, wearing a pair of mirrored aviator shades. Seung Beom Cho, a diminutive preteen from South Korea, bounced around, his bowl cut flopping, to the beat of Psy's "Gangam Style," the viral YouTube video. In each case, there was a funny disjoint between the raucous atmosphere conjured by the music and the hushed activity that ensued. One contestant, Rowe Hessler, a grizzled veteran, in his early twenties, who had stepped outside for a smoke break, to calm his nerves, entered to cheers of "Rowe! Rowe! Rowe!"

The audience numbered in the hundreds. During the solves, the silence was so absolute that you could hear the clicks of a single Rubik's Cube from anywhere in the room. There weren't enough seats to get a view, so members of the audience had gathered on tables and chairs, straining to get a look at the stage. When each solve was over, the silence dissolved into a roar of applause. The faster the solve, the louder the response. With each faster solve—the contestants sped up as the seeds got higher— the cheers grew in kind, like the response to body blows ceding ground to the cheering for an upper cut.

In the greenroom, of course, none of this penetrated. The door was sealed. The only way to find out what had happened was to wait. This was the flip side of the system: going last meant waiting longer than anybody. Over the past three days, Valk and Zemdegs had been chasing one another, as they had in the world rankings all year. In March, Valk had broken the world record for a single solve of Rubik's Cube, lowering it to 5.55 seconds, 0.11 seconds faster than the mark set by Zemdegs the year before, 5.66 seconds. It marked the first time Zemdegs had lost the record since he first broke it, in 2010, at the tender age of thirteen.

Previously, the record had been held by Erik Akkersdijk, one of Valk's compatriots, who, with a lucky solve—he got to skip half of the last layer—cut nearly two seconds off what had been the previous best, 8.72 seconds, lowering the record to 7.08 seconds. The mark stood for nearly two and a half years. It wasn't a crime to be lucky, Akkersdijk pointed out.

Still, it seemed hardly fair to have such a substantial lead on the competition. It wasn't until 2009, over a year later, that anyone else broke eight seconds. Even then, it was only just. Two cubers, one Thai, the other Polish, clocked solves in the high seven-second range.

Then Zemdegs came along.

In the spring of 2008, Zemdegs was twelve years old. He lived with his parents and younger brother in a suburb of Melbourne. In many ways, he was like any child of his generation. He spent a lot of time on the Internet, which is how he came across the video that would change his life. It appeared on the home page of YouTube. The video had been uploaded the year before by Dan Brown, a teenager in Nebraska, who had made it using a digital camera and computer in his bedroom. After introducing himself by way of "Hey world!" Brown explains, "I'm here to teach you how to solve one of society's modern-day mysteries: Ernő Rubik's Magic Puzzle Cube." The video, which has since been viewed nearly thirty million times, had just been voted the best instructional clip at the 2007 YouTube Awards, hence its appearance on the site's front page.

When Zemdegs followed the video on his own, later that afternoon, after walking ten minutes down the street to his local toy store and returning with a Rubik's Cube, you would never have guessed that he would be anything but perfectly average. He messed up several times, and had to start the video over from the beginning. Whereas most people might put Rubik's Cube down after the first solve and never pick it up again, Zemdegs immediately began to time himself. The following weekend, at a shopping mall, he was in the range of five minutes. By the end of the weekend, he had lowered that to three minutes.

Zemdegs knew that he could do better, not because he felt he had any special talent for it, but because he had seen videos of people doing so online. He got down to about fifty seconds using the method in Dan Brown's video. Then he started learning CFOP, the same method he had seen cubers like Erik Akkersdijk use, with all its strange acronyms, like OLL, or orientation of the last layer, and PLL, or permutation of the last layer. Zemdegs practiced and practiced and practiced, taking his Rubik's Cube to school, the supermarket, to visit his grandmother. Sometimes, his parents had to ask him to stop—he would solve at the dinner table or while they were trying to speak with him.

When he posted his first video, in June, it seemed like a miracle had taken place. "I am SO jealous," wrote one cuber online. In the space of a month, Zemdegs had dropped nearly fifteen seconds off his time. In the video, he solved Rubik's Cube five times, and averaged 18.46 seconds per solve, a reduction of nearly 50 percent compared to a month before. "Yeah, a lot of people don't believe me," Zemdegs replied. "But this video proves otherwise." Like plenty of miracles, it was too good to be true. In a subsequent post, the following day, Zemdegs confessed that he had cheated in the video, starting the timer after he had already solved the cross, the first step, saving him a couple of seconds. "Yeah, it's pretty obvious," wrote Joey Gouly, a British cuber whom he would later befriend. "1/5 for effort though."

Zemdegs's miniscandal obscured remarkable progress. When he posted his first legitimate video, a few weeks later, it was apparent his speed was no fluke. Zemdegs averaged 22.95 seconds. In those days, the World Cube Association had yet to expand to Australia. The first time Zemdegs attended a competition wasn't until the following year, in New Zealand. With his first official solve, he launched himself into the top one hundred cubers of all time, recording a 10.71-second solve. By the end of the competition, he had not only set the national record for an average of five solves, at 12.55 seconds, but lowered his best single to 10.05 seconds.

The following year, he set his first world record. Not even Akkersdijk had managed to achieve cubing's holy grail: a sub-10-second average of five solves. In the finals of his second competition, at the Old Melbourne Gaol, a once-notorious prison that is now part of the Royal Melbourne Institute of Technology, Zemdegs didn't break the world record for an average of five solves—10.07 seconds—he destroyed it, lowering the mark to 9.21 seconds. Afterward, a cuber in Romania altered an image of Usain Bolt and posted it online. It featured Zemdegs, grinning, a Rubik's Cube in hand, next to Bolt, making his famous pose, in front of the clock recording his world record in the hundred-meter dash, 9.59 seconds. "World's Fastest Man," the caption read. The Romanian cuber had crossed out Bolt with a big red X.

*   *   *

Every so often, a natural comes along. Someone for whom difficult things seem easy. When he was four, the parents of the violin-
ist Joshua Bell noticed him plucking melodies on rubber bands he
had stretched between the knobs of a dresser. Despite the fact that
he once managed to perform incognito in the Washington, D.C.,
metro, Bell is one of the world's foremost violinists. He has released dozens of CDs, acquired a Stradivarius, and been awarded
a Grammy. To outsiders, this sort of genius can be perplexing,
because it admits little evidence of having been developed: in fact,
its seeming lack of artifice is its defining feature.

Of course, if you actually ask these people how they do what
they do, most of them deny that talent has much, if anything,
to do with it. They talk about dedication, sacrifice, about all the
hours they devoted to honing their skills. "I've missed more than
nine thousand shots in my career," Michael Jordan famously said.
"I've lost almost three hundred games." But no one remembers
the missed shots, the defeats. What sticks in the mind are the
ineffable moments when Jordan put gravity on notice, bending
the laws of physics en route to the basket.

Unlike Zemdegs, who proceeded to break virtually every record in cubing, as if the marks were little more than stepping-
stones on the way to the ultimate limit of solving Rubik's Cube,
wherever that lay, Valk was workmanlike as he rose in the rankings. By the time Zemdegs participated in his first competition
in July 2009, Valk had already attended more than a dozen,
watching his best average fall from one minute 13.49 seconds,
to eleven seconds and change. It would take him sixteen more
competitions—and nearly two years—to get under ten seconds
himself.

Whereas Zemdegs proceeded by leaps and bounds—in 2010,
he cut the world record for an average of five solves from 9.21 to
7.91 seconds—Valk climbed upward a few tenths or even hun-

dredths of a second at a time. In 2011, at his first World Championship, Zemdegs suffered his first defeat. In the finals, he choked, settling for bronze. The winner, Michał Pleskowicz, a shaggy-haired teenager from Poland, solved out of his mind—his average, 8.65 seconds, was a personal best and broke the national record he had set earlier in the competition, all under the glare of the spotlights. (The competition took place in Bangkok, and was televised.) Still, in the semifinals, Zemdegs had recorded a 7.78-second average, the second fastest of all time. He had finally met his nemesis: himself.

Valk, meanwhile, continued to climb the rankings. By 2012, less than a year out from the next World Championship—the competition is biennial—Valk had nearly caught up with Zemdegs. His best average, 7.66 seconds, was just behind the Australian's world record, 7.53 seconds. Then, just months before the competition, Valk broke the world record for a single solve. Much the same way fans of the Twilight series vied for Bella to fall in love with either Edward or Jacob, cubers soon fell into two camps: Team Mats and Team Feliks.

In the way of athletes who know their sport isn't entirely serious, their fans are somewhat partisan. "Mats Valk is better!" I heard someone shout after one of the early heats, when Zemdegs scored a good result. The crowd surged whenever either of them took the stage, clumping so densely that, smartphones and tablets held aloft, it resembled a forest, its leaves the brightly glowing screens. The first time I tried to talk to Zemdegs, I was waylaid by a small girl from Brazil, wearing her long blond hair down and a yellow shirt with a silhouette of Michael Jackson. Like a teenybopper approaching one of her favorite heartthrobs, she tentatively stood by while Zemdegs signed her Rubik's Cube. Shortly thereafter, her father held the puzzle against a tablecloth and photographed it.

* * *

"If you get second," Valk asked, in the greenroom, "would you be mad?"

"No," said Zemdegs.

"Just wondering."

When Zemdegs asked the same question, he didn't get a response; Valk had gone back to solving. The door opened. Chris Krueger entered. "All right, guys," Krueger said, enthusiastically. "Let's go!"

Zemdegs let out a deep breath as he hoisted his backpack, which held all of his puzzles for the competition, bulging at odd angles, and put it on. "We can do this," Valk said. Then he paused. "No, you can do this," he said, turning to Zemdegs. "Seriously, you deserve to win."

If Dan Gosbee had had his way, such good sportsmanship would not exist. Or, rather, it would have no place at such an event as the World Rubik's Cube Championship. "The guy that's got the world record now," he told me, "I'd love to scramble his Cube and just give it to him and see if he can get under ten seconds. No fucking way can he do it. 'Cause I'll freak him out."

In the early 2000s, cubing was more or less just another subterranean community on the Internet. Cubers themselves were like prairie dogs poking their heads out of the ground, Cubes in hand, waiting to see if anyone else like them existed. Gosbee was the one to bring people together. "There must have been hundreds of them," Gosbee said, with characteristic pomp.

In his telling, the community wanted to revive the World Championship, but didn't have the chutzpah to get it done. "They weren't at the level where they could get it into the mainstream," he told me. "I was the guy that took it to the next level." The next level meant coverage in media outlets around the globe, TV appearances, sponsorships, and all the fanfare of having a World Championship of solving the world's most famous puzzle.

Gosbee arrived on the second day of the 2013 World Championship shortly before noon. He wore leather driving gloves and had black aviator sunglasses hanging from the neck of his T-shirt, a navy number bearing the logo of the Las Vegas Police Department. On closer inspection it turned out to be merchandise from the TV show *CSI*. He had donned a pair of white sneakers with black tube socks and was carrying a plastic grocery bag. "This is overwhelming," he said.

I had been forewarned of Gosbee's arrival by Ron van Bruchem, who waved me over when I was leaving the competition hall for lunch, shortly before my heat in the first round of the 3x3. The night before, he told me to be on the lookout for Gosbee, but cautioned me. He was a "weird guy," van Bruchem said, in a tone that was more amused than condescending. "Believe, like, half of what he says."

Now, standing by the entrance to the competition hall, van Bruchem and Gosbee were comparing bald spots. In many ways, it appeared to be exactly the sort of interaction the World Championship is designed to facilitate—bringing together cubers from around the globe. Only, there was a touch of sadness in Gosbee's eyes. Several times, he had to catch his breath. "Just being here," he said, "it's just . . . dammit."

He lived nearby, he said, in Henderson, Nevada, now that he was retired—his retirement being, as he put it, "the best thing I ever did"—but it had taken him, in his estimation, somewhere between four and eight hours to get to the Riviera. It was simply too emotionally draining. Gosbee tried to put on a brave face. "The wife kicked me out of the house so I could have some fun," he said. Still, he was evidently nursing a deep hurt. "Whatever the bad things were," van Bruchem said, "they have all been forgotten. All that's remembered are the good things." Gosbee didn't seem so sure.

For the next hour or so, in the coffee shop in the Riviera's lobby, Gosbee talked about what drove him away from cubing, and what had, at least for today, brought him back. I'd been told by van Bruchem, among others, that Gosbee was a crucial figure in the Cube's rebirth, but that he had been largely forgotten. In part, this was because Gosbee had taken himself out of the conversation. "I . . . I had a bad experience with this," he told me. "I walked away from it, just because of words." Gosbee's voice is slightly muffled, partly because of his accent—he was raised in Nova Scotia, and has a twang—and perhaps also because his mustache obstructs the words on their way out of his mouth. "It just got to a point where it hurt so much that I had to walk away from it, you know?"

Many cubers acknowledge that, without Gosbee, cubing very well might not have been revived, at the start of the millennium, or, at the very least, would have come back on a much smaller scale. "It looked like organizing a championship is a major undertaking," Jessica Fridrich, who attended the 2003 World Championship, told me. "I actually praised him a lot," she added. "I think he did a lot by organizing the first one."

In the midst of the SARS epidemic, not long after a power outage blackened much of downtown Toronto, where the competition took place, Gosbee managed to bring together nearly one hundred cubers from more than a dozen countries. "It was a huge success," van Bruchem told me, "because there were many press releases and so on and so on." There were articles in the *New York Times*, the *Boston Globe*, and a number of international papers, including the *Canberra Times*, which profiled Jasmine Lee, a young woman from Australia. "It was the hardest thing I ever did," Gosbee told me, several times.

The challenges were manifold. Not only did Gosbee have to secure permission to host the competition—"I sold it to them in a minute," he said, of his first meeting with Seven Towns, at the Macy's flagship store in Manhattan, not long after the turn of the millennium, during what he remembered as a snowstorm—but he also had to secure the funding. The final price tag for the competition was around $50,000. "The challenge was the three thousand frickin' e-mails I got from everybody's mother," he said.

This is not to say the competition went off without a hitch. As I mentioned earlier, it didn't. "It just blew up, man," Gosbee said. "I had a hundred-some people," he added, by way of explanation, "and three people scrambling the Cubes. Look at them now! They got five hundred frickin' people scrambling." This wasn't entirely accurate, but Gosbee made his point. With no prior experience, he made some logistical oversights. "The organization was really bad," van Bruchem told me. "We had no regulations."

Gosbee talked about the event as if it were a leviathan that had gotten out of his control. "It was the most exhausting thing I did in my life," he said. "It just emotionally drained me." In addition to what he describes as sniping afterward, mostly online, criticizing his way of running things, what bothered him was his relationship, or lack thereof, with Tyson Mao, when Mao cofounded the World Cube Association, the following year, with van Bruchem. Gosbee traveled to California to attend the 2004 U.S. National Championship, which Mao organized at the California Institute of Technology, where he was then a student. "When I got there," Gosbee said, "I got the sense of not being wanted.

"I wanted to smack him," Gosbee went on. "I really wanted to smack him."

What truly happened is a matter of he said, he said. "It's all me and Ron [van Bruchem] now, 'cause Seven Towns listens to us," Gosbee recalls Mao saying. "It was the comment that made me leave the Cube world," Gosbee said. "I got it over the edge and now, you know, it's Ron and Tyson and I am shit." That's how he felt, anyway. "I got to tell you something," Gosbee added, conspiratorially. "Ron was seconds away from Seven Towns telling him to leave, because of the way he was acting." It's true that, even at the best of times, Mao can be somewhat prickly, especially when it comes to delegating authority. "He hates it when people say, 'I'm older, so I have more life experience,' " van Bruchem told me.

Mao, for his part, says Gosbee was less than helpful. "I was, like, 'Hey, I'm a nineteen-year-old college student.'" He asked Gosbee for guidance. As he tells it, he received nothing but a pile of scrambles. When Mao asked what the scrambles were for, he says Gosbee told him they were extra difficult. They were designed to make it harder to build the cross, the first step in CFOP. To Mao, this didn't make any sense—he could easily generate scrambles on his own. "It became clear to me that he didn't know what he was talking about," Mao said. Eventually, he says, he started ignoring Gosbee—apparently, that much they agree on.

"I've got my regrets," Gosbee said. "But that's fine. You live with it." (In characteristic fashion, he did later admit, in a complete about-face, that he admires Tyson and thinks he deserves a lot of credit. "It wouldn't have gone this far," he said. "No way, no frickin' way.")

Still, would cubing be the same without Gosbee? When he left the community, Gosbee took with him an attitude that would have changed the nature of cubing. "Competition is about pressure," he told me. "It's just my old-school mentality, if that's what you want to call it."

In 1980, Gosbee says, he won the Canadian Pac-Man Championship. "The finals was me and this nine-year-old Chinese kid," he said. The kid might have had a chance, but Gosbee, who was about sixteen at the time, didn't let him. In his words, he played with the kid's head. "And it freaked him out," he said. "'Cause it was head-to-head competition. You fucked up the other—your competitor. Do that with a Cube. And you won't be getting six seconds on a solve. Impossible."

In Gosbee's eyes, cubing has descended to the level of professional skateboarding. Everyone, as he sees it, does the same thing and is friendly outside competition. The roots of cubing, he maintains, are the values he espouses. In the 1980s, he pointed out, it wasn't uncommon for cubers to compete at the same time, rather than staggered, as they are now. (Indeed, the first U.S. National Championship, which was featured on *That's Incredible!* and watched by millions of people on television, involved half a dozen contestants racing not only the clock but one another.) "Now," Gosbee said, "it's like everybody's hiding behind a box, you know? Sitting down, nice and comfortable, there's no pressure."

"Feliks cannot win this," I heard a cuber near me say. "It's too much for him." We were standing on tables in the Riviera's ballroom, trying desperately to get a glimpse of the action onstage. Valk and Zemdegs had entered to the biggest cheers yet, the enclosed space swelling with the sound.

Like the finalists who preceded them, Valk and Zemdegs each walked out to their own entrance music. Wearing his yellow sunglasses, Valk strode onto the stage, his long arms swinging, to something that sounded like Europop, and shook hands with the judge. Valk plays soccer—or football, rather—his lanky frame perfectly suited to his role as keeper, and he brought to mind a professional warming up for a match, buds dangling from his ears despite the earsplitting noise around him.

The emcee, Kian Barry, a history teacher from New Jersey with a Rutgers baseball cap, introduced Zemdegs by way of anecdote. Apparently, Zemdegs owned a budgerigar, or budgie, as they call parakeets down under, and he cubed so much in its presence that it started mimicking the sound of his Rubik's Cube. Zemdegs grinned, abashed.

"Watch this shit," said Marcin Zalewski. He wasn't speaking to me in particular, but I happened to be standing near the Polish contingent. They all had matching jerseys—white, with red lettering—sporting the Polish crest, a fearsome eagle spreading its wings and bearing its talons, over their hearts. Poland is notorious for its devotion to cubing—with the highest number of cubers per capita, it is sometimes referred to as "Proland."

I had met Zalewski earlier, when I sat down with him; Michał Pleskowicz, the defending world champion; and Michał Halczuk, another Polish cuber. When I asked them what they hoped to accomplish, they all gave different answers. Zalewski, who held the world record for solving Rubik's Cube blindfolded, in 23.80 seconds, said he hoped to win that event. Halczuk, who had extremely shaky hands, rendering his script nearly illegible—a requirement, his friends joked, since he was in medical school— said he wanted to win 7x7. (He failed, thanks to one bad solve, when his puzzle locked up, and he couldn't twist it.) For his part, Pleskowicz, who wore the relaxed attitude befitting the defending world champion, viewed the competition as a lottery. "There's always one person who's always just, like, 'Oh, whatever, I don't care,'" he said, "and that's the person who wins."

Valk opened with an 8.81. The crowd cheered, but he didn't react. Valk solves Rubik's Cube using CFOP, but with a unique twist. Rather than orient the last layer after the first two layers are solved, he blends the two phases together. When he finishes the first two layers, he does so in such a way that he will induce a skip. When you watch him solve, the result is like a magic trick. The Cube looks mostly scrambled, with only part of the first two layers solved, and then, presto, every step is complete but the permutation of the last layer. After rolling up the sleeves of his orange hoodie, and taking a deep breath, Zemdegs replied with an 8.39-second solve.

It was hard to escape the feeling that something momentous was taking place. The two traded solves like heavyweights going the distance. After a slower solve, a 9.52, during which he appeared to hesitate, unsure, for a split second, where to proceed next, Valk started to speed up. He followed the same routine before every solve, removing his earbuds, which are prohibited during solves, placing his hands on his knees, bowing his head, and taking a deep breath, eyes closed. Zemdegs, by contrast, sped up, tallying a 7.95 with his second solve, but then appeared to slow down. With his third solve, Valk notched the fastest of the finals, and one of the fastest in the competition, 7.61 seconds. Even Zemdegs applauded. With his third solve, the Australian clocked 8.21 seconds.

In some ways, the two resembled robots, designed to unscramble Rubik's Cube with maximum efficiency. Only later on, watching the solves in slow motion, could I detect hesitation in their movements. Zemdegs and Valk's fingers appeared so controlled, so accurate, that they might as well have been bionic. Zemdegs especially solves with notably erect posture, like an automaton. (Cubers have joked, online, that his secret is "Str8baq," the Internet nickname for his ramrod bearing.)

"I don't know how he does it with all those cameras in his face," Cameron Brown said. Like the year before, at the U.S. National Championship, Brown was selling Rubik's Cubes and other puzzles at the competition. His business, speedcubeshop.com, had, in fact, sponsored a cash prize for the winner of the main event. He had entered the competition, but his prospects had been dulled when he cut his finger while repairing his car. Most of the time, he was unable to watch the stage, on account of having to run the store, which had set up shop in the booth where Roller Derby tickets were normally sold, down the hallway.

Still, he didn't much mind. "[Zemdegs] looks like a robot," Brown told me. "I almost don't really care that I missed him solving," he added, "because it looks like I'm watching him on YouTube."

Having talked to Zemdegs, I knew this wasn't the case. "I get nervous in events I care about," Zemdegs told me. I tried to relay this to Brown, but he didn't seem to hear me.

With his fourth and penultimate solve, Valk achieved his fastest time yet. 7.31 seconds. The roars were deafening. It was hard to say what the consequence was as there was no leader board, but if he wanted to win, Zemdegs clearly had his work cut out for him. Since Valk had already notched one seven-second solve, his second guaranteed that at least one of them would be counted toward his final average. Before Valk's solve, Rowe Hessler, the American veteran, as if anticipating a killer blow, whistled the theme song from *The Good, the Bad and the Ugly*, which carried all the way to the stage.

Zemdegs answered with a 7.36-second solve, his fingers moving so fast that it sounded as if someone were firing a machine gun nearby. Zemdegs slapped his hands together. Meanwhile, the crowd exploded. It was later calculated that Zemdegs had had to notch an 8.2-second solve or better to stay in the hunt. Now it all came down to one final solve.

"It's kind of freaky," said Jeannine Michaelsen, a German TV presenter. She was filming a segment for *SportXtreme*, a news-magazine produced by ZDF, one of the country's largest public TV stations. I met her the day before, during the 3x3 heats. She and her crew—a producer, in a black velvet jacket, distressed jeans, and boots; a cameraman, who, with his paunch and balding hair, resembled nothing so much as a technically adept friar; and the sound guy, the Laurel to the cameraman's Hardy—were ubiquitous, nabbing cubers for interviews and peering over their shoulders onstage.

The idea, she said, was to cover a mental sport. "The first time I got in touch with people who can do it really good, kind of professionally, I was talking to them and they were solving them while they were talking to me. And I was so confused, because I thought, 'They cannot be listening to what I say when they parallel try to solve a Cube.'"

Michaelsen wore a peach blouse and a look of total confusion.

"Most of the sports we do," she said, "they risk their lives, they go BASE jumping, or big-wave surfing, and they experience, like, tons of things around them, and nature and they're outside, and they're forced to push themselves further and further." When I asked her how cubing differed from those sports, she said it was like comparing a black picture to a white one. "It's so reduced here and they only focus on this little Cube," she said. "And everything else doesn't seem to exist."

Arms akimbo, she turned to face the stage. "It's unbelievable," she said. "You cannot imagine how people can think so fast." She added, of the sports she typically covers, "We all think, like, 'Oh, this looks amazing,' but, of course, we know they can do it.

"But *this*? If you see this in person, it's like, 'How the fuck do you do that?'"

On his final solve, Valk sped toward the last layer, his rotations of the Cube impossibly coordinated. The last layer itself vanished only to reappear moments later completely solved. Video analysis later showed that Valk had achieved a top speed in excess of ten turns per second. For a moment, all was euphoria. The crowd banged on tables.

7.76 seconds.

Then Valk put his head in his hands and grimaced. Silence fell. The judge leaned toward Valk's Rubik's Cube, which looked oddly distended. The emcee rushed over. Together, they inspected his puzzle, their faces almost touching.

"Mats Valk, with a 9.76 second solve," Barry, the emcee announced. What had gone wrong?

After Zemdegs's final solve—his slowest of the round, 9.12 seconds—the room descended into chaos. "Who won?" I overheard one cuber ask another. "Sebastian," the other replied. "Really?" asked the first. "No," the second replied. "I have no idea."

According to Article 10f of the Regulations of the World Cube

Association, Rubik's Cube is considered unsolved if any one of its faces is askew by forty-five degrees or more. What the judge and the emcee were doing, in that awful moment, when Valk looked crestfallen, was to determine whether his puzzle had violated this rule.

With his final move, Valk had tried to realign the last layer, but the turn was never completed. The consequence for violating this provision of the rules is a two-second penalty, to be added to the final time at the end of the solve.

After leaving the stage, Zemdegs disappeared, buried in the towering mass of Marcin Zalewski, the Polish cuber, who leaned in to give him a hug. "Don't cry, don't cry," Zalewski said. At first, it wasn't apparent why Zemdegs was crying. "You've got to go to the next World Championship," I overheard his mother, Rita, shouting into her cell phone. She was presumably speaking to his father, David. "Not me—you!"

Before the results were announced, Valk hung back, signing a few autographs. He looked disappointed, but stoic—evidently, word of the result had circulated. He hadn't won. His final average, bumped up by the penalty, was 8.65 seconds, which would have tied for first place at the prior World Championship. "But that plus two," Zemdegs said, wiping tears from his eyes. "With that last result, you would have won anyway," someone told him.

This wasn't strictly true. The penalty had thrown out one of Valk's fastest solves, which would have counted toward his average. The final result was Zemdegs, 8.18 seconds, Valk, 8.65 seconds (8.06 without the penalty), and Sebastian Weyer, 8.86 seconds. Before long, in a display that would have irritated Gosbee, who didn't appear to have stuck around for the finals, Valk and Zemdegs were palling around. They stood in front of a scrim dotted with Rubik's Cubes furnished by Seven Towns and posed for photographs.

One by one, all the finalists were called to the stage. Tyson Mao had elected to allot the purse, which totaled several thousand dollars, entirely in two-dollar bills. Within a few minutes, Zemdegs was holding a bushel of cash that suggested he had just held up the casino. "Mmm," said Michał Halczuk, one of the Polish cubers, as he rubbed his sheaf of bills against his nose. "Smells like America."

CUBER'S THUMB

Chances are you saw it. So did anyone who googled anything on May 19, 2014. To commemorate the fortieth anniversary of Rubik's Cube, Google changed its doodle—the illustration on the company home page—to Rubik's Cube. If you clicked the icon, you could manipulate the puzzle, using either your mouse or the keyboard to attempt to solve it.

That day, I happened to be visiting the Liberty Science Center, in Jersey City, New Jersey, which was the first stop for *Beyond Rubik's Cube*, a traveling exhibition the museum designed in collaboration with Ernő Rubik himself and Google. It featured a number of objects from the puzzle's past, including early prototypes of Rubik's Cube, some of them made of wood, metal, and what appeared to be fishing line; as well as a robot that could solve Rubik's Cube, consisting of a metallic arm that might have been repurposed from a car assembly plant; not to mention several modern takeoffs on the classic puzzle, including the Haikube, whose sides bore words that could be rearranged into different poems, and the Masterpiece Cube, a bejeweled version encrusted with several million dollars' worth of precious stones.

My interest in the Cube was no longer topical. I wasn't just trying to write an article. I was getting hooked. The exhibit offered an opportunity to feed my growing obsession. I had started taking lessons, via Skype, with Tyson Mao, who had offered me software with which to time myself, on which I was now logging dozens of solves every day. But I wasn't the only one fiending for it. It might have been because I had never looked for Rubik's Cube before, but it nonetheless seemed that Rubik's Cube was now everywhere I looked.

For one, the Cube served as the signifier of genius, a role it appears to have always played. If life were a game of Dungeons & Dragons, where everyone had different attributes, and carried sigils to broadcast their affiliations, then geeks would have robes studded with Rubik's Cubes. Whenever Rubik's Cube has appeared in scripted films or on television, it has typically served as a sign of brilliance. Hence the scene in *The Fresh Prince of Bel-Air*, the 1990s sitcom, in which Will Smith's character gets a second look from Princeton after solving Rubik's Cube, which he finds on the desk of a white admissions officer. In this case, as in many others, the puzzle also has an egalitarian bent: if genius can overcome the odds, it must do so by cutting across stereotypes, for which only a test of pure intelligence, immune to bias, will serve. No such thing exists, of course, but Rubik's Cube is so difficult for so many people that it has become the handy stand-in for intelligence itself.

Witness the appearance of Rubik's Cube in *Thor: The Dark World*, in which it dangles from the car keys belonging to Natalie Portman, who plays an astrophysicist; or *Armageddon*, where Steve Buscemi unscrambles Rubik's Cube to demonstrate his intelligence, securing his place on the mission to save the planet from a giant asteroid. Rubik's Cube plays a similar role in *The Simpsons*, where it has appeared something like half a dozen times. When Homer has a crayon removed from his brain, boosting his IQ, he solves a basket of Rubik's Cubes while watching TV.

In recent years, as the geek has become cool, transforming from a social outcast with no romantic prospects to the incubator of billion-dollar ideas, Rubik's Cube has transformed with it. In *Sherlock*, on the BBC, the actor Benedict Cumberbatch, portraying the most famous detective in modern times, is seen to have Rubik's Cube on his desk. Not long ago, the *Wall Street Journal* revealed that Harvard graduate Ryan Fitzpatrick, then the starting quarterback for the New York Jets, solves Rubik's Cube. So do his kids. The list of celebrities with "Cube Fever," as they called it in the eighties, seems to be expanding by the day. Ryan Gosling was captured by paparazzi working on the puzzle while on the set of the movie *Drive*. Will Smith solved Rubik's Cube on *Oprah*, following his star turn in *The Pursuit of Happyness*. His son, Jaden, said during a routine press junket for their film *After Earth* that learning to solve Rubik's Cube was one of the best things his father has taught him. In his words, "The Rubik's Cube itself will just teach you about life."

Rubik's Cube has also served as a metaphor for turmoil and the intractable nature of many societal problems, especially in the Middle East. Well before I got involved in cubing, I took notice of a cartoon cut from the newspaper and posted on the wall at my favorite falafel shop, which is run by a Lebanese man. The cartoon depicts Rubik's Cube, but the sides have been changed. If you were to line them up properly, one would spell out "Mideast Peace" and the other would bear the image of a dove, carrying an olive branch. Of course, the puzzle is hopelessly mixed up.

Recently, as the world—and that region, in particular—has grown seemingly more chaotic, the metaphor has taken on newfound urgency. "It's like a Rubik's Cube is being reorganized," Moshe Feiglin, the Israeli politician, told David Remnick, the editor of the *New Yorker*, in early 2013, on the eve of an election that promised to shake up the country's legislature. "This has been like a Rubik's Cube, and we have been waiting for the pieces to click into place," a senior Obama administration official said to the press in Vienna, not long after negotiations with Iran over its nuclear program concluded.

Indeed, Rubik's Cube has become something of an emblem for the modern age: crossing national borders, irrespective of language, it represents one of our greatest aspirations—to make order out of chaos—and one of our growing fears—that, in a world becoming ever more complex, simple solutions are no longer so easy to come by.

Perhaps no instance better demonstrates this than when Edward Snowden met the journalists to whom he leaked classified documents, in Hong Kong, in 2013. "We will meet in the hallway outside of the restaurant in the Mira Hotel," he wrote to them, planning the operation. "I will be working on a Rubik's Cube so you can identify me."

The recent movie *Snowden* takes the scene even further. In the film, Snowden, played by Joseph Gordon-Levitt, conceals a thumb drive *in* a Rubik's Cube, which he uses to smuggle the documents through airport security. When he makes it through, Levitt gives the puzzle a twist. The security guard has failed to untangle it.

According to Luke Harding, the journalist whose book *The Snowden Files* served as the basis for the film, Snowden used to wander the halls of the NSA carrying a Rubik's Cube.

I hoped that the *Beyond Rubik's Cube* exhibit might offer some glimpse as to why, after so many years, Rubik's Cube was making a comeback. It wasn't just Rubik's Cube—cubing was growing, too. By 2012, the year I attended my first competition, about twenty thousand people had participated in official tournaments worldwide. Just two years later, that number had increased by 50 percent, to about thirty thousand. In 2014, the U.S. National Championship was held at the Liberty Science Center. It took place in the atrium, under Groovik's Cube, a massive, cloth sculpture, lit by LEDs, originally developed for Burning Man. Nearly five hundred cubers assembled, a tally that almost equaled the attendance at the 2013 World Championship.

Unfortunately, the exhibit raised as many questions as it answered. In large part, it was focused less on explaining Rubik's

Cube than on exploring its various possibilities. There was a wall of Rubik's Cubes for you to make your own mosaic. There was also a wooden Rubik's Cube whose pieces you could take out, examine, and mix and match, to create different colored patterns. The most popular exhibit, by far, was the robotic arm. On the day I spent wandering the museum, most of the visitors were families with small children. The kids couldn't resist watching the robot solve Rubik's Cube over and over and over. I saw one boy come to tears when his mother had to drag him away to prevent him from depositing yet another Rubik's Cube in the slot in the robot's Plexiglas enclosure.

I knew a lot less about Rubik's Cube than I thought I did. There were interviews with several figures I'd never heard of, including George Miller, a puzzle maker in a tweed jacket with a bushy white beard, who attributed the puzzle's longevity to several things I'd never really thought about. "It's got high fiddle factor," he said. It was wonderful, he noted, just to sit and twist Rubik's Cube. "There's a sweet spot," he added. Some puzzles were too large, others too small, but Rubik's Cube was just right: it fits in the palm of your hand.

The interviews, which were accessible via a tall, interactive screen in the corner, also made clear the breathtaking variety of fields to which Rubik's Cube has provided inspiration. Ryan Oldham, a composer at the University of Missouri at Kansas City, discussed a piece he had written for wind ensemble using Rubik's Cube to generate the notes. By matching certain pitches to certain pieces, he could shift Rubik's Cube and create different chords. The music sounded eerie, with clarinet riffs running spookily up and down throughout.

David Gilday, an engineer with a thick British accent, described how Rubik's Cube had inspired him to design Cubestormer II, the first robot to solve Rubik's Cube faster than a human. In 2011, the bowling-ball-like contraption, built using Lego bricks and a smartphone, was brought to the London headquarters of *Wired UK*.

In accordance with WCA protocols and in the presence of Craig Glenday, the editor of *The Guinness Book of World Records*, the robot solved a randomly scrambled Rubik's Cube in 5.27 seconds.

The exhibit also offered tantalizing clues to the mind of the inventor of Rubik's Cube. He appeared in one of the videos wearing a gray sweater, dark slacks, and a neutral expression, but with a hint of mischief in his brilliant blue eyes. His name, of course, was Ernő Rubik. He spoke English with a thick Hungarian accent, and gestured with his hands as he spoke, a sort of Eastern European version of Mr. Rogers. "I was really sure that it is interesting and it has a deep content," he said of his Cube, "and what I was not sure, how many people will share that opinion."

Over the course of several minutes—significantly longer than any taped interview of him I'd ever seen—it became clear that Rubik was actually less like Mr. Rogers and more like Willy Wonka. If it takes a genius to figure out how to solve Rubik's Cube, then it certainly takes a genius to invent it. Rubik was evidently brilliant, holding forth on the challenges his puzzle faced—it was too difficult, it manifestly wasn't a toy, he was told—and why mathematicians have been preoccupied with it for decades. Even at the end, he noted, when you are close to a solution, you often have to destroy what you've done to make progress. It was a different way of solving problems.

Rubik is known to be averse to publicity, although his reasons, the interview suggested, had less in common with those of Wonka, who worries about rivals stealing his secrets, and more to do with his own attitude toward his creation. "In my view," he said, "it's something like when you have kids." What he meant, he explained, was that your children have the potential to be many things—beautiful, strong, competitive—but that any success they have belongs to them. "So I remain all the time in the second row," he said.

And yet here Rubik was, on view, for all the world to see, a giant facsimile of his Cube parading up and down the Hudson River on a barge, in a promotional stunt put on by the museum.

Along with several visiting dignitaries, including János Áder, the President of Hungary, he made the trip to New Jersey and opened the exhibition gala, posing for photographs.

What had drawn Rubik out of seclusion? According to one of his close associates, a man named Viktor Böhm, "He was struck by the really unexpected impact of the Cube." From afar, Böhm said, Rubik watched the Cube serve as the inspiration for works of art. Like the sculptures and album covers by Invader, the French street artist, who dubbed the form, in which multiple Rubik's Cubes were used to create a pixelated image, "Rubikcubisme." Rubik also saw his Cube inspire works of science, including the search for God's Number. It took thirty years, not to mention the use of supercomputers owned by Google, whose specifications remain secret, to determine, in 2010, that any case of Rubik's Cube can be unscrambled in, at most, twenty moves. (Only an omniscient being could find the optimal solution to every case, the thinking goes, hence "God's Number.") And, of course, from the ashes of the 1980s, Rubik saw the second coming of speedcubing, abetted by the Internet. "And he started to question why," Böhm said. "And he didn't really have an answer."

If I were to draw a portrait of Rubik, it would probably come out like something by Picasso, full of angles and odd jointures, the face a mess of lines that don't quite mesh together. I had heard so many things about him. If all of them were true, it would have seemed less like the portrait of one person than of several different people. I had gotten wind, for instance, that Rubik was fabulously wealthy. One person told me that Hungarians used to leave the country, in the 1980s, carrying suitcases full of Rubik's Cubes, knowing they could resell them for a profit in the West. According to George Miller, who admits this might be hearsay, Rubik was the first person in Hungary to have a private swimming pool. I even heard that Rubik owned one of the hills in Budapest.

None of this was true, according to Böhm. "He's such a nice and charming and humble and intelligent guy," he said. "He lives very comfortably, of course. He is an architect, so he enjoys building and designing his own home." But Rubik didn't charter private jets. He didn't even fly business class. Böhm reiterated that Rubik was very humble. "And that goes for the whole family," he said. "They go for a nice holiday every other year, but they are certainly not living in a way of high-flying business people."

Still, he admitted, Rubik could have chosen differently. "At one point, he could have bought half of Hungary," Böhm said. "Because, you know, it was a controlled economy. And he was one of the few people who had very significant income in hard currency. At that point, he easily could have bought enormous pieces of land and this and that and the other."

Adding to the confusion, Rubik has been described as something of a misanthrope. When John Tierney, an American journalist who profiled Rubik in 1986 for *Discover* magazine, visited Budapest, he interviewed a colleague of Rubik's who described him as "a bit sour." Rubik didn't like talking to people, said Tibor Laczi, one of his business associates. "I really like Rubik," he told Tierney, "but I can't imagine having a real friendship with him."

Sometimes, according to Tierney, in the 1980s, on press junkets for the Cube, Rubik lost his patience. He kept getting asked the same questions. "He would try to explain why the Cube appealed to an innate human fascination with order and chaos," Tierney reported, "and all the reporter wanted to know was how long it took him to solve it (two or three minutes) and whether it was really true that the man reputed to be the Iron Curtain's first self-made millionaire still couldn't get a telephone (it was). Or they would ask, 'What does it feel like to be famous?' and Rubik would want to answer 'What does it feel like not to be famous?'"

But who wouldn't become a little misanthropic in that situation? Tierney acknowledges this, referring to an old interview in which Rubik notes that success can be every bit as destabilizing as failure. "For me it is another quiz," he said, "a new puzzle, and it is not so easy to find the proper solution."

"I'd never seen anyone enjoy success less," Tierney told me recently.

When I asked Böhm if I might come to Hungary and meet Rubik, he was polite, but not encouraging. He suggested that if I made the trip I might be able talk to some people who worked at Rubik's headquarters in Budapest. It was something.

A few weeks later, I attended my first local competition. In recent years, the largest competition in the world has been either the World Championship or the U.S. National Championship. (Although Poland has the highest number of cubers per capita, the United States has the most cubers in absolute terms.) In 2013, there were more than 350 competitions, and most of these were significantly smaller. That year, the average competition had just under thirty competitors.

In other words, Nisei Week, in downtown Los Angeles, was more typical than any tourney I had yet attended. The event took place outdoors, in the brick courtyard adjoining the Japanese American Cultural and Community Center, in the heart of Little Tokyo. The competition was shorter than most—there were only two events, 3x3 and one-handed, because it was held during the annual celebration of Japanese culture by the children of Japanese immigrants. (*Nisei* is Japanese for "second generation.")

The competition would be followed by a demonstration of *taiko* drumming. But the event itself was greeted with no less enthusiasm. The line to register snaked across the courtyard, under a large tent, passing stalls selling kimonos, toy samurai swords, and rice-paper umbrellas. The proportion of newcomers to veterans seemed higher than at any competition I had yet attended. A girl and her father, his arm in a sling, approached Michael Young, the delegate for the competition, and said they didn't know what to do.

Young told them to find their way to the stage; someone would explain the protocols. When I reached the head of the line, paid my registration fee, and collected my score sheet, I asked him in what heat I could expect to race. Young, a twentysomething rising senior at Caltech, with shoulder-length inky hair framing his face, squinted back, a bit sheepishly. "Everyone's in the same heat," he said. "We're not as organized as national competitions."

In the audience, there was a girl watching *Toy Story 3* on a tablet, a mother holding a copy of a slim book. Upon closer inspection, however, it wasn't the kind of book that you'd expect: Machiavelli's *The Prince*, the notorious handbook in which the Italian statesman offers such practical advice as publicly beheading your enemies to consolidate your rule.

Even in the most typical settings, cubing drew an atypical crowd. Sitting directly in front of me was a young man with jittery fingers. He wore a black San Diego Padres baseball hat. His T-shirt read US NAVY on the back and DON'T GIVE UP THE SHIP on the front. He was using his iPhone to time himself. He touched the screen to activate a timer, unscrambled his Rubik's Cube, and then tapped the screen again to stop it. He seemed no less nervous than if he were participating in one of the many war games inspired by the phrase on his shirt, the dying words of Captain James Lawrence, an American sailor shot by the British in the War of 1812. At one point, I noticed the young man pause, fingers literally shaking, while he contemplated a thorny problem: all but the four edges of the last layer of his Rubik's Cube were solved, and even those were correctly oriented, giving the impression that he needed but to exchange four stickers to solve the puzzle.

Ah, I said to myself, with a pang of recognition. Z-perm. *No wonder he's having trouble.* I had only recently learned the Z-permutation myself. It required executing a difficult sequence of moves, and was also easily confused with another case, in which those same four edges of the last layer were correctly oriented, but incorrectly permuted: H-perm.

They were just two of the twenty-one cases in the final phase of CFOP: Permutation of the Last Layer, or PLL, for short. In both cases, you typically have to use your ring finger and manipulate the middle slice of Rubik's Cube, a cumbersome operation that looks like you're spinning the wheel of a water mill. You have to reverse direction several times, and coordinate each twist with affiliated adjustments of the last layer itself. Altogether, the algorithms required take on an explosive sort of rhythm, when properly executed, like the bellowing of a jackhammer. Unfortunately, Z-perm* and H-perm† are so similar as to be easily confused. The first three moves of the most commonly used algorithms for each case are identical, and what follows differs only slightly.

Until now, I'd been consigned to the beginner method, which I learned at CTY. When it came to the last layer, the beginner method was, well, simple. Rather than learn a specific algorithm for each case, you simply applied the same algorithm, over and over, until it forced the right case to appear, like the NSA breaking into a phone by brute force.

What I'd been focused on was mastering F2L—short for the "first two layers," the second step in Fridrich's system. "I mean," Fridrich had told me when I visited her, "it's very intuitive. You sort of do it naturally." Maybe it came naturally to *her*, but I needed some help.

During one of my lessons with Tyson, via Skype, he advised learning one new F2L case every day. "You're learning new things, but you're keeping the speed constant," he said. Once I knew all the cases, I'd be able to solve them, no sweat, and see my times drop.

In practice, of course, learning algorithms is much harder. It takes a certain tactile memory, not unlike that required to

---

* The edges have to swap diagonally, bringing to mind the bars of the letter "Z."

† The edges have to move perpendicular to one another, like the bars of the letter "H."

memorize scales on a musical instrument. When I asked cubers at competitions, like the World Championship, if they wouldn't mind demonstrating a particular algorithm, they sometimes had trouble; the moves had bypassed their conscious thinking, and entered the murky world of knee-jerk reflexes.

Fortunately, by the time I attended the Nisei Week competition, I'd learned solutions to more or less all of the cases for F2L. My first solve reflected this: 29.66 seconds, my first under thirty seconds. Still, it's one thing to memorize the algorithms, another to put them into practice. The challenge with F2L is that you never know exactly what you're going to get. It's improvisatory, not unlike jazz. Sometimes, the algorithms are straightforward, appearing just as they do in the many lists online that allow you to pick and choose how you'll solve a particular case. Other times, however, the cases are mixed, the pieces required to solve one corner-edge pair commingling with those needed to solve another.

38.35 seconds. Even though it was nearly ten seconds slower than my first, my second solve was still a huge improvement over my second effort at the World Championship, 54.01 seconds. At Nisei Week, my next two solves—29.11 and, even better, 28.60—guaranteed not only that I would have two sub-30 solves in my average, but that I'd have a shot at averaging below thirty seconds. So long as I didn't go slower than my second attempt, that 38.35 would be thrown out.

Unfortunately, right as I reached the last layer, I found myself facing what I had chuckled at the navy kid struggling over: H-perm. I didn't execute it right, veering left when I should have gone right, with the result that I had to attempt to permute the last layer all over again. Thirty-nine seconds flat—my worst solve of the round.

Still, the average was a personal best. I'd gone from 45.23 seconds all the way down to 32.37 seconds. I had been told plenty of times that cubing is literally addictive. But it wasn't until this moment that I felt the pull of whatever neurological mechanism makes going faster not quite fast enough. I'd dropped thirteen seconds in as many months. How much lower could I go?

A few blocks away, in front of the Japanese American National Museum, a circular glassy building, stood an installation by Nicole Maloney, a Los Angeles–based artist. The sculpture, a large, metallic cube, towered over the pedestrian walkway, and some of its faces drifted in the still air. Several bore fragments of human expressions, which traded places as the puzzle turned, while others were polished metal, reflecting the faces of viewers below.

Three weeks later, I found myself at Fragrance House, a low-slung brick building in the City of Commerce, the gritty, industrial area to the south of Los Angeles. It wasn't to sample from the rows and rows of perfumes, ranging from the frighteningly generic "Let's Marry!" to the weirdly specific "Toy Story: Eau de Toilette," but to meet the owner Minh Thai.

Thai himself came out to fetch me, then took me to his office, modestly appointed with an L-shaped desk, the same blue carpet as the rest of the store, and a handful of chairs. On the way in, we passed through a fragrant cloud of incense; a statue of the Buddha, laughing, sat outside the door. The door was covered by a humongous poster advertising THE SCENT OF THE SPARTAN, a tie-in to the movie *300*.

Thai, a compact man in his late forties, was wearing a gray polo shirt inscribed with the logo UCLA DAD over the breast. He had olive skin and rimless metal glasses. When he ushered me in, there was another man in the room, with whom Thai resumed conversing, in Spanish. "I am in the wrong business actually," he told me, with an improbably cheerful grin, after the client left. "It was the right business, but now it's the wrong business!"

Thai won the first Rubik's Cube World Championship, in Budapest in 1982, the only competition later recognized as official until the World Championship was revived, in 2003. I sought him out in part because he has largely disappeared from the cubing community. (Although he no longer competes, Thai told me he still solves Rubik's Cube every night before bed, twenty to thirty times; mentally and physically, he says, it keeps him fresh.) Reclining in his voluminous armchair, his hands above his head, Thai wondered how I had found him in the first place, to which the answer was simply that I asked Ron van Bruchem for his e-mail address.

In many respects, Thai is legendary. By virtue of being the winner of the earliest tournament later recognized as official by *The Guinness Book of World Records* and the WCA, Thai held the world record for a single solve for more than two decades: 22.95 seconds. He earned his ticket to Budapest in 1981 by taking first place at the inaugural U.S. National Championship, viewed by millions at the height of the Cube's popularity on *That's Incredible!*

In contrast to today's format, where anyone who registers can show up, to qualify for the National Championship in 1981, you had to actually win a local tournament. "I see these little ten-year-old kids doing it," said one man to a reporter at the Dallas regional that year, "and I get really frustrated and want to break their wrists or something."

Unlike most of his fellow competitors, Thai had already survived a challenge thornier than Rubik's Cube. In the late 1970s, his family fled Vietnam by boat along with thousands of other refugees and landed in Malaysia, where he remembers chopping bamboo to make a house to live in. "We lived exactly like *Gilligan's Island*," he told me.

When he arrived in the United States half a year later, he spoke no English. Thai and his five siblings wound up in Eagle Rock, a suburb of Los Angeles. His father took up work in a restaurant. Thai recalls being one of only two Asians at Eagle Rock High School. Because he didn't understand what was going on, he started carrying around the dictionary. The school didn't yet have any classes that taught English as a second language.

"Let's say one day you wake up and no passport and you living in, say, Russia or Japan or something," Thai said. "But as a poor man. With no telephone. No Internet." He asked me what I would do in that situation. One of his saving graces, he said, was Rubik's Cube. He sat at the back of U.S. History, which is why he noticed Peter Valenzuela holding a multicolored cube that impossibly shifted, the sides ever mutating, like the view through a kaleidoscope.

"It was like love at first sight," he told me, with a laugh.

"This Cube is *so* good!" Thai said, holding my Cube. I had asked if we might race, to which he assented—"Just for fun," he said—before handing me his Cube, for me to scramble, and holding out his hand for mine. Thai had never held a speedcube before. In the old days, he said, they used to lube theirs with Vaseline, or whatever else lay near at hand. He scoffed when I told him how Fridrich and the other veterans to whom I'd spoken complained about stiff Cubes at the 1982 World Championship. "I think she bitch about it a lot," he said.

Still, he was delighted by how easy my Cube was to turn. He'd kept out of the loop to such a degree that he had no idea how fast cubers are nowadays. When I told him about Feliks Zemdegs, who had recently lowered the world record for an average of five solves to 6.54 seconds, Thai asked how many moves the solution required. About sixty, I said, at which point Thai practically leaped out of his seat. "You mean to tell me they are doing ten moves per second?" He shook his head. "My best is, like, three moves per second," he said.

I offered to let him solve my Rubik's Cube, but he declined. "No, I'm fine," he said. I had to admire him for this. It was like opting for a pair of weather-beaten Chuck Taylors when your opponent has just offered you a pair of brand-new Air Jordans. Not the best idea.

Evidently, Thai really didn't need the help. He took the first round, handily beating my newfangled Cube. What the time was, I can't say, since neither of us was using a timer. ("Just go," he said, summing up the rules of this desk-side duel.) Even in victory, Thai is gracious. I messed up, badly, and he offered to start the round over.* (I declined.)

The second round went to me. On my tape recorder, you can hear our Cubes twisting away. Mine gives the impression of a tommy gun—lots of moves being performed in a short amount of time. Thai's Cube, by contrast, sounds more like a Viennese waltz, stately and bouncing, as he sets up one sequence and then performs it before moving on to another.

This time, it was Thai who messed up. "I solve it wrong way," he said.

In fact, if you were to show one of Thai's solves to a modern cuber, she might agree. He uses a method that has long since fallen out of favor: Corners-First. Thai wasn't the first to use this method, and he certainly didn't invent it, but he became one of its foremost proponents in the 1980s, when he published *The Winning Solution*, a slim booklet that serves as a guide to solving Rubik's Cube.

Corners-First involves solving the corners of one face, then the remaining four corners of the opposite face, using an algorithm. (Thai is not partial to algorithms, and has tried, in recent years, to keep his number of "routines" to an absolute minimum. "If there's too many," he told me, "it kind of defeats the purpose of enjoying the Cube.") The great advantage of Corners-First is efficiency. Thai averages about fifty-five twists per solve, and he's trying to come up with routines that will allow him to clock in

---

* With the exception of his comments about the World Championship—"I had best time and best average," he said. "So for somebody to criticize, I'm sorry"—Thai was exceedingly humble. Of his victory in 1982, he said, "It's not something I brag about, talk about."

under fifty moves per solve. By contrast, my not-yet-complete version of Fridrich's system required upward of seventy-five.

Another notable user of this technique is Dan Gosbee, who modeled his Corners-First method after that deployed by Marc Waterman, a Dutch cuber from the early 1980s. Gosbee told me his variation on the method involves solving the last four corners at the same time as the final corner of the initial face. "That's all it *is*," Gosbee told me, as if this were obvious. He has never released the details of his method publicly. "I didn't have it written down," he said. "It's all in my head." ("I wasn't telling anybody about it," he added, right after telling me about it. "And that's where the frickin' problem was.")

"One more?" I asked Thai.

"One more," he agreed.

For this final solve, I focused on not screwing up, which is a lot harder than it sounds, especially when you're sitting across the table from the first world champion. Thai is extremely calm when he solves—hence the waltzlike, almost soothing sound of his Cube as he twists it. There is a composure to him that's hard to match. In person, he is affable, even gregarious, but if you hand him a Rubik's Cube, as I just did, he becomes deadly serious. The muscles of his forearms rippled as he advanced, his Cube taking formations I had never seen before. Some of them brought to mind checkerboards, the corners matching before the edges came into play.

Thai has a thick head of dark hair, graying at the temples, and a thin mustache on his upper lip. His flip phone announces calls with the jazzy saxophone solo from *The Pink Panther* movies. In amplitude and timing, his laugh is like a cannon, which he unleashes unwittingly and often. He has a zeal for life, perhaps not despite, but because of, his hard upbringing. "Nobody can break me," he tells his three kids. "We like the survivor."

There was no timer to officiate, no judge to intervene. But when I slammed my Rubik's Cube to the desk, Thai was caught with his Rubik's Cube still in his hands. "Good!" he said.

I had taken the match, best two out of three. In the end, it didn't mean much. There was no official result, but it meant a lot to me. I had just beaten the first world champion, admittedly using technology that, by comparison, would have made his puzzle look outdated even when it had just come out in the 1980s. "They don't understand what we doing," Thai said, of the average person. "They think we're crazy sometimes!"

The timing program that Tyson Mao gave me lists three numbers in the bottom right-hand corner. Your best time, followed by your best average of twelve solves, and then, finally, the average of all the solves you have yet logged. By this point, the number of solves had climbed well into the thousands, a fact I was reminded of every time I opened the program. And yet it still wasn't anywhere near enough.

On August 17, 2013, roughly a year before my visit with Thai, I recorded my first sub-30-second solve. It felt like I'd been told to expect fast solves to feel—that is, it didn't feel particularly fast. But it registered 29.98 seconds, and could conceivably have been much faster—a twenty-eight-second solve or twenty-nine seconds flat—if I hadn't taken a wrong turn on the last algorithm and had to go back to fix it.

Ten days before I visited Thai, I logged eighty-six solves in the program. By the standards of many cubers, this isn't all that much. But given the amount of time it took me not only to scramble my Rubik's Cube but to solve it, the session took close to two hours. My best average of five solves was 24.80 seconds. Altogether, the solves I did that day averaged just under twenty-eight seconds. In other words, a year after going sub-30, I had improved—my best single solve that session was 20.22 seconds—but I still had a long way, and thousands and thousands of solves, to go.

When I asked Thai if he had any advice on getting faster, he expressed doubt that either of us would ever manage to get under twenty seconds. "It can be impossible for us," he said. "Seriously. I mean, maybe for you, but for me, to bring from twenty. Right now I think I can average about twenty-two, twenty-three, but to bring it to, like, nineteen—" He said he was simply too old. "I won't try for it," he added.

According to Thai, there were three skills required to be good at cubing. The first two were physical—having good spatial recognition and being able to make good decisions, quickly. "My dad makes impulsive decisions," Thai said his daughter once wrote in an essay. He laughed, ticking off some of the situations where he is known to act quickly, from deciding what the family will eat to negotiating deals with suppliers for his business. "It's already worked out in my mind," he said.

The third skill—and this one uncannily mirrored something I'd heard Zemdegs, the year before, at the World Championship, describe—was less easy to pull off. Not thinking was the essence of this ability. "You have to be able to go into a zone," Thai said. He emphasized the word, as if the "zone" were really a place you could go, a room in your mind in which to take shelter. "It's just smooth sailing," Thai said. "You're not conscious. You're not thinking." When I told him this reminded me of what I'd heard from Zemdegs—"You don't really think, you just do it"—Thai nodded seriously. Then he brought up a martial-arts movie.

In the movie, he said, a young apprentice is exiled by his master. For seven days, after climbing a mountain, the apprentice must kneel in penance. With no supervision, of course, the student wanders into a nearby cave. There, he finds ancient instructions for using a sword. After reading them, he is approached by a little old man—the author of the form. The old man asks if he has read it, upon which the student says, enthusiastically, that he knows the whole thing. The old man asks him to perform the moves as fast as he can.

"Well," the old man says, "that's not fast enough." The apprentice looks downcast. "Now I want you to forget everything," the master says.

"Shit!" the student replies. "What do you mean, forget it?" Day by day, Thai told me, the student tries to forget everything he learned. It takes him a while—he forgets almost everything, and then remembers something, at which point the old man reminds him he is not done. Then one day, he exults. "Master, I forgot everything! I forgot everything!" The young man became the greatest swordsman who ever lived.

"Kung fu is a little bit fantasy," Thai admitted, but maintained that the point was real. "The key is in the zone," he said. "That's what his master is trying to tell him. You need to forget."

I was reminded of something else I'd heard at the World Championship the year before. The second night of the competition, Zemdegs, Valk, and another world-class cuber, a German teenager named Cornelius Dieckmann, gathered onstage. Upward of one hundred cubers assembled to hear them lecture. "So, everyone get a Cube, if you can," Zemdegs said, "and I want you to scramble it and solve the cross and F2L." There was a rustle like the sound of a rainstick turning upside down.

I was attempting to take notes, but even I picked up my Cube and did my best to follow along. "So, I'll wait another fifteen or twenty seconds," Zemdegs said. It took me at least thirty seconds to get the job done, but I managed to catch up in time for his next instruction. He wanted everyone to examine the OLL—that is, the orientation of the last layer case—but not in the typical manner, looking only at the top of the Cube. "Look at the whole thing," Zemdegs said. He meant the sides as well—the motley assemblage of colors that ringed the sides of the last layer like so much paint splattered around the edge of an unframed canvas.

"Now what I want you to do," he continued, "is to close your eyes—everyone close their eyes—and execute their OLL algorithm and keep their eyes closed." This was a challenge, like asking a billiards player to line up a shot and take it with her eyes closed. "Now," Zemdegs continued, "keep your eyes closed and try to do the PLL." This was even harder—like asking the billiards player to take the next shot with her eyes *still* closed.

"Oh, wow!" I heard as I opened my eyes. Onstage, Dieckmann, who had dutifully followed along, had almost solved his Rubik's Cube. It lay on the table, resolved but for one twist of the last layer. "So this is a pretty fun exercise," Zemdegs said, "and I'm using it to demonstrate a kind of sixth sense that comes with solving."

Both Zemdegs and Thai stressed that this sort of superhuman ability—which all the best cubers seem to possess—doesn't come easy. "This isn't something that can be taught," Zemdegs added as the crowd tittered, looking at Dieckmann's Cube. "You can learn it by practice."

Zemdegs takes Allen Iverson's "We're talking about practice" meme to heart. "If I get a message from someone asking how to get faster," Zemdegs said, "the most likely answer that I give is, 'Practice.'" He added, "One thing I do often is just pick up a Cube when I get home and maybe watch TV or something and just solve the Cube in a relaxing way."

Likewise, Thai indicated that only after a great deal of practice will "the zone" permit access. The martial artist of whom he spoke—the hero of *The Smiling, Proud Wanderer*, a 1970s novel by Louis Cha, a hugely popular Chinese-language writer, and its many film adaptations, including *The Legendary Swordsman*, the one Thai saw—had to learn the form *before* he could forget it. "First," Thai said, "you have to be good at it, prepare and everything else. And after that, put yourself in a zone. To compete."

On September 24, 1981, the *New England Journal of Medicine* published a letter from Douglas Waugh, a doctor in Ontario,

Canada. He had written in, as many physicians do, to describe a novel ailment, which he himself had contracted. Many of the other letters in that issue were standard medical fare: that is to say, obtuse to the general reader. "If hybridization occurs with a malignant cell line," wrote a scientist in Corpus Christi, Texas, "there is a danger of introducing oncogenic viruses into recipients." In other words, the technique under discussion might actually induce cancer rather than treat it.

But Waugh's missive was starkly topical. It played out like a little story: Not long before, Waugh began to experience pain in his thumb. At first, it seemed as if he had contracted gout. The thumb was swollen and gout is a form of arthritis, in which joints suddenly swell and ache. He visited his own physician, who tentatively agreed with his diagnosis. The treatment was phenylbutazone, an anti-inflammatory drug that is now used exclusively to treat horses. Still, Waugh couldn't resist describing, in excruciating, anatomically precise detail, the nature of his ailment: "The condition is characterized by a localized, exquisitely tender swelling on the volar surface of the left metacarpophalangeal joint."

I didn't know what any of that meant when I felt a twinge in my thumb in the weeks following my visit with Minh Thai. In fact, I had yet to read Waugh's letter. Like Waugh, I assumed, initially, that my pain—it rose sometimes to a throb, at others falling to a low boil—had some more distant cause. Only I came to discover that the cause lay right under my nose. "The correct diagnosis," Waugh wrote, "was made a couple of days later when I picked up my cube and jammed it against the painful metacarpal." Waugh, like me, was a Rubik's Cube addict.

The injury came about, most likely, because I was practicing. So much, in fact, that the sound of cubing—the telltale *click-clack, click-clack*—had become the soundtrack to my life. Once, visiting my parents, I woke my mother in the middle of the night. Apparently, the percussion had penetrated through my door, wended its way down the hall, and roused her.

*　*　*

Waugh's problem, he admitted, was simply technological: he had, by his own admission, a cheap Rubik's Cube, in every sense of the word. His puzzle, he wrote, "tends to stick when its pieces are rotated." He had originally gotten hooked when he bought his wife a Rubik's Cube and found himself competing for her attention. Whereas hers was "top-of-the-line," his was shoddy, made in Taiwan. It was cheaper, but the price was ultimately dear. "Treatment on an interim basis has consisted of swiping my wife's racing cube," Waugh said. Even though his ailment would soon likely disappear—he planned to purchase a new Cube, as soon as stocks replenished—he ended the letter by noting, soberly, that a cure for "cube addiction" had yet to be found.

In truth, I could easily have stopped solving Rubik's Cube then and there and been no poorer for it. I had already gone under thirty seconds in competition, at least for a single solve, which is faster than most people would ever hope to accomplish. While I was hardly at the top, I was nonetheless respectably in the middle. At the time, about thirty-two thousand people had competed worldwide. My best average, 32.27 seconds, was good enough for a five-way tie with two Americans and two Chinese for 17,002nd place overall. Still, I also understood, in a visceral way I hadn't before, what Waugh meant by his diagnosis of "cuber's thumb."

In particular, the part about "cube addiction."

I kept cubing. I couldn't really help myself. The best way to moderate the pain, I found, was to cube in small increments, a few solves here, a few solves there, throughout the day. It became a compulsion. Going a day without solving produced a longing, like I'd imagine a caffeine or nicotine withdrawal. I really was an addict. Without my Cube, I felt like something was missing. That practice was paying off only made it more painful. In February 2015, four months after beating Thai, two and a half years after my first competition, I recorded my first sub-21-second average.

My goal—going sub-20—seemed within sight. A few solves later, my average fell to within a hairsbreadth of the promised land: 20.19 seconds.

It wasn't in competition. But still, it felt like I'd almost made it. I could solve Rubik's Cube faster than I could tie my shoes. By the time someone saw me, solving in a coffee shop, or elsewhere out in public, and looked again, I was either done with the puzzle or nearly there.

I never got any free sushi, like Cameron Brown, who once ate himself sick after solving the Cube at a sushi bar. (It had been placed there for decoration.) Nor did I meet the love of my life, as Toby did at a competition (more on that later). But cubing was fast becoming part of my identity. Cubing wasn't just something I did. I was a cuber.

And then, all of a sudden I picked up my Cube and felt anew what Waugh meant by a "localized, exquisitely tender swelling." It was as if someone had yanked a tendon wide open, the tissue crying out in pain. I tried to learn new algorithms. But, even then, it was starting to look like I might never be able to pick up where I left off.

SCHOOLED

"**S**o, you use a lot of F turns," Tim Sun said.

I wasn't sure if this was good or bad. We were sitting in the café at the student union of Columbia University, where Sun and I met in college. At the time, I had no idea he was a cuber. I knew he could solve Rubik's Cube, but had never heard of the World Cube Association or cubing, and so had no idea that Sun was one of the best cubers in the world. Over the course of 2009, he broke the North American record for solving Rubik's Cube with his feet nearly half a dozen times. Even though he didn't compete much anymore, he still ranked among the one hundred best in the discipline worldwide. He could also solve Rubik's Cube one-handed and blindfolded. His regular—that is to say, two-handed—solves weren't too shabby either. He boasted a best average of 10.10 seconds. Currently, Sun was back at Columbia as a graduate student.

"It's probably better to rotate," Sun said.

Barrel-chested, with jet-black hair that swoops across his forehead, Sun has better spatial recognition than most. He plays competitive badminton—a master of calculating angles and trajectories in his head. In graduate school, he was putting the same skills to use, pursuing a doctorate in computer science. A few months after our meeting, some of his research would receive widespread attention—he helped to design a computer program that can produce a model of any three-dimensional object and instruct a 3-D printer to turn it into a twisty, Rubik's Cube–style puzzle.

I asked Sun to explain what he meant. I knew what F turns were—every cuber did. The letter *F* corresponds to the front face and denotes one, ninety-degree clockwise turn. To perform an F turn, you flick the face in question with your thumb, the same way you might adjust the dial on a thermostat.

Sun demonstrated there was a simple alternative. If you rotated Rubik's Cube on its vertical axis, so the front face shifted to the left- or right-hand side, it became a matter of simply turning your wrist rather than using your thumb. He picked up my Cube to demonstrate. Instead of adjusting the front face with his thumb, he rotated the puzzle once, so that what I had been targeting—an empty slot in the first two layers—was now flush with his left hand. With a practiced, smooth movement, he manipulated that face in concert with the last layer until the desired pieces fell into place. It looked as easy as twisting a door handle.

Just like that, the movement that had been giving me so much trouble—it hurt to perform inverted F turns, or F' turns, in particular, since they involved my ailing right thumb—was rendered essentially moot. "You're using F' more than you probably need to," Sun concluded. "That's probably why your thumb is . . ." He trailed off, glancing at the offending appendage. Sun suffered periodic wrist issues, but nothing serious.

Sun couldn't help unscrambling my Rubik's Cube the rest of the way, and I couldn't help but notice how controlled his movements were, how subtle and accurate, like the footsteps Andy Warhol once painted, showing the feet of someone dancing the fox-trot. Sun rarely turned anything but the sides and the last layer of Rubik's Cube, rotating the puzzle when I would have kept the orientation fixed and resorted to F turns. "I see a lot of other cubers use F turns a lot," Sun added, handing my Cube back to me. "I think it has a lot to do with newer Cubes. Because back in the day, you could never solve it."

When Sun started cubing in 2005, the only thing on the market that wasn't a plain old Rubik's Cube was Rubik's DIY, a kit that gave you the opportunity to assemble the puzzle yourself, which allowed for a certain amount of customization. "Even when I started competing," Sun said, "people were still using store-bought Rubik's Cubes." The puzzles were so stiff that regularly deploying F turns would have been unimaginable.

The upshot was that certain styles of cubing were encouraged. "A lot of newer cubers," Sun said, for a moment casting off the guise of the millennial and picking up the mantle of a crotchety old veteran, reminiscing about something like the golden age of radio serials, "they turn really fast, but they don't look ahead that well." He still solved the way he had learned, by turning slowly but never stopping. It was no longer necessary, Sun admitted, to look ahead so well if you could turn so fast.

"Nowadays, ten turns per second," he snorted, "that's average for these people." But for someone like me, who could neither turn very fast—I averaged about three turns per second, not much slower than Sun—nor look ahead very well (at least not yet), the lesson was clear: I had to get back to my roots, to master the basics.

"If you want to get sub-20," Toby Mao said, "you've got to learn your algs, man." We were sitting in the offices of Scribd, the digital publishing start-up, where Mao was working as a software engineer. The offices looked modeled after the set of *Silicon Valley*. The truth was probably the other way around: a suit of armor stood by the entrance, below a zip line that spanned the main suite. Around the corner lay the commissary, stocked with every breakfast cereal and every board game you could think of. Mao was clad in a black, white, and red hoodie, representing the dojo where he and his fiancée, whom he met cubing, train in jiujitsu. (They planned to eschew the formalities at their upcoming nuptials and not only time the vows, but inaugurate the noble sport of cube-jitsu, in which the first opponent to solve Rubik's Cube or get the other contender to submit wins the match.)

Mao didn't really cube competitively anymore, but when I asked if he could still go sub-20, he sounded almost offended. "Of course!" he sputtered. When I asked if he thought I could go sub-20 by the 2015 World Championship, which was slated to take place five months later, in São Paulo, Brazil, he did a double take. "You can do it no problem!" he said.

Mao sympathized with my injured thumb. He'd injured his own thumb rock climbing and was never able to return to the sport. Instead, he'd taken up board games. When I arrived, he was playing a card game called Netrunner, which simulates the experience of hacking into a major corporation. One player is the hacker; the other, the corporation. (You can do almost anything in the game, including hiring escorts to seduce and befuddle the chief executive.) But Mao hadn't lost his touch with Rubik's Cube. "I'm really slow now," he said, "but I can still do it, probably do it in fifteen seconds."

After reminiscing for a while about CTY—"I hated that class!" Mao said, reminding me it was his mother who had signed him up, thinking it would improve his college applications—I asked if Toby might watch me solve Rubik's Cube. I'd already handed him my Cube, and he'd demonstrated a few techniques—another way, for instance, that I could avoid using my thumb. (When I told him that I'd asked Sun for advice, Mao agreed with Sun's verdict. "In my day," he said, "using the thumb was considered a newb move.") But Mao said he didn't need to see me solve to know what the problem was.

"Don't be lazy!" he said. "That's why you're not sub-20."

What Mao meant was that I had to master Fridrich's system: I was literally trying to run, fingers flying around the Cube, before I could walk. "Learn your algs," Mao said. "And then, after that? F2L. *Slow* F2L. And smooth, right?" The goal was to remove any pauses, any hesitancy, in my solving.

"And that's it," he said. "There's no magic. It's hard work."

The San Francisco Bay Area is one of the world's leading hubs for technology and innovation. Virtually everyone knows this. It is also, perhaps unsurprisingly, one of the leading hubs for the study and resolution of Rubik's Cube. Toby still lived with his parents in Hillsborough, the tony suburb in Silicon Valley where he grew up (understandably, he and his fiancée made that decision to save money). His older brother, Tyson, lived with his wife, a chemical-engineering-PhD-turned-product-manager, just up the street. The brothers once organized competitions at Crystal Springs Uplands, the private school where Toby used to lift weights with the janitor. But the crown jewel of the region, cubing-wise, sits across the Bay, nestled in the rolling hills of Berkeley: Cal, the University of California's flagship campus, its soaring campanile, which you can see for miles, tolling out the hours with its carillon bells.

In the 1960s, the student-led Free Speech Movement famously shut down the campus. Thousands of students gathered to advocate for free expression. One of the protest's leaders, Mario Savio, was soon being followed by the FBI; one night, the governor gave permission to start mass arrests, which only further enlivened the demonstrations. Eventually, the protests ended, but not before radically transforming the campus, to say nothing of the nation itself. (When Ronald Reagan successfully ran for governor of California, he promised to "clean up that Berkeley mess.")

One of the less well-known effects of the counterculture at Cal was that students could now create their own courses. In 1968, Eldridge Cleaver, one of the leaders of the Black Panther Party, guest-taught Social Analysis 139X: Dehumanization and Regeneration of the American Social Order. The program, known today as DeCal, short for Democratic Education at California, has provided an outlet for students whose favorite subjects would not otherwise be taught. Recent offerings include everything from Philosophy in *Calvin and Hobbes* to Fetch Is Going to Happen: Mean Girls and Modern Society to Learn to Solve the Rubik's Cube.

The latter course, formally known as Math 98/198, has two sections. The first is for beginners. The second is for those who already know how to solve the Cube and want to get faster. Both sections are taught by members of the Berkeley Rubik's Cube Club. Every year, far more students want to take the course than there is room to teach—total enrollment is usually capped around a hundred to a hundred and fifty students. Selection is by application only.

I first heard about the course from Vincent Sheu, the former president of the Cal Rubik's Cube Club, whom I met at my first competition: the 2012 U.S. National Championship. In the world of cubing, Sheu is a legend, not only for being the only person to have tied a world record for the third time (2x2 single, 0.96 seconds, along with Rowe Hessler, the American veteran, and Erik Akkersdijk, the Dutch master), but also for his eloquent and outspoken advocacy on behalf of the puzzle. Once, at a basketball game, Sheu was caught solving his Rubik's Cube live on ESPN, right behind Bill Walton, in the Cal student section. "All of us are talented in our own way," he said later, in a video produced by the Cal athletics department.

When I finally made it to Evans Hall, huffing and puffing after a long walk uphill, I wasn't sure I had arrived at the right place. It was only a few minutes before five o'clock, when the class was scheduled to begin, but I didn't see anyone solving Rubik's Cubes. 10 Evans, the lecture hall listed on the syllabus, appeared to be occupied by a psychology course. (I could make out PLEASURE ≠ GOOD on the blackboard.) Across the hall was a statistics class.

I took a seat at one of the chairs in the hallway and looked around. Clusters of students were chatting here and there, but from what I could overhear, the topic was limited to their plans for spring break.

And then, all at once, the hall began to echo with the sound of cubing. Everywhere I looked there were people solving Rubik's Cubes. The tenor of the conversation had changed, too. Where previously the students had been discussing road trips, now they were passionately debating optimal solutions to the cross. The hall gradually filled with more and more students, all of them carrying Rubik's Cubes. "Everyone's cubing?" said one, depositing his backpack on the floor.

"What do you think?" another replied.

Solve the Rubik's Cube is a complicated course, but grading it is not. For each section, three elements factor into the final grade. The first is attendance. The course meets once a week. Miss four sessions, and you will automatically fail. The second is the midterm. For the beginner students, this involves solving the first two layers of Rubik's Cube, with no time limit. For the advanced students, it means doing the same in less than two minutes. The third is the final. If you're in the beginner section and you can't solve Rubik's Cube within ten minutes, given five attempts, you fail. For those in the advanced section, the requirements are much stricter: solve Rubik's Cube five times in a row, with no solve exceeding one minute and fifteen seconds.

There was a palpable air of nervousness in the room when everyone settled into their seats. 10 Evans is a huge lecture hall, but the clicking of Cubes and rustling of packs made it feel quite small, as if the space had constricted. The instructors, a diverse band of undergraduate and graduate students, about half female and half male, hung around the stage, wearing green zip hoodies, signifying their membership in the Cal Rubik's Cube Club.

"It's quiz day!" said the president, hopping onstage.

I had met Chia-Wei Lu before, at the 2012 U.S. National Championship. There, he was ebullient, charming, and rakishly handsome, his black hair cropped close on the sides and long on top. Kicking off the midterm, Lu, a senior in the biology department, was no different. With practiced ease, he started mixing up the Cubes of the students in his group. (Since there are so many students, the course is split into smaller groups, each with its own instructor.)

Lu is one of the fastest cubers in the world. "I can do, like, three of you at once," he said to his students, mixing up their Cubes so fast it was hard to tell what his fingers were doing. The first student to whom he returned the puzzle, a young woman wearing a fake-fur vest, took it, but shrank back, as if she'd just been handed a spider, and emitted a faint cry of surprise.

Once his students had solved the first two layers, Lu set them another challenge: he solved the first two layers but for two adjacent edges in the second layer, which he swapped. To solve the case, the students would have to remove each edge and put it in the correct position, taking care not to unscramble the rest of the first two layers. "Okay, you're done," Lu said to one student, who then sighed with relief and actually crossed himself.

Not everyone had an easy time of it. One student, in sweatpants, flip-flops, and a San Francisco Giants hat, looked at the second case with the flipped edge pieces and shook his head. He rotated the puzzle a few times and shook his head again. But, after about a quarter of an hour, Lu got up in front of the class to make another announcement: "So all of you passed the quiz—awesome!"

It's hard to say exactly what Rubik's Cube teaches, because there is little it does not. You can use the puzzle to study mathematics, from geometry (the Cube is a platonic solid, after all) to group theory, an esoteric subject that is crucial in computer science. The Cube has been used in lectures on quantum physics and lessons for elementary school students on problem solving. But, perhaps more than anything, the puzzle teaches discipline.

Once the quiz was over, the class remained broken into groups. Each instructor began to teach his or her charges a new algorithm or two as they worked toward completing the last layer of the puzzle. One instructor in particular stood out. He was wiry, with a kind of coiled energy, like a welterweight doing battle with a particularly resilient foe. As I would later find out, this instructor was a graduate student in computer science named Jianneng Li. His students, four young men and two young women, sat watching with rapt attention.

When one student ran into trouble, confusing the first and last moves of a particular algorithm, Li summoned the group's attention. "Sometimes, when you cube for so long," he said, like a coach in the dugout giving a pep talk to his team, "it's difficult to remember how hard it was at first. So if someone is having trouble, be patient!"

One of his students looked up at me, presumably expecting I was the teacher. I offered that I might be able to help her. Instead, she held up her Rubik's Cube, which was completely solved. "I did it!" she squealed, her face glittering with delight. I gave her a high five and asked if she'd ever solved the puzzle before. No, she said, and admitted that, since Li had solved the first two layers for her, it probably didn't count.

When I looked back, she had already scrambled the puzzle. Industriously, she put the first two layers back together, and began wrestling with the last layer once more. Her face bore a look of determination. I asked her, when she took a break, why she had elected to sign up for the course. Well, she said with a laugh, she wanted to leave campus with a tangible skill.

*   *   *

A few minutes later, I got a lesson of my own. I asked Lu, who had finished with his students, if he wouldn't mind critiquing one of my solves. "I like your movements," Lu said, to my surprise. "Very smooth," he added. "It's just, like, *controlled*." Of course, my goal wasn't to solve beautifully, but quickly—I had only a few months until Worlds, after all.

Fortunately, Lu had a couple of pointers. For one, I had to stop rotating the Cube so much—shifting it from one orientation to another in search of my next move. Evidently, I'd taken Sun's advice too far. "It would be fine," Lu said, "if you could just shift it and do a trigger."

I professed ignorance to the term. Whatever Lu had just done to his Cube, a blur of motion on the right side, looked entirely unfamiliar to me. "Do you know why it's called a trigger?" Lu asked.

He removed his right hand from the puzzle. "It's 'cause you trigger a gun," he said, yanking his index finger a couple of times. When he returned his right hand to the puzzle, and performed the same motion, his Cube cycled quickly through a range of permutations, taking the puzzle from my case to solved and back again.

Lu also showed me that I'd been holding the puzzle wrong. While my left hand was in neutral grip—another term I'd never heard before—my right hand was in trigger grip. Neutral grip, also known as home grip, Lu explained, was when you had your thumb on the front face, and your other fingers on the back. Trigger grip was holding your thumb on the bottom, and your index finger on top.

The upshot was efficiency. Most of the time, Lu said, if you stayed in neutral, you wouldn't have to change your grip on the Cube, allowing you to proceed without interruption. When I started from neutral on my next solve, I found that it was a lot easier to turn the puzzle.

"I wish I'd taken your course!" I enthused to Lu.

"Yeah," he said, grinning. "It's hard to change your habits."

* * *

Later that night, after class was over, the instructors decamped for one of the student dives lining Telegraph Avenue. Their usual haunt—Thai Noodle, after which the WCA scrambling program, TNoodle, is named—was full, so they wound up at another Thai restaurant farther south. It must have been a familiar sight— the waitstaff didn't seem particularly impressed—but a pair of middle-aged women at the next table gawked. We passed our Rubik's Cubes around in a circle, scrambling the puzzles belonging to our neighbors, before passing them back. I got a handicap: my cross was already solved.

When someone counted down, we began solving. On my first attempt, I messed up badly, which led to my handicap increasing: now, it was agreed, I'd be allowed to start with not only the cross, but the first pair solved as well. This was a blow, if a small one: earlier, while demonstrating my technique to Lu, one of the female instructors, who was about my speed, looked over and grinned. "Wow," she said, impressed by my F2L technique. On the following solve, I got a little closer to not finishing last. Then a little closer still.

The following day, I found myself to the south, at Stanford, in the heart of Silicon Valley. Compared to Berkeley, cubing's presence at Stanford, or "The Farm," as the bucolic campus is affectionately known by its students, is surprisingly weak: there is no class on the subject, and the number of cubers is drastically smaller. Partly, this is because Berkeley is larger: it has nearly forty thousand students, compared to Stanford's relatively small population of about sixteen thousand. Jeremy Fleischman, a ginger-haired one-handed specialist and one of the former presidents of the Cal Rubik's Cube Club—the winner of the beer race at the 2012 U.S. National Championship—who now works as a software engineer in the Bay Area, has a different idea: "My pet theory," he says, "is that their students have too good work ethics to get involved in a new hobby like cubing, whereas Berkeley attracts the smart people who are also kind of slackers."

I don't think the word *slacker* fits any of the cubers I met at Cal—Lu, for instance, speaks five languages, including Mandarin, Tagalog, and Japanese—but, compared to my afternoon appointment in the Stanford Mathematics Department, virtually anyone would seem lazy.

Shotaro Makisumi, a doctoral candidate in his midtwenties, is slight and unassuming. He rises at 4 a.m. and goes to bed at 8 p.m., when the evenings of most graduate students are just beginning. He does this because, he finds, it's easier to contemplate the problems to which he has devoted his life without any distractions. These are mathematics so abstruse they literally cannot be described. "All I can say about what I do is it's about symmetries and it's incredibly beautiful," he told me. "Just trust me." When I said I believed him, he came across chagrined. "Sounds like I'm in some cult," he said.

Makisumi, of course, is "Macky," the wunderkind who spurred Tyson Mao to imagine that cubing might be more than a hobby pursued on the Internet. With his ebony hair arranged in a spiky formation, indigo jeans, and orange gingham shirt, he resembled Amadeus Cho, the Marvel superhero whose brain is his most potent weapon. That day, the only opponent was my Rubik's Cube, which Makisumi had offered to help me defeat.

The mathematics department is located at the northeastern corner of Stanford's quadrangle, in a sandstone building whose interior has been recently remodeled. Since it's the math building, it doesn't need many frills. The lounge, on the uppermost floor, where Makisumi and I met, boasted a number of comfortable chairs, a couple of chalkboards, and one of Makisumi's fellow students, who was staring at one of the chalkboards with a vacant expression. Makisumi told me the department had not long ago unintentionally played host to a number of vagrants, who lived undetected on the premises for several weeks before anyone realized they didn't attend the school: they looked just like the graduate students.

Makisumi didn't cube much anymore, like Toby, but he still retained his profound ability to unscramble Rubik's Cube in less time than it would take me to properly scramble it.

According to Makisumi, there are two kinds of cubers: those who twist fast and pause often, to figure out their next move, and those who turn slowly but smoothly, never pausing. When I asked if he belonged to the latter, he replied, "I almost represent the school." As Tim Sun and Toby Mao had hinted, the latter school had fallen out of favor. "I don't want to say look ahead became less important," Makisumi said, appraising these developments. "But I feel like sub-20, these days, you can do just by turning fast."

Unfortunately for me, turning fast was no longer an option. Even if I could unleash a barrage of twists, I didn't think my thumb would have allowed it: the soreness had extended to the tendon between my thumb and forefinger. There was no guarantee I'd be able to turn fast, and even a chance that I might never be able to cube again if I didn't learn how to solve more judiciously. The space bar on my laptop, which I used to start and stop the timing program, was starting to wear thin, just where my right thumb made contact. The keyboard looked unremarkable but for that key, which appeared to have been exposed to a small quantity of acid: a growing hole revealed the circuitry underneath.

In other words, I didn't have a choice: it was either go old school or go home. Fortunately, Makisumi is a skilled teacher; looking ahead is a lot harder than simply applying algorithms as fast as possible. When I asked Makisumi to demonstrate how he would approach a particular case for solving the first two layers, he asked me to try it myself. Only with a small caveat: instead of solving the four pairs, of corner and edge pieces, one at a time, he suggested I try doing two pairs at once. He didn't mean solving them at the same time. He meant solving them in sequence, without ever pausing to figure out the next move.

"This is just a training method," he said. "So I see these two—this pair and this pair." He pointed to four separate pieces that would eventually become two pairs. They were about as close together as four Lego bricks in a pile left behind by a child after a temper tantrum. "You should be able, even without turning, to calculate where this pair is going to be," Makisumi said, indicating the second corner and edge.

"Let me think about it," I said. There was a long pause. I could visualize the first two pieces linking up, coupling like a pair of railcars, and then I lost it. "Um . . . it's going to be somewhere over here?" I hazarded, pointing to the far side of the Cube. It wasn't even close.

"This piece is going to be over here," Makisumi said.

"And I just know that?"

In response, Makisumi put my Rubik's Cube behind his head, where he couldn't see it. "So you put this corner in," he said, "so now you know the corner is here." He pointed to the exact spot where the corner had, indeed, migrated. "The corner is still in the same orientation," he said. I wasn't entirely sure what to make of this, but he wasn't wrong. The corner had simply migrated without changing its orientation, like a car that's moved parking spaces but is still facing the same direction. "Now, if you know that," he said, "you can just keep going." Makisumi solved the two pairs we'd been discussing, all the while keeping the Cube out of sight. It was like watching a blind person pick up a bow and hit one bull's-eye after another.

"Wow," I said.

"But that should be almost automatic," Makisumi replied.

I wasn't sure where to begin. I had so many questions. How was such a thing possible? This wasn't like blindfold solving, where you memorize a configuration of the puzzle and proceed from there; Makisumi was literally seeing the Cube move inside his head. It's clichéd to describe someone as having eyes in the back of his skull, but in this case it seemed literally true. I asked Makisumi if he thought I could go sub-20 by Worlds. He did. When I told him Toby's advice, that I should first master the remaining last-layer algorithms, he demurred. "I would focus on F2L more," he said.

"And look ahead." Makisumi speaks quietly, with a laconic style, and carefully enunciates each word. This may be a relic of having learned English as a second language, or simply his natural perfectionism. (Makisumi also speaks immaculate French.) Realizing that I was hoping for a more elaborate answer, he added, "Until you get to twenty seconds, at least. You don't want to rush. There should be no stop between pairs."

"Yeah," I replied, "I'm not there yet!"

While we spoke I was scrambling my Cube, going through the motions I'd been practicing since I was fourteen years old. It was hard to come to terms with the fact that I would essentially have to relearn everything I knew. No motion, no algorithm, would escape suspicion. It was time to figure out what my solves were really made of.

Makisumi watched my hands like an entomologist tracking a butterfly. "You honestly don't have to turn that fast," he said. "You just need, like, three moves a second."

"That's probably not much faster than I'm doing right now," I observed.

"If you could do that—"

"But not stopping."

"Yeah, you'd easily be sub-20."

The two of us looked at my Cube.

"But that's the hard part," Makisumi said.

* * *

"I talk about this a lot," Weston Mizumoto said, "but it's making good decisions, right?" He held his Rubik's Cube in one hand, deciding what to do with it so quickly that his fingers resembled the legs of a spider, scurrying up the wall. If the cubers at Berkeley are less driven, but greater in number, those at Stanford seem to be more distinguished, although there are certainly fewer of them. Mizumoto, a junior studying computer science, had just finished designing his own operating system, logging twelve hours a day on the project. He was also a distinguished concert pianist, not to mention one of the fastest one-handed solvers in the world.

Wearing a white linen shirt with the sleeves rolled up, teal shorts, and tortoiseshell glasses, Mizumoto gave off a distinctly California vibe. He spoke like a character parodying a twenty-something on television, interjecting *like* into every sentence. But his laid-back demeanor was probably more in line with the "Stanford duck syndrome," which the *New Yorker* once defined as seeming cheerful while paddling furiously to stay afloat.

When Mizumoto was more serious about piano—"I consider myself a cuber first, and then a pianist, and then a programmer," he said—he would spend hours dissecting a single passage. He scored victories at piano competitions across Southern California, where he grew up. (It's also how he met his girlfriend, a concert pianist studying at Juilliard.) In high school, he told me, his summer vacations essentially boiled down to cubing, as much as eight hours a day. "To the point where my fingers were, like, bleeding," he said.

If Makisumi is the wise elder, Mizumoto is the twenty-first-century guru, dispensing advice on YouTube. For a while, Mizumoto told me, his ultimate goal was to have something named after himself. "I thought it would be really cool," he said, "if I could just think of a set of algorithms, or a way of doing something, that people would call 'The Weston Something.'" He waved his hands, as if sketching a banner in the air.

While it never quite happened—for a while, cubers in Southern California called his style of one-handed turning the Weston Style, although, as he freely admits, he borrowed it from the Japanese—his influence on the subsequent generation of cubers shouldn't be understated. In 2012, when Mizumoto failed to defend his title in the one-handed event at the U.S. National Championship, he was distressed that he'd never so much as heard of the challenger. "And then the guy came up to me later that day and said, 'I learned everything I know about one-handed solving from your videos,'" Mizumoto told me. "I was, like, 'Okay, I like this guy now.'"

I met Mizumoto in the late afternoon at the Stanford student café. His talk of deliberating over every possible choice sounded eminently familiar: I, too, had played an instrument—the clarinet—and studied it for years, playing in bands and orchestras from the time I was in elementary school until I reached college. "If you're practicing the same thing over and over again," Mizumoto said, sounding like one of my old teachers, "you're probably not going to improve very fast, because you're practicing the wrong thing, right?"

He used to videotape all his solves, he said, and watch them in slow motion. That way, it was easier to spot mistakes. With every twist, he asked himself the same question. "If I had unlimited time to think about this, would I have made the same decision? And if it's not the case, then you made the wrong decision."

To me, this seemed like an impossibly high standard to which to hold one's solves, but Mizumoto explained there were other benefits. The more you solved Rubik's Cube while paying close attention, the more likely you were to stumble upon something you didn't know before. "It feels like there are a bunch of these secrets," he said. "And your goal is to find all of these secrets."

For instance, there was more than one way to solve the cross. I knew this, but Mizumoto threw the fact into fresh light. He watched me attempt a solve. Then he stopped me. In this instance, the cross was all but complete: one of the four arms was in the correct position, but incorrectly oriented, the white sticker pointing away from the white center, rather than matching up with it. Mizumoto showed me that I could twist the upper *two* layers of the Cube together to orient the edge, saving me a move. "There's little tricks," Mizumoto said, with boyish glee. "If you know them, all of a sudden you have new abilities."

Still, as I suspected, there was no shortcut to getting faster. "There's no way you can get good at cubing without spending hours and hours on it every day," Mizumoto said. When I told him that I had never completed more than sixty or seventy solves in one go, a tally I was unlikely to repeat anytime soon, owing to my thumb, he responded as if I'd just informed him that I was having trouble mastering the alphabet. "Oh," he said.

Mizumoto told me he'd heard Kevin Hays, the American Big Cube specialist, tell some young cubers at a competition that if they wanted to be fast, they couldn't treat cubing as a hobby. To Mizumoto, this pronouncement had the ring of truth. "It's not just something that you do when it's fun, right? It's something, like, I'm going to do ten averages of one hundred today whether or not they're good, whether or not my hands hurt, I'm just going to do it."

Before eight in the morning on a Saturday, most students at Yale are fast asleep. The streets of New Haven are empty and the halls of the old Gothic campus are completely silent. One morning in April, I followed the only noise I could make out: a faint clicking, like the sound of locusts, which gradually rose as I entered Linsly-Chittenden Hall. It was the first time I'd attended a competition in eight months, my first chance to test my thumb and newfound knowledge, to see if the lessons I'd learned would pay off as I hoped they would.

You know you're getting into cubing when you find yourself, on a Saturday morning, doing just that. Scores of cubers, most of them kids, accompanied by their parents, had gathered in the building's main lecture hall, a wood-paneled room with windows by Louis Comfort Tiffany and decades' worth of graffiti on the desks, including geometric figures, snippets of Latin, and the phrase *No War*, for the Yale spring competition.

For the first time, I volunteered to help run the event. The organizers, a pair of Yale undergraduates, were extremely harried. They were using a small table jammed in the corner to scramble puzzles, and needed judges to sit onstage and monitor each solve. Even though I had yet to read the rulebook front to back—it extended to some twenty different articles—this was my fourth competition, so I knew what the protocols were. That's what I told myself.

My first contestant, whose name I had to bellow, was a boy who couldn't have been more than twelve years old. He had close-cropped sandy hair and wore a large hooded sweatshirt with the sleeves rolled up. When he sat down, I asked him if this was his first competition. He meekly nodded. I showed him how the timer worked, and told him that, when he was ready, I would unveil his Cube and give him fifteen seconds to inspect it. The boy picked up his Cube, touched the pad, and started his solve, fingers flying, while his family looked on proudly from the audience.

Then I realized something had gone horribly wrong. The timer, which was facing the audience, wasn't moving. Already I could see his mother, holding a video camera, furrowing her brow, perplexed that the red numerals hadn't budged. That's when I glanced at the timer and realized I had failed to reset it: it still bore the mark of the previous attempt.

It pained me to have to interrupt the boy, his face a mask of concentration, the tip of his tongue sticking out of his mouth, to tell him that his first attempt, his first official solve, was null and void. Fortunately, since it was my fault, the organizers dispensed an extra attempt, but I had to shuttle the boy off the stage. His Cube would have to be rescrambled.

As luck would have it, my own round got off to a better start. I was in such a rush, trying to find a seat onstage, taking a pause from judging, that I was hardly thinking about what I had to do. Without really being conscious of it, I followed the same motions through which I'd just led several contestants, activating the timer and unscrambling the Cube: 20.96 seconds, a personal best in competition by nearly eight seconds.

I didn't even have time to figure out what had gone right—I was called to the stage immediately afterward to attempt my next solve—but I did have time to start worrying about what might go wrong. The next couple of solves were probably more reflective of where I was than where I wanted to be: hovering in the low thirties, not much faster than I'd been eight months before. The arc of my injury had brought me back to the same place; the average worked out to 31.38 seconds, an improvement of just under a second.

In the audience, later, I found myself consulting with a number of other cubers. We'd all had things go wrong, in one way or another. Andy Smith, a teenager from New Jersey whom I'd met at the U.S. National Championship nearly three years before, had forgotten his signature noise-reducing earmuffs. In order to distract himself, he'd taken to eating potato chips and Sour Patch Kids from the vending machine in the hallway. Since eating relaxes your body, his thinking went, it no longer has the capacity to get anxious. Evidently, his strategy had flaws. During his penultimate solve, Smith, who won the 2013 U.S. National Championship, messed up. His final average, 9.64 seconds, kept him just off the podium. Third place went to a cuber who clocked in at 9.63 seconds.

Fortunately, Smith is the kind of guy for whom even the most stinging of defeats is only temporary. Besides, something crazy had just happened to him: he'd been invited onstage at a concert by Logic, the hip-hop artist, who'd become enamored of Rubik's

Cube. "This is Logic's Cube!" Smith said, pulling out another Rubik's Cube. Apparently, he'd accidentally taken it off the tour bus. Smith appeared to be more excited than if he had won the competition. (Later that year, Logic would release his second album, *The Incredible True Story*, which includes the tongue-in-cheek line, "Man, bitches love the Rubik's Cube.")

Smith knew what I hoped to do, and how far I was from getting there. What were my splits? he asked. I honestly replied that I didn't know. What he meant, he explained, was, did I know how long it took me to solve the different phases of CFOP—the cross, the first two layers, the last layer. "What are you slow at?" he asked. He had a point: until I had benchmarks against which to judge myself, how would I know what needed to be worked on?

Before the end of the competition, Smith asked me to scramble my Cube. I figured he'd ask me to solve two pairs without looking at them. Just as Makisumi had. Then Smith darted his hand forward, covering my Cube before I'd had a chance to even inspect it. What did you see? he asked.

Nothing, I replied.

That's what we need to work on, he said.

ST. ERNŐ

When I attended my first Rubik's Cube competition, in the summer of 2012, I made sure to seek out the most veteran cuber in the room. If anyone had anything to say about Ernő Rubik, I figured, it would be one of the graybeards. Perhaps there would be a lead, or even a story or two. The oldest cuber at the competition, Lars Petrus, had indeed met Mr. Rubik.

"I guess I got his autograph, shook his hand," Petrus said. "I haven't really talked to him. He's not much for the, you know, the limelight and the celebrity lifestyle."

When I asked Petrus to whom I might speak to learn more about Rubik, he replied as if I'd just asked for help finding the Ark of the Covenant. "Oh, I don't know," he said. "You're not going to get to talk to Ernő Rubik, because he barely talks to himself, it seems."

Petrus, the dour Swede who competed at the 1982 World Championship, is not one to sugarcoat things, but even I found this excessive. Surely, Rubik had talked to someone?

If he had, I could find little evidence of it. Virtually all of the cubers I approached over the next three years gave one of two responses: Either they had not met Rubik, and saw little chance of ever doing so, or they had, and had nothing to tell me. "The first time I met him was obviously in Budapest, at the World Championship," said Jessica Fridrich. "And that was the last time I met him."

Perhaps because of the language barrier, she surmised—neither of them spoke very good English at the time—they didn't interact much.

The story was the same with Minh Thai. "I did the Cube in front of him," Thai recalled. Rubik's response was brief, albeit complimentary: "Pretty good." Like many cubers, Thai had collected Rubik's signature, but not much else. "I'd like to meet him again," Thai said. He'd saved the press kit from the 1982 World Championship, which had this to say about Rubik:

Life for the Professor has never been quite the same since he invented his Cube.

He is a boyish looking 37 year old with pale blue eyes and sandy hair who wears his cords, high-necked white pullover, leather jacket, Beatle cap and scarf with a casual laid back style.

He is also rich and getting richer, as global sales of the Cube continue to soar and he is one of the busiest Ambassadors visiting toy capitals of the world promoting his Cube.

His English has improved dramatically since he attended a private tutor in London last year, which has helped him enormously to spread his gospel of the Cube across the pages, and on the television screens, of the world's media.

When he's not touring and teaching, he spends as much time as he can with his wife and two small children.

He enjoys Science Fiction novels and films ('Star Wars' was a particular favourite, and 'The Empire Strikes Back'), poetry, and listening to the cool relaxing vibes of Count Basie and Duke Ellington on his Hi-Fi.

At weekends, he enjoys boating and walking in the privacy of his country cottage at Lake Balaton.

When he's asked about money, the chain-smoking Professor

says he leaves that to others "to work out." He still drives a baby
600cc Fiat.

In the photograph included with the press kit, Rubik is dressed
in a dark suit and striped tie, holding what appears to be a cigarette in one hand and his Cube in the other.

More contemporary cubers like Tyson Mao hadn't fared any
better. "I shook his hand," Mao said. "He didn't say much to me."
I learned this the night I spent at Mao's house in Hillsborough,
during my trip to the San Francisco Bay Area. "This is the box of
shit I'm allowed to keep," he said, referring to his wife's insistence
that he reduce his Cube footprint. It contained a number of his
most prized possessions, including a pair of first-generation Rubik's Cubes, from the 1980s, still in their cylindrical packaging.
"The reason why I brought out this box was simply this thing,"
Mao told me, removing a slim cardboard parcel, whose flaps
he unfolded to reveal a portrait of Rubik, signed by the man
himself.

For a long moment, neither of us said anything. To me, anyway, the whorls of Rubik's signature felt almost holy, as awe-
inspiring as the knuckles of some long dead saint.

In the photograph, Rubik was dressed casually, in a red long-
sleeved shirt and faded purple vest with quilted shoulders. His
expression was entirely neutral, his lips forming a flat line, his
brows neither arched nor furrowed. "I mean," Mao said, finally,
before putting the picture away, "it's up to him to decide how he
wants to interact with his people."

Rubik was born in the air-raid shelter of a Budapest hospital
during World War II, on July 13, 1944. His father, Ernő Rubik
Sr., was a noted aeronautical engineer, with special expertise in
the design of gliders. Rubik once said that he can still see planes
designed by his father in the skies above Budapest. His mother,

Magdolna Szántó, was a poet, making Rubik the union of art and science in the most literal sense.

This, anyway, is what I've cobbled together from the handful of accounts I've found of his life. Unlike, say, Steve Jobs, about whom there are biographies, documentaries, and even feature films, the biographical literature on Rubik is scant. This is not an accident. According to Viktor Böhm, Rubik's associate, Rubik is not only humble and modest, but also extremely averse to publicity. "Basically," Böhm said, "he was a recluse in his native Budapest. And many, many requests, of course, found him, for interviews and books and biographies and movies and all the rest of it. Which he basically immediately turned down."

The most substantial article yet written about him was authored by John Tierney, the American journalist, in the March 1986 issue of *Discover* magazine. "At first, he didn't want to talk to me at all," Tierney recently said. Indeed, the inventor rebuffed him. Initially, he gave Tierney a manuscript about his life, and suggested he read it, but eventually Rubik relented and allowed Tierney to follow him around for a week. The result, "The Perplexing Life of Ernő Rubik," runs to some five and a half thousand words. "This is going to collapse," Tierney remembers thinking. "That was a really hard piece to do," he said.

In Budapest, Tierney reported, there were two schools of thought about Rubik. One held that he had been turned into a bit of a curmudgeon by his own success. "One moment," Tierney writes, "he's a professor of design who makes $150 a month and has never been outside the Iron Curtain; the next he's the richest and most famous man in Hungary, beset by money-grubbing communists and capitalists alike." The other theory was that, as Tierney put it, Rubik was a "taciturn, suspicious loner" long before he invented the Cube.

Rubik, Tierney said, preferred not to discuss either theory. Even though he presumably understood the conventions of the celebrity profile, the inventor seemed either unwilling to help

Tierney fathom his subject, or perhaps had reconciled himself to the difficulty of doing so. "It's very hard to say the truth," Rubik told Tierney. "Usually we are only saying part of the truth."

In 1967, Rubik graduated from the Budapest University of Technology and Economics, where he studied architecture. After lecturing in the department of drawing and design, he returned to school, this time at the Academy of Applied Arts, taking a second degree in 1971. Shortly thereafter, he signed on to teach interior design.

In 1974, as Tierney has it, Rubik was still living at home with his mother in a two-bedroom flat. His room was filled with geometric constructions in cardboard and wood. One day, he happened to be playing with a set of wooden blocks and got it into his head to try to attach them. He used elastic bands at first. Surprisingly, it worked—he could twist the contraption—but his model's shortcomings soon became apparent: the bands snapped.

Rubik's solution, as Tierney puts it, was "brilliantly simple." After cutting and sanding the blocks, he carefully assembled them so they supported one another. Then, Rubik applied adhesive paper to the sides so he could keep track of what happened when he twisted it. "It was wonderful," he later wrote, "to see how, after only a few turns, the colors became mixed, apparently in random fashion."

But when Rubik tried to put each color back on the appropriate side, he didn't know how. It was, he later said, "like staring at a piece of writing written in a secret code." Only, and this is the extraordinary thing, it was a code that he himself had invented.

Rubik allowed Tierney to quote from "Rubik on Rubik," an unpublished manuscript that he had written in English and apparently told the story of his life. Rubik doubted whether or not the public really wanted to read his autobiography. He told Tierney that he had secured a publisher, but hadn't yet had the time to make the requested revisions. (Tierney assured him that no American celebrity would have any such misgivings.) "Rubik's memoirs aren't unlike the Cube," Tierney reported. "Highly abstract, often tedious, yet in their own way engaging and revealing."

Rubik seems never to have published the manuscript—for all I know, he destroyed it—meaning that Tierney's quotes are all we have to go on. Insofar as he quotes it, the manuscript was somewhat florid. Rubik described his parents' divorce, which took place when he was in college: "The waves surged high, but they did not reach me." His favorite activities were solitary: kayaking on the Danube and solving chess puzzles. His best friend, he wrote, was Renni, a stray Irish setter.

According to multiple accounts, it took Rubik at least a month to solve his puzzle. During this time, according to one story, which may well be apocryphal, Rubik's mother brought food to his room. After two weeks, he came out and put the Cube on the table, and said it was impossible. His mother cried, "You fool!" She pointed out that the puzzle had begun in a solved state: it had to be possible to return there. In the end, Rubik managed to unscramble his Cube. "I remember how proudly I demonstrated to her when I found the solution of the problem," he wrote of his mother in the manuscript. "And how happy she was in the hope that from then on I would not work so hard on it."

Rubik has a way in interviews of answering and yet not answering questions at the same time. For instance, why did he invent his puzzle? Multiple sources report that he wanted to challenge his students. Others directly contradict this. Yes, he showed his Cube to his students, Tierney reports, but Rubik hadn't built it for them. More recently, Rubik contradicted himself, telling CNN, in his first video interview in years, that he designed it for his students, while searching for a suitable task to assign them.

When I finally managed to contact him, Rubik himself only succeeded in muddling the picture further. In 2013, at the World Championship, I met one of his associates, Holly Riehl, the stateside liaison for Seven Towns, the London-based firm to which Rubik has assigned the rights to his Cube. She offered to relay my questions to him by e-mail.

"How would you describe your intentions in building the puzzle?" I asked.

> At its birth almost 40 years ago, the Cube was first and foremost an object of art: creating a new meaning for Platonic solids in the form of a design-object speaking to human universals of perception, cognition and emotion.

Rubik was certainly a genius, and eloquent, but he was starting to remind me of Isaac Newton, the famous physicist, whose maid is said to have once found him boiling his watch and holding an egg.

As I read on, though, I realized that Rubik was neither absentminded nor obtuse: he simply couldn't be reduced to one side alone.

> Objects of arts have multiple sources of inspiration and if they succeed, they become the inspiration for others. I was obviously inspired by the science and engineering behind three-dimensional/descriptive geometry among many other things. It is also true that I was genuinely frustrated as a young professor at the difficulty of explaining the transformations of shapes to my students and that I relished using the Cube in class. In that sense, a first "application" of the Cube was undoubtedly in education.

＊ ＊ ＊

For Rubik, the point is not so much the destination but the journey. Perhaps the clearest indication that Rubik may never be figured out is the narrative he uses, in the excerpts quoted by Tierney and in the introductions to a handful of books, to describe his relationship to his Cube. It is not one of finding the answer, but of struggling with it.

Once, in the introduction to a French book on Rubik's Cube, the inventor wrote that he liked to play games, but that his favorite opponent was not another human being, but nature itself. "I think the Cube arose from this interest," he explained. In "Rubik on Rubik," as quoted by Tierney, Rubik likened the Cube to a force of nature: "There is something terrifying in its calm state, like a wild beast at rest, a tiger in repose, its power lurking."

In 1986, Tibor Laczi, one of Rubik's chief associates, told Tierney, "Most Hungarians that come here want to look at shops or buy jewelry or visit a bar or a striptease." Laczi was describing Rubik's first visit to Austria, which was more permissive than neighboring Hungary. "Rubik went back to his hotel," Laczi said. "He was always that way, even after the money started. He never liked to be away from his family for long or spend money on himself. The only thing he did was start smoking better cigarettes. There was no drinking, no women—he just went back to his hotel room to read."

"They were such an odd couple," Tierney told me. Laczi was gregarious and charming, Rubik taciturn and aloof. "Everyone made money on the Cube except the Hungarians," a playwright who dramatized the puzzle's rise told Tierney. Before Laczi, anyway. "He was what Rubik needed," Tierney said. The first time Tierney met Laczi, the latter sported a diamond ring.

According to a rare interview that he gave in 2009, on the website of the European Union, Rubik loves to read. "I indulged myself in books from the moment I learnt to read," he said. "Books offered me the possibility of gaining knowledge of the World, Nature and People. I have a special interest in science fiction." In the interview, Rubik listed about a dozen luminaries who have influenced his work. They included everyone from Isaac Asimov, the science-fiction writer, to Leonardo da Vinci.

"What do you see as the Cube's virtues?" I asked Rubik, in my email.

> As noted, the Cube relates to human universals in a very simple and immediate manner. It crosses all cultural or age barriers and disregards socio-economic differences. It is languageless: it never needed a users' manual, anyone who touches it understands the challenge instantly.
>
> The Cube also embodies the tension of our most basic contradictions: simplicity and complexity, dynamism and stability, pleasure and frustration and so forth.
>
> Over the years, the Cube has also become a universal symbol for bewildering complexity and triumphant human intelligence and problem solving skills. As such, going back to its origins, the Cube can be immensely helpful in developing emotionally engaging, immersive learning experiences for younger and older students—something I am ever more interested in exploring.

"My favorite cocktail," Rubik once said, "is what is mixed of Beauty and Truth—I call it Harmony."

By the time of Tierney's visit, in 1986, Rubik had purchased a villa. "It was the grandest house in Budapest, I think," Tierney told me. (He added that, by American standards, it was nothing special.) Until then, Rubik had been living in his father's house with his wife and two children. (They were later joined by two more, for a total of three girls and one boy.) I once heard a rumor that Rubik lived in a castle with one floor for every one of his children. This is not true, but given the state of Hungary at the time, it might as well have been. "Here was the first great tangible reward," Tierney wrote. Rubik took him on a tour, showing him the three-car garage, with a Mercedes inside, the glassed-in porch, and the swimming pool and sauna in the basement.

Tierney noticed something was missing. "Where's the dining room?" he asked.

"I eliminated that," Rubik replied. "We'll eat right there." He pointed to a corner of the kitchen. Tierney wondered aloud if Rubik planned to have many guests over for dinner. As Tierney tells it, Rubik puffed on his cigarette and frowned. "I hope not," he said.

Before heading to Europe, I reached out to Böhm again, to ask whether or not Rubik would be available for an interview. While Böhm himself would be in Budapest, he replied that he wasn't sure about his boss. Böhm didn't close the door entirely, but neither did he leave it open. Still, I'd managed to solve Rubik's Cube, hadn't I? How hard could the man himself be to puzzle out?

YOU CAN NEVER LEAVE
A CUBE UNSOLVED

Ron van Bruchem pointed skyward. "How do you like my lamp?" he asked. It was springtime in the Netherlands, and the sun set early. In the darkness, we could see a handful of apartment blocks rising, their frames outlined by windows aglow. At first, I couldn't make out what he was pointing to; I didn't have my glasses on. But after squinting for a moment, I could discern a light that didn't resemble its neighbors. It wasn't one color, but several, and appeared to be much larger than an ordinary lamp.

Van Bruchem lives in Almere, the largest city in Flevoland, Holland's newest province. Almere lies in a polder, that is, a spit of land reclaimed from the sea, by dint of dredging. Upon entering his apartment, van Bruchem ushered me into his living room. I saw the lamp sitting on the windowsill for what it was: a giant facsimile of Rubik's Cube. The rest of the room was similarly appointed. There was an homage to *Golconda*, the surrealist painting by René Magritte, in which men in bowler hats and dark coats float like balloons, receding into the distance, only with actual pieces of Rubik's Cube extruding from the canvas in place of the figures. This hung above what appeared to be an ordinary cabinet from IKEA, divided into three rows and three columns.

Van Bruchem had filled the nine cubbyholes with organizers in shades of various colors, such that it called to mind, even from a short distance, Rubik's Cube.

Some years ago, van Bruchem started dating Hanneke Rijks, the mother of Mats Valk, who, at the time of my visit, still held the world record for a single solve. Rijks is a woodworker with a shop in Amsterdam and holds a graduate degree in mathematics. Her clients include the Dutch royal family. She has also restored furniture in the Amsterdam branch of the Hermitage. Her own sculptures have won prizes at competitions. "It's called *Hungarian Sardines*," van Bruchem said proudly, displaying what resembled an enormous wooden tin of sardines, which he'd plucked from atop the cabinet. The tin had been pried open, a thin piece of warped, light-colored wood serving as the lid, revealing a mass of cubies—the small, colorful constituents of Rubik's Cube— bobbing in a bath of hardened resin. *The Hidden Cube*, van Bruchem added, showing me another sculpture made by Rijks, this time a wooden block, about the size of Rubik's Cube, one corner of which appeared to be peeling away, revealing Rubik's Cube, hidden inside.

Van Bruchem splits his time between Almere, where he maintains an apartment to be close to his daughter, and Amstelveen, a suburb of Amsterdam, where he and Rijks own a flat in which she lives with Valk and his sister Natalia. "It's funny," van Bruchem said, pointing to a number of paper cubes on his bookshelf whose sides had been shaded using colored pencils, "she made . . . for Mats, his world record." The cubes were arranged in descending order, starting with one the size of a grapefruit: the scramble. On they went, from the cross to the last layer, representing each stage of Valk's world-record solution, shrinking until the puzzle was solved and the size of a lychee fruit.

The tour included the water closet, where Rijks had carved a wooden projection bolted to the wall that was designed to resemble Rubik's Cube with one half open, the better to access the toilet paper hanging inside. Van Bruchem had strategically placed Rubik's Revenge (the 4x4) and the Professor's Cube (the 5x5) atop the trash can. "I cube a lot on the toilet," van Bruchem once told a blogger, "and sometimes a piece pops into the toilet." He added, "I have cubes everywhere in my house, even in the shower."

I had been told by George Miller, the well-known puzzle inventor and collector who appeared on video at the Liberty Science Center and whom I met in person during my trip to the Bay Area, that Holland is the most puzzle-crazy nation on earth. Van Bruchem seemed determined to prove it. He had a complete set of *Cubism for Fun*, the triannual newsletter put out by the Nederlandse Kubus Club, the oldest continuously operating society devoted to Rubik's Cube in the world. Once a year, the club holds Dutch Cube Day. Since the dissolution of the craze for Rubik's Cube in the 1980s, the club has expanded to welcome aficionados of other puzzles. In photographs, the event looks like something out of Harry Potter's Diagon Alley: tables and tables of puzzles, from Rubik's Cube and its descendants to wooden entanglements of every size.

In the hallway, where a placard hung commemorating his one-hundredth competition, a mark he'd reached in 2013, van Bruchem started rummaging around his small closet. What remained of his puzzle collection fit into a couple of cardboard boxes. He told me that his ex-wife had thrown out most of his puzzles. He pulled out a few specimens of Rubik's Cube, including one made of clear plastic. "I have some stuff here," he said. "It's really boring."

"She didn't really like puzzles?" I ventured.

Well, van Bruchem said with a sigh, he thought she wanted to hurt him.

When I first met him in 2013 at the World Championship, van Bruchem pointed out that anyone could start an organization to supplant the World Cube Association. "There is no legal entity 'WCA,'" he said, using air quotes. "So anyone could start a new 'World Cube Federation,' or whatever." The situation could easily become like that in boxing: there are different organizations that each claim to administer the world title. "I mean, it's the WBC, or the WBO, or the WBF, or whatever," van Bruchem said. "No one knows the difference anymore."

In fact, there have already been attempts to knock the WCA off its perch, most notably in China, which has seen the rise of the Chinese Cube Association, or CCA. (It's not all that surprising, considering that the WCA has only five delegates covering the entire country, that some enterprising person spotted an opportunity.) But the WCA has something that no other organization can match: van Bruchem, and his zeal for Rubik's Cube. Every year, van Bruchem, frequently accompanied by Rijks, travels to some far-flung country to help organize competitions, like a missionary spreading the gospel of Rubik's Cube.

Thanks to his efforts, the influence of the World Cube Association has expanded to more than a dozen additional countries, from Iran to Iceland. As a result, van Bruchem has wound up in front of village assemblies in Tamil Nadu, where the elders questioned the value of cubing—wouldn't it distract the children from their studies?—not to mention the Trans-Siberian Express, with a suitcase full of Rubik's Cubes.

Van Bruchem is one of the most fun-loving, easygoing people you are likely to ever meet. "Tyson and I, we've never been friends," he told me, at the 2013 World Championship. "We have very different personalities, and, uh . . . I think, at the moment, it's really, really the worst ever." Then he chuckled. What to someone else might be a dispiriting situation—conflicting with the cofounder of the organization to which you've devoted much of your life—was, insofar as van Bruchem expressed himself, just a minor inconvenience, or at the very least, a temporary one.

Part of this might have to do with van Bruchem's upbringing.

He was raised by the Salvation Army. There isn't much he hasn't faced in the way of adversity. And yet van Bruchem typically signs his e-mails "Happy Cubing!" He qualified for the most elite track of the public education system, the Voorbereidend Wetenschappelijk Onderwijs, which lasts six years and involves intensive study of Latin and Greek. After graduating from the University of Twente, he started working as a software engineer at Rabobank, the multinational financial services company head-quartered in Utrecht that specializes in agribusiness.

Van Bruchem, who is in his early fifties, is still in the IT de-partment, but now serves as the business architect. With a budget in the tens of millions of euros, he decides what projects the de-partment should pursue. "I love my job," he says, but admits that it sometimes keeps him very busy. One morning, he showed me his schedule: a flurry of blocks, representing meetings, took up all the space on his e-calendar from 7 a.m. until 5 p.m. Several of the blocks overlapped, meaning that he was supposed to be in two places at the same time.

In addition to his work cubing, van Bruchem travels for his job with some frequency: he's visited the United States more than seventy-five times. But neither a dearth of sleep nor con-flicting responsibilities can dampen his spirit. When he picked me up from the airport in Amsterdam in his blue hatchback, van Bruchem kept up a running commentary, telling me about the scenery. We passed one apartment complex he described as the Compton of the Netherlands, a lamentably disadvantaged area with high rates of crime and low social mobility. After crossing the bridge to the polder, van Bruchem joked about living several meters below sea level. "If there's a big flood," he said, with a chuckle, "my house is gone!" Not even the street signs escaped his attention. "Ah, it's Bob Marley Street!" Almere is divided into quarters; in the Muziekwijk, where he lives, every street name is musically inspired. His apartment, for instance, is just around the corner from Michael Jacksonplein.

*   *   *

In a lot of ways, Ron van Bruchem and Tyson Mao are complete opposites—Mao is brash and headstrong, van Bruchem gentle and easygoing—but together, they make an effective team. Their chemistry was on full display when they dealt with Mátyás Kuti, the Hungarian cuber who famously cheated in the multiblindfold event.

"It's all about punishment, yeah?" van Bruchem said, of the American judicial system, which he finds puzzling. "So Tyson was about 'expelled for life,' and so on."

One of the other board members at the time, a Japanese veteran named Masayuki Akimoto, was more concerned that those who lost to Kuti and were denied the chance to be world champions have their honor restored.

"We are like, 'Okay, he is still young,' and his parents didn't teach him to behave well," said van Bruchem of his response, and that of the other European officials.

In the end, the resolution, which led to the satisfaction of all parties, involved a combination of all three approaches to wrongdoing: Kuti's tainted victories and world records—only those where it could be proved there was solid evidence of malfeasance—were vacated. He was also banned from competition for several years, and those who lost to him were retroactively elevated to the proper status. (Although, since Tyson told me Kuti never returned the prize money, their titles were largely symbolic.)

When I first met van Bruchem, he was preoccupied with what would happen to the WCA in the future. "I hope that we can keep everyone together," he said. "Instead of, like, there's going to be more unions, or whatever. That would be really sad, if that would happen."

The more cubing grew, the harder it would be, van Bruchem figured, to keep it growing. "Will people still start cubing," he wondered, "knowing that they have to practice for four years to become world class?" Mao was no longer concerned—he was moving on, after all—but van Bruchem still felt deeply invested. "It feels a bit like my child," he said.

"I think—I hope—that it will never die," he added. "Because the craze in the eighties was much, much bigger than it is now. But it only lasted two years. And now we're already in our eleventh year, and still growing."

Van Bruchem rushed through the door after a day at work. "Honey," he cried out. "I'm home!" I was in his living room, working on—what else?—my PLLs, the algorithms for permuting the last layer. Just weeks before, at the competition at Yale, I'd messed up the A-permutation, one of the most frequently encountered cases, which involves flipping the Cube over and rotating several faces in concert. The A-perm calls to mind the interlocking gears through which Charlie Chaplin travels in *Modern Times*, one face affecting the other, spinning and spinning and spinning around.

Memorizing algorithms, I was discovering, is a lot like memorizing scales. First, you have to pick one: there are scores of different options for every case. In Fridrich's day, as she told me, algorithms were by necessity boutique affairs, generated by hand. But now computers allow you to produce dozens of alternatives, optimized for whatever you like—the fewest moves, the easiest to execute, and so on. Then you have to practice the algorithm slowly, over and over, letting the rhythm of the movements sink into your fingers, at which point, hopefully, you can do it with your eyes closed. Then you start incorporating the algorithm into your solves, pausing, if necessary, to execute it when the proper case appears, even if it takes longer, at first, than whatever you used to do.

I had also started timing my splits, as per Andy Smith's recommendation. The cross took me about four seconds. The first two layers, about fourteen seconds. The last layer, about nine seconds. When I visited Berkeley, Chia-Wei Lu, the president of the Cal Rubik's Cube Club, who gave me a lesson, said I needed to get my F2L—meaning the cross *and* the first two layers combined— down to about ten seconds.

Thanks to the efforts of Rob Stuart, a towering Australian who goes by the handle Brest on the Internet, the splits of all the best cubers are common knowledge: Stuart watches videos of record-breaking solves over and over, reconstructing them from scratch. As if he were providing commentary for *SportsCenter*, he spells out the solutions, move by move, and then gives detailed analyses of each step.

Valk's world-record solve, for instance—5.55 seconds—took him forty-five moves (forty-nine if you count it as executed) for an average of about eight moves per second. If you were to set a metronome to the equivalent speed, it would be about 480 beats per minute. Prestissimo. The fastest jazz songs ever recorded top out just below 400 beats per minute. But not every phase of the solve was equally long or equally quick: the cross (plus the first pair, since Valk, along with most advanced cubers, solves both at once) required thirteen moves, which he completed in just over a second and a half.

The rest of the first two layers demanded thirty-three moves, which Valk completed in just under four seconds; the last layer, twelve moves and close to two seconds. In other words, Valk's time was unevenly distributed, just like mine. He spent most on the first two layers, and roughly the same on the cross and the last layer. Since I had yet to master the required algorithms, my last layer was twice as slow as my cross, although, like Valk, the sum of my cross and last layer more or less equaled the time required for the first two layers.

In other words, I had a lot of practicing to do. Some days, my splits were faster than others—I once recorded myself solving the cross and first two layers in just thirteen seconds. Other days, my splits were abysmally slow. By this point, I was using a timing program on my iPhone designed by Chinese cuber Jichao Li: the eponymous ChaoTimer, which I had downloaded from the App Store. The timing program worked like the StackMats used in competition. You touched the screen to activate the timer, including the fifteen-second inspection, after which you touched it again to start the solve, and once more to end it. More than once, I spent so much time trying to plan my cross, during inspection, that I failed to activate the timer in time: the resultant DNF, or Did Not Finish, felt doubly embarrassing, because I wasn't even in the pressured environment of competition that makes such mistakes commonplace.

When he was practicing, I asked van Bruchem, did he ever have up and down days?

Van Bruchem shrugged. He has a jutting chin, which gestures when he speaks, underlining his words. He also has a thick guttural accent, presumably because Dutch is a very throaty language. "That means your look ahead is not going well," he said. "Go slow! Or just don't cube. You don't want to build bad habits."

While van Bruchem got back to work—he had another meeting that night, into which he teleconferenced, his Rubik's Cube lamp illuminating the room—I sat on the couch and started solving slowly, deliberately not paying attention to the timer. It was much harder than I expected to keep twisting—as Makisumi and my other gurus had advised—without stopping. Like trying to stay on a balance beam, moving forward one step at a time, all the while struggling not to fall off. The goal, of course, wasn't to get to the end quickly, but it was hard to set aside that impulse—I wanted to finish the solve so badly. I had to remind myself, especially while going through sequences I knew, that it was more valuable to slow down and look for the next steps than to satisfy the urge to feel Rubik's Cube smoothly glide through my fingers.

Earlier, I noticed that the paper cubes representing Valk's world-record solve lay atop a printout of the actual solution.

Scramble: D2 U' R2 U F2 D2 U' R2 U' B' L2 R' B' D2 U B2 L' D' R2

x y' // inspection
F R D L F // cross
U R U' R' d R' U R // 1st pair
y U2' R' U' R // 2nd pair
U L U' L' d R U' R' // 3rd pair
y' U' R U R' U R U' R' // 4th pair (VLS)
R2' U' R' U' R U R U R U' R U2' // PLL

It blew me away how simple it was. The layperson, obviously, would have no idea how to make heads or tails of it, but I was beginning to understand the language of cubing well enough to get an inkling of what it meant. Since I had my Rubik's Cube with me, I tried following along, rehearsing the solution like a kid trying to imitate Michael Jordan's jumper, raising up straight at the ankles and letting the wrist fly just so: it was thrilling to experience what Valk had done, retracing his steps, so to speak, inch by inch. It read like poetry: Valk had reduced what is an enormously complex operation (solving Rubik's Cube) into a series of steps so simple that even I, who had yet to go sub-20, could grasp what had made the solve so quick.

Valk's solution didn't require anything out of the ordinary—just a single F turn during the cross. Most of the moves were U and R—turns of the upper and right-hand faces. In the same way Mozart sounds kind of elementary but is actually quite complex, Valk had woven together the simplest of moves into an awe-inspiring solution.

I ran through it over and over, as if I *were* reading a poem. With each attempt, I got the impression that more than I realized lay beneath the surface. For instance, Valk had somehow managed to keep the edges of the last layer almost all oriented while he solved the first two layers. It was hardly an accident that he skipped the orientation of the last layer and proceeded straight to permuting it. By the time he reached the last slot, the last layer was all but oriented.

With a few simple twists, he solved the final corner-edge pair of the first two layers and simultaneously oriented the last layer. This was his special technique, which had earned him the prize so coveted by Mizumoto: an eponymous tactic. It was called Valk Last Slot, or VLS, for short. All that was left for him was to tackle the A-permutation, one of the simplest PLLs, which he completed from the reverse. It was like watching a basketball player score thirty points' worth of uncontested layups, driving to the basket and dropping buckets at will.

When van Bruchem finished his conference call, he came over to see what I was doing. He pulled out his Cube—or, rather, one of his Cubes—and decided to show me something. (He also turned on the television. By his own admission, van Bruchem watches, on average, ten movies a week; the selection that night was *8mm*, starring the inimitable Nicolas Cage, as a detective who tries to figure out if a snuff film in the estate of a recently deceased man is real or not.) The move was called the sledge-hammer, van Bruchem said. And once I learned it, I would be able to do as Valk did, at least to some extent, and influence the orientation of the last layer.

Van Bruchem scrambled his Cube. Then he solved the first two layers: all that remained was a single pair, on the left-hand side, facing him. The last layer, he noted, had nary a single edge already oriented. The yellow face, which was the last layer, in this instance, had only the center piece, which was always oriented, since it couldn't move, facing skyward.

Then van Bruchem inserted the lone pair that remained into the first two layers. He did this not as I would have, by moving it out of the way, bringing the slot up, and inserting the pair. As if he were swinging a hammer, he slammed the pair down to the bottom of his Rubik's Cube, then swung it back up. At this point, presto: the last layer was no longer devoid of yellow squares. In addition to the center, two edges were now oriented, like the limbs of a lowercase r.

"In the beginning, it's a bit hard," van Bruchem said, reversing the move so the pair sprang back into place. The oriented edges disappeared, like footage of a vase shattering in reverse. He showed me how my normal technique would have resulted in the edges remaining on the sides of the last layer, rather than migrating to the top. I would have been left with one of the dreaded "dot OLLs," cases that typically involve a lot of moves, since the algorithms have to orient all four of the last layer's edges. "But, later," he added, performing the sledgehammer with all the confidence of a construction worker shattering a cinder block, "it's automatic."

Van Bruchem also introduced me to the "Sexy Move." Twist the right face ninety degrees clockwise, then the upper face of Rubik's Cube ninety degrees clockwise; then reverse the first turn, rotating the right face ninety degrees counterclockwise, followed by a ninety-degree counterclockwise twist of the upper face. In the lingo, the "Sexy Move" was R U R' U'.

"Why is it sexy?" I asked.

"Because it's just sexy," van Bruchem replied.

As if to demonstrate the point, he started applying the Sexy Move over and over, starting from the solved state. The front right-hand slot of the Cube cycled rapidly through a number of different states, first separating the corner and edge, then bringing them together in the wrong order, and then bringing them together in the right order, the corner flying backward to meet the edge like an iron filing drawn to a magnet. (I realized this was no different from the trigger Chia-Wei Lu had demonstrated, only different terminology.)

While Nicolas Cage prowled the screen, doggedly pursuing a

lead, I started over, beginning from a random state before progressing to the cross. I paid close attention so I could transition without hesitation to the first two layers, which I then solved, one corner-edge pair at a time. "Nothing wrong with that," van Bruchem said.

"Really?" I asked.

"Really," he said.

A few days later, van Bruchem and I took the train to Amstelveen, where Rijks and her two children met us for dinner at their apartment. They live not far from the city center, in a three-bedroom flat, appointed with more of Rijks's artwork and souvenirs of her travels with van Bruchem. On the wall hung a collage made of all her past credit and ID cards, framed like a painting. The cards were arranged by color, evoking the multicolored nature of Rubik's Cube. Different clusters of cards provided splashes of various hues, from indigo to carnelian. Opposite, framing the television, was a wooden shelving unit, stocked with puzzles and books. These included monographs on M. C. Escher and Kazimir Malevich, the Russian Formalist painter, whose stark compositions almost foreshadow the simplicity of Rubik's Cube. There were also encyclopedias of mazes and optical illusions. Rijks had displayed several sculptures, including an entirely functional wooden Rubik's Cube. The original *Hungarian Sardines*, a wooden tin so large it could have baptized a newborn, sat on the dining table.

As I saw it, even if I never met Rubik, it was still worth traveling to Europe just to get a little more face time with Valk. At competitions, he is usually so deluged with autograph requests that it's hard to corral him for an interview. After dinner, we hung out in his room. Since I had first met him at the 2013 World Championship, Valk had filled out. He no longer reminded me of Gumby. There was a faint dusting of stubble on his chin. He lived at home, as is not uncommon in Holland, while attending university in Amsterdam, where he was majoring in business analytics—a mash-up of economics, computer science, and mathematics. Not much had changed, he said. He still played soccer, for the same club, leveraging his lanky frame in the role of keeper. But he had less time to cube, thanks to his school-work.

Valk's sparsely appointed room had a cabinet for all of his trophies. (One was so tall it had to be laid on its side.) In the last two years, Feliks Zemdegs had managed to speed even further ahead, cutting his world-record average from 7.53 to 6.54 seconds. He and Valk were one and two, or two and one, depending on how you looked at it: Valk still had the record for a single solve, 5.55 to Zemdegs's 5.66, but Valk's average was nearly a second behind, at 7.45 seconds. Still, he was only the second person to have broken 7.5 seconds.

The two had most recently competed against each other in South Africa in late 2014. They headlined tournaments in Cape Town and Johannesburg. These days, they were both sponsored, which was another notable development: cubing had progressed to the point where the top contenders were outfitted with free puzzles, and sometimes even flown to competitions. Valk had been offered a salary to switch exclusively to solving Yuxin Cubes, an upstart brand, but declined. He told me he would get only eight and a half to nine-second solves on the puzzle, a significant step down from his usual times. At first, both Valk and Zemdegs were sponsored by Cameron Brown's speedcubeshop.com, but Valk had since switched his allegiance to thecubicle.us, a business run by Phil Yu, a recent Georgetown Law grad, out of the East Coast.

Valk had even started to give demonstrations: The managing director of a local company had learned of his hobby, and offered to pay for his travel to the upcoming World Championship in São Paulo. He also hired Valk to give periodic lessons and demonstrations to his employees. Once a month, Valk said, he found himself in a room full of suits, demonstrating his talents. "They mostly say it's impressive, like, what I can do," he said, with a chuckle. "But, for me, it's just, like, something I do on a daily basis."

I was curious what these lessons consisted of—had solving Rubik's Cube unlocked the secrets of free enterprise? In just an hour, Valk admitted, you couldn't teach anyone to solve Rubik's Cube. What you could give them was a few life lessons—for instance, that the solution to a problem is often further away than it initially appears. He manipulated his Cube in a flourish, the twists and turns echoing in his small room like coins spilling to the floor. It looked almost solved—all of the pieces were in the right place, only flipped. "It's close to solved," he said, "but this is one of the hardest states." Known as the superflip, it would take twenty moves to unscramble—the most of any state. "So, something that is close to being solved," he said, twirling the Cube, "may still be really unsolved. Stuff like that.

"For me," he added, "it's just fun." He didn't go to competitions any longer to break records or win trophies. "We went to South Africa," he said of the competitions he had recently attended with Zemdegs, "and we had so much fun not only cubing, but also swimming in the pool, playing table tennis." (The two of them also teamed up to solve what was then said to be the world's largest functional Rubik's Cube; they had to keep flipping it, like auto mechanics, since it was too heavy or too cumbersome to lift. It took them just under seventeen minutes.)

For Valk, anyway, this was one of the essential lessons of what it takes to be good at cubing. "Spatial awareness, that's really important," he said. "But there's also something; I don't know how you say it in English." I expected him to say "look ahead." But Valk settled on something quite different. "Um . . . like social skills?

"And that's why there are some people who just go for prac-tice," he continued, pronouncing the last word a bit distastefully. "They won't reach the real top level, because they don't know what's behind it." I had been under the impression that Valk, like most cubers, was all about practice. Earlier in our conversation, when I asked him for advice on solving the cross, he said there was nothing to learn: I just had to practice it over and over and over.

But in his view, cubing in isolation didn't pay dividends in the long run. "You won't get the knowledge from just practicing, yeah?" he explained. "I mean, you don't know what you need to learn. And it's just too much to figure it out on your own. So you need other people to help you—and you can help other people, yeah?—to get more knowledge."

The following day, I took the train east, traveling to Enschede, by the German border, to meet two of the most veteran Dutch cubers. They greeted me at the station, just across the tracks from the stadium where the local football team plays. One of them, a woman in middle age, with a warm smile and blue eyes, immedi-ately brought to mind Mrs. Whatsit, the charming, angelic woman in Madeleine L'Engle's *A Wrinkle in Time*: she was clad from head to foot in roughly woven gear—a cream-colored, floor-length skirt; striped sweater the color of a stormy sea; and cerulean hand-bag, slung over one shoulder—and seemed piercingly intelligent. The other, a rangy man with a mop of graying hair, had a slightly disheveled aspect, as if his red cable-knit sweater and jeans were not just protection against the springtime chill but preparation for a countryside ramble.

We got in the man's car—a red station wagon, crammed with assorted gear—and drove to the University of Twente, which they had both attended, a few minutes away. In the 1980s, the two of them spent a good deal of time exploring Rubik's Cube in the

Games Club, a warren of rooms now located in the basement of a building that the man noted was much less confusing than it used to be. The building itself, he remarked, was once something of a puzzle, with thirteen floors of narrow passageways. In fact, it was so hard to navigate that it had had to be renovated: too many people were getting lost.

We took seats at the student café, a semi-professional affair with leather banquettes overlooking the garden. The café gave onto a strange work of art: a giant clock tower, immersed in a pond, just the shingled turret poking out. It called to mind the floods so common in Holland's past. The clock itself was half-submerged and covered with mildew, its reflection in the water creating a shimmering whole. "So, what did you bring?" the woman asked, opening her bag and divulging a pile of Rubik's Cubes, papers, and various buttons on the table.

The man emptied his bag. He had just brought one Rubik's Cube. It looked unremarkable, but it had a distinguished parentage: it had once belonged to Erik Akkersdijk, the Dutch cuber. In fact, the man said, giving it a twist, it was the very same Rubik's Cube that Akkersdijk had used to set his single-solve world record of 7.08 seconds. The woman pulled out a pile of diagrams on graph paper that showed drawings like those Jessica Fridrich had inscribed in her notebook. They were neat enough to have been spat out of a computer, but they were entirely hand-drawn, even more neatly than Fridrich's little blue squares. "I drew these things a thousand times," the woman said.

When I met Dan Gosbee, the gregarious Canadian impresario who put together the first modern World Championship in 2003, he spoke reverentially about a man named Marc Waterman. In the 1980s, Gosbee said, Waterman had developed a method of solving Rubik's Cube corners first, not unlike many early cubers, but one that had blazingly fast results. When I looked him up, I learned that Waterman, indeed, had averaged under twenty seconds in 1987. (Admittedly, not in competition.) With a few tweaks, Gosbee said, Waterman's method could rival the best layer-by-layer solvers—that is, Zemdegs, Valk, and company—in the world.

Now, Waterman, the man with the mop of gray hair, was sitting across the table from me, twisting and turning his Cube in a manner that I had never seen before. It resembled the solution Minh Thai employed, but was somehow different, with lots of jerking at the wrists. Waterman was curious how fast I was. When I told him that I had almost breached the twenty-second barrier before I was waylaid by injury and that my times had consequently gone up, he said we were probably now the same speed. After years of working as a farmer, he had taken to data analysis for the Dutch forestry service, leaving him without much time to practice. I noticed a mischievous glint in his eye I hadn't seen when we walked in the door.

"I was never much of a speed cubist," said his companion, Anneke Treep. The two had become friends when she was a high school student. She discovered Rubik's Cube in the summer of 1980, when it was displayed prominently in a department store in Amsterdam. The Cubes were hanging from chains, like so many exotic lamps, to prevent anyone from stealing them. When she requested one for her birthday a few months later and received it, she immediately set about working out how to solve it, and succeeded without any assistance in just a few weeks. "I've always been very interested in just all kinds of patterns," Treep said, "whether it be embroidery patterns, or the Islamic tiles, like in the Alhambra—"

"Or mazes," Waterman said.

"Or mazes," Treep acknowledged. She used to draw mazes herself, on sheets of graph paper, and give them to friends to try to puzzle out. "So that has been sort of the common thread through all these things that I loved to do and still love to do." Only a few months into her cubing obsession, she met Jost van

Rossum, another teenager, and the two of them fell to cubing, going to contests at local toy shops. They cofounded the Dutch Cube Club, the one still active today. "Here," she said, "this is the first newsletter." She slid an old piece of paper, in black and white, with neat little drawings of Rubik's Cube, across the table. "This was all done by typewriter, my mother's typewriter, and these were all drawn with pen and ink, by hand."

By their own admission, neither Waterman nor Treep is nearly as enthusiastic about Rubik's Cube as he used to be. "Although I still see the beauty of it," Treep said, fingering one of her puzzles. At a certain point, she said, she simply had to move on—there weren't any new patterns for her to explore. She meant this literally. In the 1980s, along with a couple of friends, including Kurt Dockhorn, a teenager, and his brother, Hans, who had access to a primitive computer, and Guus Razoux Schultz, the first Dutch national champion, whose drive as a competitive swimmer had begun to bleed over to cubing, she set out to explore all the possible variations of solving Rubik's Cube layer by layer.

This is why van Bruchem will never refer to CFOP as the Fridrich method: several months before Fridrich and her friend, Luděk Marek, deciphered the mysteries of the last layer, Treep and company proofread a book by Frans Schiereck, *De Hongaarse Kubus!*, or *The Hungarian Cube!*, which outlined the basics of solving Rubik's Cube layer by layer. In the ensuing years, they went even further, delineating not only the orientation and permutation cases but the nearly 1,200 possible arrangements of the last layer, devising an algorithm for each of them.

When I told Treep about van Bruchem's quibble, she laughed. Neither she nor Waterman had ever asked for credit—for them, as for Fridrich, who has never claimed to have invented the method, and has (correctly) pointed out that other people applied her name to it, cubing is as much collaborative as it is competitive. "It's not about one person," Treep says.

"It's the same thing with my method," Waterman added. Unbeknownst to Gosbee, another Dutch cuber, named Daan Kramer, did most of the work, but had never been recognized for it. Waterman laughed. "He is very hard to find on the Internet!"

"It's more like a sport than it was in the eighties," Waterman remarked. He didn't lament this change—it was just a fact. "I think it's similar to chess," Treep said. "If you are getting started in chess when you are six or five years old now, you really have the desire to become really, really world top because you know that there is so much to learn ahead. And we didn't have anything ahead of us that we had to learn."

Still, some things never change, as Waterman demonstrated when we finished our meal. That gleam still in his eyes, he suggested casually that we all race. We cleared the table, and prepared to time ourselves. We all went at once, the idea being that we would complete five solves. Whosoever had the fastest average would be declared the winner. I let Waterman, who hadn't lubed Akkersdijk's puzzle in a long time, use one of my Cubes, which was much easier to turn.

To my surprise, I came in first. Even though Waterman started breathing down my neck—he got faster almost every solve, dropping from 39.56 seconds to 20.38—I managed to stay consistent. My final average, 27.63 seconds, just squeaked by Waterman's average of 29.70. (Treep, with a best solve of fifty-nine seconds, and an average of one minute and twenty-one seconds, remarked, happily, "It's not much worse than it used to be!")

"Wow," Waterman remarked, "you are very steady, Ian." I'd never considered this a virtue before—what good did being steady serve if you were consistently slow?—but Waterman had a point: I'd only won because my three counting solves were all in the twenty-seven-second range, while his ranged from twenty-two to thirty-nine seconds. "I think you turn the Cube a lot faster," he said, "but you use more moves than I do." We shook hands all around.

"Congratulations!" Treep said, beaming.

That night when I returned to Almere, van Bruchem and I cubed into the wee hours, long after the sunset. Like a married couple, we had settled into a routine. More or less every night, we turned on a movie. Then out came the Cubes. A few nights earlier, it had been *Mud*, starring Matthew McConaughey. That night, van Bruchem told me it was important to pay attention to my finger pressure. If you looked at slow-motion videos of Valk and Zemdegs, he said, well, sometimes Zemdegs's fingers shook a bit, but neither of them gripped the Cube very hard. They had a light touch, as if they were handling eggshells.

It was really the same lesson all over again—to go fast, you have to go slow. There will be no hesitation during this solve, van Bruchem said, turning his Cube toward me. Indeed, it was utterly smooth, like a choreographed ballet, the delicate interplay between his fingers and the Cube's various parts belying the fact that it had never been rehearsed, because it couldn't have been—it was a new solve, a novel scramble, just like every attempt. He said the cubers in countries to which he traveled often had the wrong idea. Van Bruchem grabbed his Cube so tightly his fingers whitened. Then he jerked his hands around, as if the puzzle were trying to buck him off. "And I will still beat them," he said, "because that's a fourteen-second solve, and they can't do that." In other words, even his slow solves were fast.

Tonight, my last night in Holland, the film on tap was *Hellbender*, a truly execrable production about which I gleaned little, other than that demons seemed to show up with some frequency. "You should have looked ahead," van Bruchem said when I paused during the first two layers, sounding almost like my old band teacher, irate that I was making the same mistake again.

But that was nothing to the sound he made when I attempted to leave the room. "Ach!" he cried out. He pointed to my Cube, lying scrambled on the coffee table, next to his coasters, a set of plastic squares designed to look like the faces of Rubik's Cube. He seemed alarmed, as if I'd just been passed by a black cat and broken a mirror on my way to the shower. "You can never leave a Cube unsolved!" he said.

PROOF

It's very, very hard to find me as a person.

—Ernő Rubik

Rubik Studio, Ltd., occupies a stately house in the twelfth district of Budapest, across the street from the leafy paths and greenswards of Városmajor Park. If you were to look up the address—74 Városmajor Street—online, you wouldn't be able to see the house, even on the street view setting of Google Maps. The building is set back from the road, behind an office complex that also counts a number of small businesses, including a boutique law firm, a mobile applications company, and several investment partnerships, among its tenants. Inspect the marquee outside, however—a column of metal plaques—and you will notice, second from the bottom, in bright red paint, RUBIK STUDIO, LTD.

There is also a rear entrance, accessible by a long, narrow ramp. This is how I entered the facility, one foggy afternoon in late April. The ramp is exceedingly difficult to navigate if you're in a car, as I happened to be. It takes a sharp, almost ninety-degree turn before approaching a large, metal gate that must be opened electronically. Then it turns to cobblestones, and you rattle all the way down to a parking lot the size of a postage stamp. It is actually easier to reverse down the driveway, performing all the hairpin acrobatics while looking over your shoulder, than to proceed straight and face the prospect of turning around at the bottom.

This, anyway, is what János Kovács said. He drove expertly, wending his black Volkswagen sedan into the lot, registering his disapproval of a driver who had almost hit us on the street, going the wrong way. With his bald pate, ringed by close-cropped graying hair, small and neatly trimmed mustache, broad-shouldered physique, and penchant for dark sport coats, Kovács could easily pass for an Eastern European secret agent. In fact, he is one of Rubik's longest-serving, most loyal, and reliable colleagues. In 1990, when the Cube was at its least popular, Rubik founded Rubik's Studio, and Kovács shortly signed on and stayed for almost three decades. Kovács eventually became the firm's director, but then left to found his own company, which now has an agreement with the Studio to produce and distribute Cubes in Hungary and several neighboring countries.

I had been introduced to Kovács by Ron van Bruchem, who surmised that Kovács might be more amenable to meeting in person than Rubik himself. Indeed, I arrived in Hungary with still no assurances that I would be able to meet the inventor, although I had been told that a rendezvous might be possible. In the meantime, Kovács offered to show me around. He was even so generous as to put me up in his house, a rambling stone pile in Budaörs, a town to the south that climbs up into the mountains. Kovács, who is in his midfifties, grew up in the house, and has since added several stories. You can see the passage of time in the styles of the different floors, from the wine cellar, which dates back centuries, to the uppermost floor, which is coated in eggshell stucco. Like most of Budaörs, the building is very old: the first people to settle there arrived some five thousand years ago. Locals have turned up everything from Bronze Age artifacts to Roman coins. Inevitably, the ancient has given way to the modern: the highway cuts through town, and even the oldest structures have found new purpose. Not long ago, Kovács told me, he threw out all the wine and filled the cellar with his latest vintage of Rubik's Cubes.

Kovács is a man of constant activity. I tried counting, and failed to find five minutes in which his phone did not ring. At the time, he used a black iPhone 5. The phone was normal in all respects but for the speaker. Kovács had framed it with two white stickers, either repurposed from some forlorn Rubik's Cube or else drawn from his cellar, where he has rolls of stickers, stacked as if they were bales of hay. When I asked him the purpose of the stickers, he replied that his phone's video camera often turned on and off without any apparent reason. He suspected a connection between the attempts to video the proceedings of his life and the suspicious glitches he frequently encountered on his computers, even his personal laptop. The stickers were intended to thwart any would-be onlookers. "Lots of people want the Rubik's," he said.

After parking his car—a diesel stick shift, with black leather upholstery—at Rubik's Studio, Kovács pulled out his keys and unlocked the building. The front door was a work of art: the slab of white-painted wood was interrupted by two columns of portholes, inset with glass, each covered with an elaborate metal curlicue, painted cobalt blue. Inside, the house smelled of old wood and tobacco.

After ushering me into his office, Kovács took to chatting with his secretary in rapid-fire Hungarian. The shelves were stuffed with papers and puzzles. There was a map of Europe on the wall. Apparently, Kovács was already late for a meeting—he had to bustle off to another part of the house—leaving me to explore the premises.

For decades, this had been the heart of Rubik's operation—not only the focal point for designing and distributing puzzles, but also his career as an architect. Stepping into one room, I noticed both walls were mounted with glass cabinets, which extended to the window and were filled with so many colorful designs and pictures that they formed a wraparound mural: one side, on the left hand coming in, was devoted to Rubik's Cube, and the other to the work of A+D Studio, the architecture firm of which Rubik remains a principal partner.

I turned my attention first to the piece on the left, the one depicting Rubik's Cube and related paraphernalia: old advertisements, design sketches, news clippings. At first glance, it looked like a chronological retelling of the puzzle's history, proceeding from left to right like a narrative scroll. On the left-hand side, it began with a snapshot of the first World Championship in 1982. The black-and-white photograph conveyed the bizarre, circuslike atmosphere of the whole affair. The stage was empty but for a single stand, at which Lars Petrus, then a twentysomething college student, was captured either midinspection or at the very beginning of his solve. The emcee, a dark-haired man in a pale suit, was caught looking at his cue cards, while another official, a sturdily built man in black boots, strode across the stage, his head inclined toward the leader board. The press crowded the stage. One photographer even went so far as to hide behind a flowerpot. Off to the right, almost as an afterthought, the photograph included the judges, a row of several men and one woman in formal attire at a long black table, fronted by several planters bedecked with flowers. The men all wore light-colored suits, with the exception of the judge closest to the middle of the table, who likewise distinguished himself by hunching forward, his clasped hands throwing the lower part of his face into shadow. I recognized him instantly.

The mural, it turns out, was not chronological, but a mixture of images not unlike Rubik's Cube: unruly, disordered, but no less interesting for being so chaotic. It included a miniature reproduction of a Rubik's Cube mosaic depicting Jim Morrison, the frontman of the Doors, in his famous, shirtless pose; blown-up covers of books on the puzzle in different languages, from Dutch to German to Hungarian; and perhaps the most provocative advertisement for Rubik's Cube I have ever seen, featuring a young woman wearing a string bikini attempting to solve the puzzle amid crashing surf. The images themselves were arranged in a grid, the interstices filled in by colored squares, as if they had simply replaced the stickers on a giant Rubik's Cube.

Roving over the composition, my eye was drawn to a sketch roughly in the middle.

It depicted Rubik's Cube, partially disassembled, hinting at the mechanism inside: you could see the pieces lining up to create a rough semblance of a sphere, and the axles of the core supporting the centers, allowing movement along three different axes. The artist had striven to demonstrate the puzzle's capabilities, including lines stemming from the sides of the puzzle, delineating the x, y, and z axes, along with arrows around each axis pointing in both directions, showing that the puzzle could be rotated every which way. The sketch was drawn expertly. It appeared to have been freehanded, some of the lines a bit wavy, others jutting into space, but its judicious use of shading and perspective made it seem almost tangible. It had been photographed with an actual Rubik's Cube sitting on the page, and the two couldn't have been more alike. But for the fact that, in the sketch, Rubik's Cube was exposed, like an architectural diagram, the missing pieces drawn at its base, the two objects were the same shape, the same size, and even shaded in the same direction, the light pointing from left to right. At the bottom, the sketch was dated "81.06.22." Next to the date scrawled a loopy signature, which looked a bit like musical notation, the line rising and falling from the top of the staff to the bottom and back again: Rubik, Ernő.

On the other side of the room, in the glass cabinet on the right, were framed photographs of some of A+D Studio's projects. They ranged from sport stadiums to commercial offices to museums to embassies. The style was often modern, with plenty of steel and glass, but also whimsical, such as the Kecskemét branch of the

SPAR supermarket, which had corrugated metal siding in cream and carmine with a conelike turret projecting above the building. There was nothing to suggest any overlap between Rubik's Cube and this or any other building, but when I consulted the website of the firm, I couldn't help noticing that every page was structured around the same basic format: a three-by-three grid, consisting of nine squares. In other words, what you see if you look at Rubik's Cube from the side, with all but one face obscured.

The rest of the house was quiet, like a mausoleum. I walked gingerly up the staircase, trying not to disturb the silence. The railing was painted gray with a slight hint of blue, and a modern lamp, a large white orb on a long metal filament, hung in the stairwell. The top floor—where A+D Studio was housed—was locked, but on the next floor down, I encountered a paunchy man who spoke as much English as I did Hungarian, which is to say none.

The man was sitting near a large model of Rubik's latest creation: the Touch Cube, a digital version of the puzzle whose sides are essentially tablet computers, on which you drag your fingers this way and that. The man was hunched over his desk, overlooking the parking lot. When I told him that Kovács had brought me and pointed to the car, he seemed to hear only "Kovács." Summoning me with a big pawlike hand, he walked me down the staircase and started jabbering with Kovács's secretary. While the two of them discussed whatever they were discussing, I turned to examine the room. There were any number of Rubik's Cubes lining the bookshelves, including one for which I couldn't help reaching. It was beautifully machined and extra large, perched on a plinth that touched only a single vertex, so that it appeared to stand like a spinning top. When I picked it up, it fell apart. Evidently, it was ceramic, two pieces designed to mesh together. "No toys, no toys," the secretary said, taking the pieces out of my hands. With a disapproving look, she gently but firmly shooed me back into the foyer.

* * *

The twelfth district of Budapest is sometimes referred to, although perhaps only in travel guides, as "The Hollywood Hills" of Budapest, since it extends up into the hills and contains many fine residences. It is the only district of Buda, the western side of the city, that does not abut the Danube River. In the way stands the first district, also known as the Castle District, after Buda Castle, the rocky promontory overlooking the Danube atop which the Hungarian kings of old built their palaces. The Castle District is a haven for tourists, with shops everywhere you go. In one of them, I found a magnet that resembled Rubik's Cube, only patterned to recall the Hungarian flag, striped red, white, and green. In the same way New York City has dozens of outlets merchandising the Statue of Liberty in every conceivable form—T-shirts, mugs, key chains, and the like—Budapest seems to have no shortage of wares piggybacking off Rubik's Cube.

One of the highlights of the Castle District is the Fisherman's Bastion, a terrace overlooking the Danube whose name derives from the fact that it was once defended by local fishermen. (The modern version was built in the late nineteenth century, and refurbished after World War II; it resembles a Disneyland-style confection, with soaring turrets and arches.) Much the same way that the history of Budaörs is visible in Kovács's house, the history of Buda Castle is ingrained in the Fisherman's Bastion. You can descend a spiraling staircase to emerge in a drafty medieval chapel, and pay a few forints to watch a film about the history of Hungary, advertised aboveground with posters of fearsome warriors on horseback.

The film begins with a narrator intoning, in various languages, depending on the dial to which you tune your headset, an old Hungarian proverb. "Hungarians are considered the last ones to enter a revolving door," he says, while the globe slowly rotates on the screen. "But Hungary is the home of world-famous inventors," he continues, at which point the globe transforms into a planet-sized Rubik's Cube, which solves itself.

The film also mentions that Hungary has produced many artists and scientists, but Rubik's Cube is the only work singled out. (This despite the fact that Hungarians invented the ballpoint pen, the helicopter, and the AC transformer. Not to mention that George Soros, the billionaire investor; Judit Polgár, the best female chess player in history; and Béla Bartók, the pioneering composer, were all born in Hungary.) When I finished taking notes, I struck up a conversation with the young woman running the projector. She was excited to hear that I wanted to learn about the origins of Rubik's Cube. Most Hungarians, she said, were aware that the puzzle was invented by a Hungarian, but most foreigners had no idea. She also knew that Rubik was not just the name of the puzzle, but of its inventor. This, too, she thought was a well-known fact in Hungary. When I asked her if she knew much about Rubik himself, though, she drew a blank.

When I shared that I hoped to meet him, she looked even more puzzled. How was that possible, she wondered—was he even still alive?

While staying with Kovács I received the e-mail I had been hoping for the entire trip. It was from Viktor Böhm, the associate of Rubik's who had helped him organize the exhibition at the Liberty Science Center and generously replied to my questions about Rubik.

The e-mail simply said:

Shall we meet at Szép Ilona restaurant at 12:30 on Wednesday?
V

I showed the message to Kovács, who raised his eyebrows. He remembered the article Tierney had written, but couldn't recall any writer spending much time with Rubik since.

* * *

A few weeks before my visit, Kovács moved his production facility from Rubik's studio to another location, a suite of rooms in a tall, nondescript building about four miles south. Kovács drove us over so I could meet one of their Cube ambassadors. The offices smelled strongly of plastic. This is where they made the Cubes, Kovacs told me. I passed one room in which a man with salt-and-pepper hair shared a table with several massive rolls of butcher paper, to which had been applied innumerable little stickers, in the signature hues of Rubik's Cube. In another room, a number of employees were assembling different facets of the puzzle. One woman had a pile of silvery cardboard, which she was folding to make the bases for the display stands.

Kovács often employs local cubers. Typically high schoolers, for whom helping to assemble puzzles is a part-time job. Some of them graduate to the performance team—a troupe that is hired by tour groups to give foreigners a taste of Hungary's perhaps least recognized but most widely known cultural export.

Balázs Bernát, or rather Bernát Balázs—in Hungarian, the surname comes first—was one of the team's starring members. He studied electrical engineering at a local university. For a while, in high school, he worked on the lowest rung of the assembly line, applying stickers to Rubik's Cubes. This involved taking sheets cut from those rolls of stickers, a pile of blank Rubik's Cubes, which were as obsidian as the monolith in *2001*, and applying nine stickers at a time, one color to each face.

"I was competing against myself," he said. "I wanted to do more a day, because I get paid better." He would line up twelve Cubes—a single batch—and time himself, to see how fast he could sticker them. First, it was twelve minutes. After a while, he got down to nine.

Bernát is tall, with black half-rim spectacles, a neatly trimmed goatee, and gray eyes. He showed me around the office, answering my questions about the processes involved in producing Rubik's Cubes. (In competition, he himself uses Chinese-branded puzzles, as do most of the cubers in Hungary.) Bernát clarified that the puzzles Kovács makes are not those sold in Toys "R" Us. Rather, they are specialty Cubes, sold only in Hungary, using the same technology as the original model. The Cube is made of tougher plastic, and the stickers are slightly less bright. (It is just as hard to turn as the original.) The Rubik's Cube of today is mass-produced in China, but this throwback is assembled entirely by hand in Budapest: an artisanal Cube, if you will.

Bernát once attempted to break the Guinness world record for the number of Rubik's Cubes solved in twenty-four hours. He did so along with several Hungarian cubers, one of whom eventually succeeded. Bernát himself injured his wrist about halfway through. Every fifteen minutes or so, he was forced to resort to solving one-handed. Fortunately, his wrist injury had recovered—it only twinged now and again—but he understood my predicament, cubing-wise: I wanted to get faster, but also to ensure that I could keep cubing.

"What do you average?" I asked.

"It depends," he said.

Most of the time, he hovered between ten and twelve seconds. It was reassuring to see Bernát cubing so quickly: in the week following his injury, he told me, his hand was all but unusable. He couldn't even hold a pencil. To his surprise, he didn't have to write any essays or participate in any tests. His teachers let him off the hook, perhaps because of the respect accorded the Cube in Hungary. In any event, Bernát didn't end up having time that day to give me a lesson.

Instead Kovacs had given Bernát the assignment of making sure I arrived at lunch with Rubik on time. They didn't want me to show up at the wrong restaurant by accident—the signage in

Budapest is mostly in Hungarian. Bernát and I left the offices and took the tram, a rattling, Soviet-era contraption, until we arrived at Széll Kálmán Square, which was undergoing a renovation that might best be described as a demolition derby with occasional pauses for a jackhammer solo. We had to circle the square, skirting the construction, to transfer to the bus, which began traveling up a grand avenue into the second district, a leafy enclave of well-appointed dwellings.

On the bus, I asked Bernát about Rubik. Had he ever met him? Once, he said, but only briefly. He had had a question relating to his job—before every performance, he gave a brief account of Rubik's invention of the Cube, and he wasn't sure at which school Rubik was teaching at the time. "He's still like a professor," Bernát said. "I asked a simple question and he gave an answer in five minutes which was more confusing than before."

The school at which Rubik taught—the Academy of Applied Arts, now the Moholy-Nagy University of Art and Design—was just up the street from the restaurant. And, according to what Bernát said Rubik had told him, it also served as the inspiration for his Cube. "He wanted to show his students that it is possible to make a body that can turn in all three dimensions," Bernát said.

Whether or not this was true would be resolved shortly, I hoped. As the bus approached the station, which bore the same name as the restaurant, and the neighborhood—Szép Ilona—Bernat added that he had once attended a public event at which Rubik's presence was required. Rubik made a brief appearance, and then virtually disappeared. Bernát had looked away only to find Rubik gone, as if he had special powers, like Batman leaving Commissioner Gordon perpetually in the lurch.

I disembarked the bus and turned around. I expected to see a tall, white building with ornate iron balconies, elaborate moldings, and neatly trimmed hedges: Szép Ilona Vendéglő, just as it appeared online.

What I did not expect, still, despite the assurance from Böhm, was to find a well-dressed older man sitting on the patio, his silver hair gently ruffled by the wind, the steep cant of his eyebrows and sharp line of his jaw marking him indisputably as the inventor of the greatest puzzle in the history of the world. And he was looking directly at me.

It's hard to meet your heroes, harder still if you are also trying to report on them. I had brought along my usual equipment—a tape recorder, a notebook, and a camera—but wasn't sure how to record this encounter. I didn't want to disturb Rubik in any way, to throw him off-kilter, like a physicist who changes the very nature of the particle she's examining by simply examining it.

Quite by accident, Rubik and I were dressed almost alike. We each wore blue sweaters over collared shirts. His was duotone, dark blue beneath the shoulders, periwinkle from the shoulders to the neck. He also had on a faded cargo vest, which might have once been blue or purple, and a checkered scarf, thrown casually about his neck. When he stood up, later, I could see that Rubik had donned a pair of black jeans, the same color as my slacks.

Sitting next to him, in the corner of the patio, was Viktor Böhm, wearing neatly pressed trousers, a striped shirt, and a tangerine sweater. He had on a pair of loafers, and had carefully parted his hair. Böhm splits his time between London and Budapest. He holds a PhD in moral and political philosophy and was also a research fellow at New College, Oxford. Before linking up with Rubik, he worked with a number of other Hungarian geniuses. Böhm was a senior executive of George Soros's Central European University and an advisor to Judit Polgár, the greatest female chess player in history, and to Maestro Ivan Fischer, the principal of the Budapest Festival Orchestra.

At first, the conversation was light. When the waiter arrived, I asked Böhm what he had ordered to drink—he had a small glass of liqueur sitting by his plate. This was Unicum, he said, a

Hungarian aperitif not unlike Jägermeister in that it's made from fermented herbs. Rubik nodded when Böhm said that it has medicinal properties. The two of them chuckled when I took a sip and gagged. It's what I imagine liquor made of tobacco would taste like. It's a bit like broccoli, Böhm said, an acquired taste.

By the time I recovered, Rubik hadn't said much, so I asked him a question. Did he know that his puzzle was featured in a video at Buda Castle? With a bemused look, he replied that he did not. Pulling out my notes, I offered to recount the episode, quoting the line with which it begins: "Hungarians are considered the last ones to enter a revolving door."

That's a proverb, Böhm said. I asked if he wouldn't mind elaborating. Well, Böhm said, it's *half* a proverb. The other half is that Hungarians somehow exit the door first, even though they enter last. I asked if this was because Hungarians were especially talented. No, Böhm replied. It's generally understood to be the result of subterfuge.

Rubik chuckled at this, as he had several times, but he still was more or less mute, quietly eating bread. Fortunately, I had prepared for this. From my bag, I withdrew a puzzle. Immediately, Rubik's eyes fixed on my hands. The puzzle was nothing like his Cube. I figured there wouldn't have been much point in showing him something he already knew.

The Cast Marble looks, and feels, like a paperweight. It's a rectangular metal prism, about one inch by one inch by half an inch, the color of gunmetal, inside of which is a metal orb. I had received the puzzle as a gift from George Miller, the puzzle collector and designer who appeared in the videos at *Beyond Rubik's Cube*, the exhibit at the Liberty Science Center.

The goal of the puzzle is to take it apart and put it back together. There are only four pieces—two that make up the prism, and two that constitute the marble—but I had yet to figure out how to solve it. I wondered if Rubik would have any more luck.

Rubik immediately identified the mechanism, carefully teasing the puzzle this way and that with his fingers. Any thought of noshing was clearly gone. His entire being seemed willed into the little piece of metal between his fingertips. Evidently, he said, his voice deep and resonant, a slight accent to his English, it depended on how you aligned the marble.

"It looks absolutely hopeless," Böhm said.

When the appetizers came, Rubik barely noticed. He was still deep in thought, contemplating the Cast Marble. Aside from a brief mention of Barrochal, an Italian sculptor, he stayed mostly mum. Putting down the puzzle for a moment, he asked if I'd ever heard of Barrochal. I couldn't say that I had. Böhm pulled up a picture on his phone: in the 1980s, the sculptor had created homages to kouroi, the ancient Greek sculptures of young boys, but that were themselves puzzles, with Rubik's Cubes concealed in their heads.

Böhm engaged me in a seemingly unrelated conversation. He wanted to know what I thought of sports that were, as he termed it, "technical" sports. That is to say, they were sports in which technology had come to play a decisive role in the outcome. At this point, Rubik looked up. In such sports, Böhm pointed out, well-thought-out regulation was crucial, to ensure a level playing field. Surely I had heard of the debacle in swimming, a few years ago, when technical suits allowed formerly plebeian athletes to set world records?

I allowed that I had. "I know this is a touchy subject," Böhm said, "but what do you think of standardized Cubes?" I struggled to respond, partly because I wasn't entirely sure what to say, but also because some of the bones from my fish soup had gotten lodged in my throat.

I had been warned about the soup beforehand, and sure enough, it was in the traditional Hungarian style. This meant, apparently, that the fish had been cooked, almost whole, and placed in a tomato sauce. Fortunately, clearing my throat gave me time to formulate my response. I felt like a politician, trying desperately to appease two different constituencies.

This wasn't a topic I was even sure would come up. Obviously, it was of great importance to both sides—to cubers, and to Seven Towns—but I was reluctant to introduce it myself, at least not so early in the conversation. Fortunately, I'd spent quite a lot of time thinking about it.

Cubing wasn't like other sports, I said, making any comparison to swimming inexact. Yes, there were engineers who made better suits, and their innovations were now hampered by regulations for good reason—swimmers who had signed with rival sponsors couldn't wear the suits, and a few milliseconds could mean the difference between victory and defeat.

No one in cubing hides technical secrets from anyone else, I pointed out. If the community had formed along the lines Dan Gosbee imagined, it would be exactly like professional sports, with cutthroats hiding their best moves and trying to throw off their competition. Only cubing took the other, more communitarian path: if anyone gets a technical edge, everyone gets it.

Cubing also didn't run afoul of the debate about natural human performance, as the imbroglio involving swimsuits did. There is nothing natural about solving Rubik's Cubes in the first place—the puzzle was invented, unlike the act of swimming, which arose out of necessity. If everyone gets faster because the puzzles get better, everyone benefits.

I thought I had comported myself rather well, standing up for cubers while not stepping on anybody's toes. Rubik and Böhm nodded politely, and began to tend to their entrées, steak frites, with a slice of cucumber, and a mound of curly, fried something or other on top.

Then Rubik spun into action.

* * *

In many ways, Rubik is like his puzzle. His exterior is prickly, even a little bit aloof, but something about him draws you in. It might be his eyes, so blue they could have been carved from a piece of sea glass. They are just eyes, but they seem to contain multitudes.

Once he started talking, he didn't stop. Evidently, he had been gathering his thoughts for some time. Or he could speak off the cuff with all the polish of a lecturer with a sheaf of notes. What is a sport? Rubik asked. I didn't bother to answer. It was a rhetorical question. Sports are composed of two elements, he said, the body and the brain.

In some sports, Rubik noted, the brain was supreme. In chess, for instance, the body was extraneous. The game can take place entirely at a remove. Your opponent can be halfway across the world or sitting across the table from you. You can play chess with a computer.

In other sports, Rubik pointed out, the body was all that mattered. Weight lifting might require some thought, he admitted, but it involved less strategy than brute force. You either had the physical strength to hoist the bar or you didn't.

These are just the poles, Rubik said. One purely mental, the other purely physical. Most sports lie somewhere in between. The Cube, for instance, he said, was both physical and mental, sharing the two qualities in nearly equal measure, to a degree unique among sporting activities. You couldn't solve the Cube without a strategy, nor could you compete at the highest level without a great deal of physical training. It was simply too demanding.

I wasn't sure where Rubik was going with this, but I was curious to find out. Hearing him speak gave me a glimpse into his thinking. His words carried the trace of the mind that formed them. Like the sketch in the office, they were highly analytical—I felt as if I'd signed up for a lecture on sports theory—but full of energy. If the Cube were the embodiment of his thinking, then this was the raw material, the source of so much confusion and delight.

It was at once confounding to listen to him, because he never slowed down, unspooling one thought after another with the speed of film whirring by the lens of a projector, and yet thrilling to hear him think aloud.

Sports fell along another spectrum, he said. This one was bounded by two different poles. Winning and record keeping. Soccer, for instance, was almost purely about winning. You only had to score more goals than the other team. But in sports like swimming, where victory is reduced to a single metric—time— records assume an outsized importance. In other words, record-driven sports are more narrowly focused—from the shot put to bobsledding—while sports driven by winning are more expansive.

In this context, Rubik said, his Cube presented a theoretical problem. Records are due partly to luck. I thought about cutting in. There are rules in place to minimize the effects of chance— being ranked by the average of five solves in competition, for instance—and I didn't want to underestimate Rubik by assuming he wasn't aware of this. He had a point—cubing was inextricably bound up with luck. But so are many sports. Just ask Diego Maradona, the soccer star who recently kissed the referee who allowed his hand ball against England in 1986, securing a victory in the quarterfinals of the World Cup.

While I was pondering Rubik's remarks, he had knifed sideways, like a fish darting in a different direction. "In one way," he said, "I can say it's an unfinished object." I listened for a moment, and realized Rubik was talking about all the ways his Cube had grown beyond his wildest dreams—appearing on fashion runways, in mathematics lectures, inspiring a generation of puzzle makers like George Miller, making cameos on the silver screen, fueling the obsessive nature of cubers around the globe. "In another way," he said, "I can say it's an absolutely finished object."

I had ordered venison, one of the house specialties. It came with boiled potatoes and a tureen of forest berries, stewed into a steaming compote. By the time Rubik finished his disquisition, I realized I hadn't eaten any of it. After I cleaned my plate, hurriedly—Rubik and Böhm had already finished eating—I asked if Rubik wouldn't mind posing for a picture.

"Ah, yes," he said. "For proof."

FIRST PLACE

The Hungarian National Rubik's Cube Championship happened to be scheduled for the first weekend of May, only a few days after my lunch with Rubik. The WCA sponsors relatively few competitions in Hungary, despite it being the birthplace of Rubik's Cube, several people told me, because Rubik himself is wary of bad competitions. He is concerned with quality control: he wants the competitions that take place there to be big, to be spectacular, to strengthen the brand. I signed up just in time—the field was capped at 150 competitors.

Consequently, according to Kovács, the venue was typically the Hotel Gellért, a ritzy establishment on the bank of the Danube, just down the road from Buda Castle. The baths of the hotel were once used to film part of the Cremaster Cycle, the wide-ranging film series by the critically acclaimed artist Matthew Barney.

This year, for reasons that were not entirely clear to me, the National Championship was to be held in Lurdy Ház, a soaring modern complex that was like a mall on steroids, including everything from a sporting complex to shopping boutiques. It would be the first of two—the first time since the founding of the WCA that more than one tournament would take place in Hungary in the same calendar year.

One reason, perhaps, that Hungarian cubers wouldn't have to travel to neighboring countries, like Slovenia, Austria, and Italy, so often for their fix in 2015 was that Olivér Perge and Niki Placskó were involved. The couple, a pair of twentysomethings, had become the first cubers of Hungary, so to speak: they organized competitions within the country and around Eastern Europe, acting to spread the gospel of cubing as vigorously as van Bruchem.

I met the two of them at their apartment, in the ninth district, where they hosted me for dinner. They live in a spacious two-bedroom apartment in a building that would fit into a Wes Anderson film: the interior courtyard rises like a movie set, the balconies all weather-stained iron with elaborate banisters.

Outwardly, Perge and Placskó are polar opposites. Perge stands over six feet tall, and once played semiprofessional basketball. Placskó is hardly short, but next to Perge she looks small. His close-cropped hair is the color of wheat. Placskó's tresses are jet black and extend to the middle of her back. In terms of personality, they are also an odd couple. Perge is excitable, boisterous, his mouth a torrent of references and jokes that his friends only sometimes get, since they involve American politics, which he follows with a devotion few Americans could match. By contrast, Placskó is quiet and polite, and sometimes rolls her eyes at her boyfriend's jokes.

When Perge himself competes, which he does often—he once set the world record in Rubik's Magic, a puzzle the WCA no longer recognizes, at 0.83 seconds; and the world record for Rubik's Clock*, a puzzle it still does, at 6.93 seconds—his fingers exude nervous energy, which sometimes paints him into corners.

Clocking up an average just at the end, Bernát told me, is

---

* Patented by two men named Christopher C. Wiggs and Christopher J. Taylor, Rubik's Clock was licensed by Rubik in 1988. It resembles a clock, but with a three-by-three grid of nine tiny faces, each with a single hand, which you have to align at twelve simultaneously.

known among cubers in Hungary as Jesusing Up, because that's what Perge always does. Since he used to have long, flowing hair and pronounced cheekbones, his nickname was "Jesus" in his basketball-playing days. In fact, you can find a video on the Internet of Perge dunking the basketball, looking for all the world like the Messiah in a pair of Air Jordans.

Placskó, on the other hand, is methodical with her solves. She proceeds without slowing down or speeding up, with the upshot of being extremely consistent, if not quite as fast as Perge. In 2014, she set the national record for an average of five solves of Rubik's Clock; the standard deviation of her three counting solves was less than 0.05 seconds.

For dinner, we made a traditional Hungarian confection of potatoes and chicken. For my part, I doused some broccoli with oil and garlic and put it in the stove. I couldn't help noticing that Perge and Placskó had a pair of Rubik's Cubes in the kitchen. Those were salt and pepper shakers, they told me. They no longer used them, because when their friends came over, they always tried to solve them, twisting them rapidly, which resulted in a quantity of salt and pepper spilling on the floor.

Perge and I retreated to their room. He watched me complete a few solves and shook his head. My F2L was horrible—I kept slowing down and speeding up, like a car driven by someone who's just learning how to shift gears. (He did admit that, sometimes, "your F2Ls were, like, perfect," but this was the exception, not the rule.) And I executed what I did know too slowly. "You are like Niki," he said. "Maybe afraid to turn fast."

Fortunately, Perge showed me I was on the verge of speeding up. If I just learned a few more algorithms, I'd be able to cut down my time orienting the last layer by as much as 50 percent. Until now, I'd been orienting the last layer—the penultimate step of every solve—using a mishmash of algorithms I'd picked up from Toby a decade ago.

When you orient the last layer, Perge explained, you arrive

at one of four different possibilities: either none of the edges are oriented; two of the edges are oriented; all of the edges are oriented; or the entire face is oriented, and you can skip straight to the final step, switching any pieces that are out of place—that is, permuting the last layer.

When I ended up with the first of these four—that is, with no edges oriented—it sometimes took me four tries to get to the final step. The first time Perge (and Placskó) saw me pull off a four-look OLL (that's the technical term), they looked at me as if I were mentally deficient. I should never have to do more than two algorithms to orient the last layer, Perge said.

The first algorithm should orient the edges, he said. Then the second algorithm should orient the corners. There were only three cases for edge orientation: either no edges were oriented, two were, or all of them were. One algorithm would suffice for each of the first two cases. There were seven algorithms for orienting the corners. He assumed I already knew most of them. "We will see," he said.

Indeed, I was familiar with the plurality of OCLLs, that is, algorithms for the Orientation of Corners of the Last Layer. There was the Sune, which I knew as the Jesus Fish: a cross with one quadrant filled in, a figure that resembled the Ichthys, the early Christian symbol. (And there was the anti-Sune, the mirror image of the Jesus Fish.) The list also included the bow tie (a pair of overlapping squares, like an extremely neat bow tie) and one whose name I didn't know: a yellow cross with irregularly placed yellow squares around it.

The algorithms that I didn't know—the double-Sune, headlights, and chameleon, so called because it resembled the head of the lizard, with two squares (the eyes) poking to either side—Perge offered to teach me, then and there. It was easier than I thought. The double-Sune was basically what van Bruchem called the Sexy Move twice, bookended by a four-move setup. Headlights, a configuration of two squares pointing forward, like the headlights of a car, required a relatively easy counterpoint involving the top and bottom layers of the puzzle. And the chameleon invoked another variation of the Sexy Move, this time using a wide-angle grip that subsumed the middle layer into the algorithm.

It was at this point that I smelled smoke. I had forgotten all about the broccoli in the oven. That's good, Perge said as I removed the pan, acrid smoke rising faintly from the blackened heads and stems. If you want to average sub-20, he said, you *need* to do that. "If I could tell you all the times my mother said, 'Dinner is ready!' And I said, 'Five minutes!'"

My visit to the birthplace of Rubik's Cube coincided with an eruption of interest in the puzzle, a major event that made headlines everywhere from the *New York Times* to the *Today* show. On the afternoon of April 25, 2015, at a table in the cafeteria of Central Bucks West High School in Doylestown, Pennsylvania, Collin Burns, a lanky teenager with a passion for astrophysics, broke the world record for solving Rubik's Cube. He lowered Mats Valk's two-year-old mark of 5.55 seconds to 5.25 seconds. The reaction was immediate. Daniel Goodman, a cuber in the audience, was filming the solve, and within a second of its completion, Burns staring openmouthed at the timer, Goodman shouted, "What? What? What?" as if he were bearing witness to some extraterrestrial invasion, following that up with the exclamation, "World record!"

The last American to hold the world record for a single solve was Toby Mao, when it was nearly twice as slow, at 10.48 seconds. That was in 2006, well before cubing had started to bubble up again in the public consciousness; having been primed by the Cube's increasing presence on YouTube and social media, the story of Burns's record-breaking solve went viral, as did the video, which promptly attracted upward of two million views.

Olivér Perge had subsequently appeared on RTL, a major

commercial broadcaster. This was apparently not enough. The day after I met Rubik, I got a call from Bernát, who told me that M1, the Hungarian equivalent of the BBC, wanted its own segment, analyzing the record. They were sending a car to pick him up that morning. Did I want to come?

I met Bernát outside his dormitory, where a yellow cab arrived to ferry us to the station. The car zipped along the Danube, passing by the Chain Bridge and Buda Castle, while Bernát rummaged in his knapsack, inspecting his Cubes. He'd brought about a dozen, by my count. To be honest, he said, he wasn't entirely sure what he was going to say. He'd never met Burns—he'd never even heard of the guy until he broke the world record.

He asked me if I knew anything that might be useful. In fact, I did—I'd met Burns at the Yale competition only a few weeks before. I told Bernát he was homeschooled. "So he's a genius?" Bernát asked. I laughed, and explained that homeschooling wasn't all that uncommon in the United States, but that Burns was certainly smart—he was already taking classes at the University of Pennsylvania at just fifteen years old.

To explain how Burns had broken the world record, Bernát had looked up the solution. It had already been reconstructed on the forums. The solve had taken forty-four moves to Valk's forty-five. Burns had managed to solve the first two layers about half a second faster. He hadn't rotated his Cube, which can add time to the solve; Valk had rotated his puzzle twice.

But, to Bernát, anyway, that wasn't the most important part. He pulled up the solution on his mobile phone and started leading me through it. Burns is color neutral, like Zemdegs, meaning he can start his solve on any side; in this case, the most propitious was white. The Cube was arranged in such a way that, when you solved the first two layers as he did, you didn't have to rotate the puzzle. Doing it myself, using my own Cube, it seemed easy.

Then, Bernát said, Burns did something he'd never seen before. When Burns reached the OLL—a case known as the freeway, or highway, or OLL 55—he used an algorithm with which Bernát was unfamiliar. The case looks like a freeway, bordered by traffic lights: there's a yellow bar in the middle of the last layer, facing upward, and the sides of the last layer are yellow, too: the road and the streetlights. Whatever Bernát used to solve the case, it didn't have the effect that Burns's technique did: when Burns finished twisting, the last layer was not just oriented, all the stickers on top pointing in the same direction, but entirely solved.

The headquarters of M1 are modern, a glass and steel building in the third district, in the northernmost reaches of Budapest. The presenter showed Bernát to the stage, where they took seats at a conference table. Bernát started to arrange his puzzles on the surface. He had mixed some of them, such as his 5x5, like chessboards, if chess were played with half a dozen sides.

When the segment began, the station aired the YouTube video in question, at which point Bernát caught my eye and grinned. I couldn't hear everything that was said, but it was clear that Bernát was trying to explain what Burns had done to break the world record.

The presenter was following gamely along, asking questions from a clipboard on her lap, but it seemed that whatever Bernát was doing went a little over her head. When he reached the algorithm Burns had used to solve the last layer, I wondered if Bernát himself knew what he was doing—he fumbled his Cube a bit, and wound up apologizing, before swiftly rectifying the situation and solving it.

The segment ended and Bernát had to sit there for a minute until the next news update concluded. I asked him how this compared to his other TV appearances. It went fine, he thought, but he was annoyed with himself for messing up the OLL.

* * *

In the Budapest metro, you can see traces of Rubik's Cube. They're subtle, hints of color, nods to the design. But if you look for them, they're easy to find: in the station Móricz Zsigmond körtér, the walls of the platform are divided into brilliant rectangles. They remind one of the colors of Rubik's Cube: red, white, blue, green, yellow, and orange.

Take the M4, or green line, two stops farther, across the Danube, and you'll notice another Rubik's-themed work of wall art, this one in the staircase leading to and from the stop at Kálvin Tér. It looks like the sort of mosaic that, up close, is supposed to be nonsense, and at a distance, form something intelligible. In this case, words, dark tiles interrupting little white squares, paying homage to the hymns sung in the Protestant church for which the square is named. But if you look closely, you'll see the words aren't black, as they first appear, but the agglomeration of tiny little squares of many colors: red, yellow, blue, green, and so on. They happen to be almost the exact size of those on the sides of Rubik's Cube.

I once asked Kovács about these displays, and he told me they were indeed homages to Rubik's Cube, but inexact ones. There were some purple squares in the station at Móricz Zsigmond körtér, for instance, and the mural at Kálvin Tér was abstract. They didn't want to pay the licensing fees, he said.

After Bernát and I left the TV station, we played a round of miniature golf. If you want to see competitive fury on the links, forget Tiger Woods in his youth: just put two cubers in a Soviet-era Putt-Putt, with concrete greens and metal ramps, and watch the chaos unfold.

We played two rounds: the first went to Bernát, who managed, improbably, to land a shot that required dropping the ball through a hole in the net suspended several feet beyond the starting point. (There was a ramp, with such a steep angle that my shot rolled backward.) The second round came down to the final hole, a pinball-like attraction that involved sending the ball up one of several passages, which I managed to do successfully. Bernát was less lucky: his final shot caromed back to the start, ceding the second round to me.

Bernát received a text that a major news agency had already written up his TV appearance online. Word of the record likewise continued to spread around the world. I later went to the post office to mail a few postcards, and Perge happened to call me, as breathless as if he'd won the lottery. It was Fox News, he said. They had managed, in a single sentence, to misspell both *Collin Burns* and *Rubik's*, rendering the two as *Colin*, with a single *l*, and *Rubix*, with an *-ix* at the end.

Later that afternoon, Bernát and I took the train to Fővám Tér, right by the Great Market Hall, or Nagycsarnok, a towering nineteenth-century building in which you could find Rubik's Cube for sale—including the special vintage version produced by Kovács, which was labeled *Bűvos Köcka*, or *Magic Cube*, the original Hungarian epithet for the puzzle.

Afterward, having admired the great quantities of sausage and ornate Hungarian lacework on display—single tablecloths, embroidered with flowers and abstract designs, were selling for hundreds of dollars—we walked up nearby Váci Street, a tourist trap if ever I had seen one. We used to busk here, Bernát told me.

He and a friend would arrive together. One looked out for cops while the other cubed. They earned fifteen thousand forints, the equivalent of about one hundred dollars, in two to three hours if it went well. They did this when they wanted beer money. But not anymore, Bernát said. They were too old for this stuff, he explained, with a wistful note to his voice.

Twenty minutes later, we arrived in front of the Vigadó concert hall, the site of the 1982 Rubik's Cube World Championship.

It stands on the bank of the Danube, on the Pest side, facing the Castle District. The concert hall was closed, but we posed for pictures outside; the façade, with its five soaring arches, and statues of men and women playing lyres, in homage to antiquity, looked exactly as it had in 1982, when Minh Thai captured the title.

Lurdy Ház, the venue for the Hungarian National Championship, was located in the same district as the Pesti Vigadó, only farther south, a few hundred meters east of the Rákóczi Bridge. When I arrived there, that evening, after parting ways with Bernát, it was to find a pair of burly men putting together tables the spitting image of Rubik's Cubes: they had six sides, each covered with a range of vinyl matting, appropriately chipped to give the impression of an actual puzzle.

Along with Perge and Placskó, they were accompanied by a rail-thin young man with a shock of raven hair wearing an Avengers T-shirt: Bence Barát, a name I'd only ever before seen on the rankings of the World Cube Association. Barát, who has participated in three World Championships, winning five medals, has the reputation of being a master of the Big Cubes—the 5x5, 6x6, and 7x7—and has the résumé to prove it; he has set multiple world records for the 7x7.

"I fucking love cordons," Perge said.

He was crouching in front of me, affixing velvet ropes to stanchions. When he finished, he pretended to snap pictures. There were always parents who thought their kid was the best cuber in the world, he said, shaking his head. Nearby, a Rubik's Cube sailed through the air.

There are a lot of things that go into setting up a competition. You need timers, tables, judges, computers for entering the scores into the WCA database, scramblers, medals, an area for competitors to warm up, and you also, perhaps most importantly, need good lighting. If you can't see your Rubik's Cube because it's too dark, or the stickers shine in your face like headlights because it's too bright, your times—and those of your competitors—are bound to suffer. This is why Barát had chucked his Cube at Placskó, who caught it neatly and set to work cubing in different parts of the room.

The two of them tossed the puzzle back and forth, every couple of minutes, as if they were playing a game of hot potato, testing first the corners of the stage, then the middle of the room, until finally they decided the lighting was adequate.

During a break, Barát started timing himself. I figured that wasn't a bad idea. The timers take some getting used to. There's a slight lag between the time you touch the timing device and the activation of the clock. If you wait too long, you might get a penalty. My average was twenty-four seconds, or thereabouts—a twenty-five-second solve, followed by twenty-three-, twenty-four-, twenty-one-, and twenty-seven-second solves—a whopping seven seconds faster than my current PB.

If I could do that during competition, I would be stoked: only five seconds until I reached the land of sub-20, where I had yet to tread. Of course, it still remained to be seen whether I *could* do that in competition. The other night, Perge told me to practice until I collected a sub-20 average of twelve solves every single day. "But official times are always slower," he said. "It's pressure," he added, with a shrug.

Mayday: in the United States, it signals distress, as when pilots blow an engine. Elsewhere, of course, May Day is the ancient holiday once used to celebrate the rites of spring, and, later, the rights of workers. (Efforts to shift Labor Day in the United States from September 1 to May 1, known as International Workers' Day, have so far been unsuccessful.)

In Hungary, as in most European countries, May 1 is a holiday. Ironically, on a day celebrating workers, when no one is required to work, Bernát had to show up for work: entertaining tourists in the square outside St. Stephen's Basilica, a magnet for sightseers and the Roman Catholic faithful alike. The church, located in the fifth district, is tied for the tallest building in Budapest (regulations prevent any new construction from rising higher than its ninety-six meters), and its reliquary is said to contain the right hand of St. Stephen himself.

When I arrived, around ten in the morning, Bernát and his friend Norbert, the one with whom he used to busk on Váci Street, had already set up, their Cubes arrayed like piles of treasure on one of the table-sized Rubik's Cubes that would be later used at the competition. Norbert, a slight young man clad in a suit jacket, blue gingham shirt, and jeans, sat with Bernát on a ledge overlooking the square, chatting to a pair of young women who organized the tours and smoking a cigarette.

Before long, drawn by the sight of the puzzles, a boy wearing a blue Windbreaker approached the table. What were we doing? he asked. Solving Rubik's Cube, Bernát told him. The boy's eyes bulged out of his head when Bernát completed a fourteen-second solve.

The boy asked if he could give it a try. Like a clown making animal balloons at a party, Bernát handed the boy his Cube and pulled another one out of his pocket. The official tours started to stream past a few minutes later, their members gawking openly at the sight of Bernát, Norbert, and, well, me, solving Rubik's Cube.

"That's next, that's next!" one of the guides said.

When the first group emerged from the basilica, some of its members stampeded down the steps to stake a spot in front of the table. At this point, I retreated to the ledge to watch the performance. Bernát was wearing the same suit as when he appeared on TV and carried himself with supreme ease, as if he'd done this hundreds of times before.

Bernát requested two volunteers. He handed them his Rubik's Cube and Norbert's. While the volunteers scrambled the puzzles,

Bernát asked the audience to guess how fast they could solve them. Like an auctioneer, he called out the different responses. "A minute? Thirty seconds? As in three-zero?" The lowest estimate was twenty seconds.

"Let's see if we can beat twenty seconds," Bernát said.

As he and Norbert prepared to activate the timers—they were going to race—the audience crowded close.

"No," one woman said as they resolved the first two layers. They were neck and neck.

"Shit," muttered someone else, as they neared the end of the solve.

"Thirteen," Bernát said, after he put his Cube down. "Well, fourteen for me. Norbert was faster."

The next group, from Kuwait, consisted largely of men with strong aftershave, aviator sunglasses, and shaved heads, and women in silken head scarves. There were lots of exclamations in Arabic. One of the Kuwaitis asked if the puzzle's inventor was still alive and if he had made a lot of money. Yes, Bernát said, and not as much as he could have.

"It's not like poker," interjected the tour-company photographer. "This is real knowledge. Poker is also luck. And you can't make money from knowledge."

The Kuwaiti man nodded. "This world is unfair," he said.

Bernát was a consummate showman. He made each performance, which lasted about twenty minutes, rise like a crescendo. The audiences loved it. They mobbed him for pictures, selfie sticks extended, elbowing each other in their haste to document the affair.

The pièce de résistance was the last solve, which Bernát introduced casually, as if he were simply remarking there wasn't a cloud in the sky. It was a sign of how rapt his audience was that they failed to look up, even when biplanes soared above the Danube, doing loop the loops that echoed down the narrow streets.

"What are you looking at there?" asked a woman from Iran.

"I'm going to solve it with a blindfold," Bernát said.

With some groups, it wasn't even necessary to introduce the premise. The last group, from the United Arab Emirates, *demanded* that he solve Rubik's Cube blindfolded, as if to prove to themselves that it wasn't all some elaborate joke. "Well, I can try," Bernát said, "but I've never attempted it before."

"Lies," Norbert said, behind a cupped hand. "He can do it."

Before arriving in Hungary, I spent a week in Germany, visiting friends. I kept practicing Rubik's Cube, day and night. One evening, at the dinner table, while explaining how the puzzle worked to some guests, I noticed that one of the orange stickers had turned suddenly and inexplicably brown. I had never seen anything like it. The only square affected was the center of the orange face: the rest were tangerine, as before.

Now, following the performance, I pulled out my Rubik's Cube, to twiddle it idly, as I'd gotten into the habit of doing. During the performance, I'd kept it in the mesh pocket on the side of my backpack, the one normally designed to hold water bottles.

It looked, at first, as if someone had taken a waffle iron to the orange face. It was jagged with dark lines, like those from a griddle. I freaked out. That's not too strong a word for it: according to the regulations, the colored stickers of any puzzle must not be distinguishable from one another. Here, we had a glaring problem: this was my only competition Cube. I didn't have any other stickers, nor had I ever replaced the stickers on my puzzle before.

If I didn't think of something to do, and fast, I wouldn't be able to compete tomorrow.

"Make sure you scrape that off," Perge said. "If there's too much jizz on the puzzle, the new stickers will slide around." It was later that night, at Perge's apartment. He had offered to help me replace my orange stickers. Perge had a wide selection to choose from. He even had a special tool for removing the old ones, a kind of plastic blade designed to slide up under the vinyl and peel it off. Underneath lay a mess of crusty yellow gunk, or, as he liked to call it, the jizz.

We had rendezvoused at his apartment, along with Placskó, to go over the final details for the competition. At one point, after Barát joined us, Perge and I left to get döner kebabs for dinner. When we returned, Barát was right where we had left him: on the edge of Perge's bed, solving Rubik's Cube, hunched over his phone, with the timer out. "This is what you need to do if you want to go sub-20," Perge said.

After testing my Cube, Perge decreed that it needed additional lubrication. It was one of the newer models, the MoYu WeiLong, which had recently superseded the DaYan ZhanChi, in much the same way the Firebolt replaced the Nimbus 2001 as the broomstick to envy in the Harry Potter books.

"Okay, let's lube," Perge said, after dinner, leading the way into his bedroom. He used a QiYi, another Chinese model. "That's not a sentence I like to say a lot to another guy," he added, "but when you need lube, you need lube!"

Since I didn't have any events the first day of the competition, I offered to help out. It felt polite, in the same way it is to assist the host with the dishes when you've been invited over to dinner. Only no amount of dishwashing could ever measure up to the amount of work that goes into running a Rubik's Cube competition.

I had only assisted with one competition before, at Yale, where I managed to botch a young cuber's first solve by failing to reset the timer. Still, that meant I had more experience than some cubers present at the Hungarian Nationals; by now, I had attended more than half a dozen competitions.

If you volunteer to help at a cubing competition, there are

four different things you can do: judge, scramble, enter scores, and run. The latter is the easiest: you literally "run" puzzles to and from the scrambling table. To be a good runner, all you have to do is keep a watchful eye—solves finish at different times—deliver the puzzles to the scramblers, wait to pick them up, and then call out the names of the cubers whose puzzles you now hold.

Unfortunately, Hungarian is one of the most confusing languages known to man.

"Barnábas?" I yelled. "Barnábas Turi?" It was hard enough to make my voice heard over the temblor of all the Cubes twisting. My gross mispronunciations of the competitors' names made it even harder. One of the competitors sitting nearby urged me to shout, "Sarnabas."

Don't, Perge said, sweeping by and throwing the cuber a dirty look. He's trying to get you to say "shithead," Perge explained.

The cuber in question, Barnábas Turi, eventually showed up and nodded, wearily. It must have been like having the given name Richard, and everyone calling you Dick.

That night, the Hungarian cubers gathered in the food court to go over the day's events. I had the chance to meet a young man with floppy brown hair named Hunor Bózsing, whose aquiline nose and limbs suggested aspects of a bird of prey. He has extremely long, talonlike fingers, which allow him to manipulate Rubik's Cube with one hand in ways that most people can only accomplish using ten digits. Earlier that year, at the Slovenian Open, in Maribor, he had solved Rubik's Cube in 6.84 seconds, breaking the national record.

I asked him to watch one of my solves and critique it. "That wasn't a bad solve," Bózsing said, with characteristic bluntness. "You didn't do any stupid things."

His main advice had to do with the first step, the cross. "That's my trick for winning competitions," he said. For ten minutes before he solved onstage, he practiced solving the cross, making sure to plan it out entirely beforehand. "I never turn the Cube" during that period, he said. If he memorized it, he didn't have to look at the cross while he solved it, and could examine the rest of the Cube, to look for the first pieces he would use during F2L.

When I told him my goal was to go sub-20, hopefully in time for the 2015 World Championship, now just ten weeks away, he nodded. He remembered when he was still trying to go sub-20 himself. "It's, like, yeah, having a record, or breaking a world record," he said. "And, uh, until you have it, it's your dream goal." But, once you'd crossed the barrier, it was like turning Super Saiyan in Dragon Ball Z—after you'd done it, it was no longer the challenge it once was. "Like, if you fuck up a solve," he said, "it's still sub-20."

26.89 seconds. Not bad. Nearly five seconds off my personal best. The first time I'd averaged under thirty seconds in competition. The night before, Perge had said that my goal should be not to embarrass myself. What he meant was that I shouldn't aim too high: better to go slow.

To my great surprise, 26.89 seconds was sufficient to make the second round—the first time I'd ever advanced beyond the first round of a competition. The cutoff was generous—the top three quarters moved on—but I wasn't anywhere near to being on the bubble. If I'd been averaging what I had just weeks before, at the Yale competition, I might not have made it: the final cubers to get into the second round clocked averages in the low thirties.

This is where I hoped I'd be—two weeks earlier, when I visited Valk, in the Netherlands, I told him that I hoped to average around twenty-five seconds in Hungary. That would leave me only five seconds to cut before the World Championship. "You'll probably do pretty bad," Valk said. He figured I'd average in the thirties again. Only later, when I had more experience under my belt, would I get into the twenties. So it was sort of like breaking through? I asked. Exactly, he said. Once I'd gone as fast in competition as I was at home, I'd just keep getting faster.

"That's really important," he stressed, ". . . to go to competitions. A lot. As much as possible. And not just 'I'll practice and practice and go to Worlds.'" He shook his head. "No, just no."

My first solve of the second round was 27.30 seconds. Worse, in fact, than my first solve of the first round—22.56 seconds. Still, I figured it was best not to give up hope. That I'd managed a twenty-seven was actually not so bad: I'd had to permute the last layer twice, and made a couple of small mistakes during the first two layers that wasted a few seconds, at least.

The second solve gave me occasion to use a PLL I had recently learned, for the Y-permutation. The Y-perm, as it's known, transposes two corners and two edges, tracing a figure not unlike the eponymous letter. It blends together two different algorithms used during the orientation phase: Mounted Fish, so called because it resembles a striped bass on the wall, followed by Tying Shoelaces, which involves looping pieces in and out of the first layer and the last layer, as if you were binding threads together.

Some PLLs are awkward—I was still having trouble learning the N-permutation, which implicated so many different movements that I couldn't keep them straight in my own head—but the Y-permutation felt natural. When I told Perge, beaming, what I'd just done, he cocked his head, said, "But why?" and then guffawed at his own terrible pun.

My average for the second round was 25.67 seconds. I was now only five seconds away.

"Ah, you made a really stupid mistake," Perge said, after my last solve. In six moves, I could have solved the orientation case, skipping at least half a dozen steps. He demonstrated the algorithm, building a block of four squares, and then another block.

"Ah, well," I said, grinning. "At least I didn't do an embarrassing average!"

* * *

"I'm competing for best of the rest," Bernát said. The finals produced the usual suspects: Bózing, who held the national record for a single solve; Milán Baticz, the national record holder for an average of five; Dániel Varga, a towering twentysomething whose beard and scowl brought to mind Shane Smith, the bad boy CEO of Vice News; and Bernát, who had qualified fourth, just behind Bózsing, with an 11.01-second average.

In the 1980s, speedcubing was serious business in Hungary. According to a pair of veteran cubers to whom Kovács introduced me and whose comments he translated, competitions began at the village level, a winnowing process that took the better part of a year to crown a national champion. One of them set aside his career as a professional chess player, thinking that Rubik's Cube would become just as lucrative. The other actually earned more placing second at the National Championship than he did in six months working his normal job as a quality-control engineer.

The prizes at the 2015 Hungarian National Championship were hardly so spectacular. I had helped Placskó arrange them, tying together the various medals and placing the small trophy for the winner of the main event in a place of honor. The winners themselves were a relatively small bunch—the same people kept going up to receive their prizes, hanging medals around their necks until they brought to mind Michael Phelps after the Beijing Olympics, his neck wreathed in gold.

Barát alone collected twelve medals, nearly one for every event contested. It was enough of a prize, I figured, to have met Rubik. The Hungarian cubers universally expressed amazement that I'd had lunch with the inventor. (They are jealous, said Baticz, who took second in the main event, behind Bózsing.)

Then I heard Perge call my name. First place, Perge said, goes to Ian Scheffler. He paused. In the event of longest distance traveled to the competition!

CHAPTER 12

7 LAMBTON PLACE

The famous blue door from *Notting Hill*, the movie starring Hugh Grant as the owner of a small bookstore and Julia Roberts as the Hollywood actress who purchases one of his books and falls in love with him, is the door of an actual residence in London. It stands at 280 Westbourne Park Road, in Notting Hill, unsurprisingly, just around the corner from the tchotchke-filled boutiques that line Portobello Road.

Scores of tourists drop by the door these days to pose for selfies. It is safe to assume most of them have no idea they are only paces away from the headquarters of another, equally beloved enterprise: the manufacture and sale of Rubik's Cube. Seven Towns, Ltd., the firm that controls the brand, operates out of a small town house a few blocks away, not far from the Helmut Lang and Club Monaco boutiques, tucked in a cul-de-sac at 7 Lambton Place. Unless you were to look carefully, you would probably miss it: there is a sign out front, but the planters jutting out from below the windows on the second story, spilling ivy like so many waterfalls, more or less obscure it.

In the world of speedcubing, Seven Towns, Ltd., occupies a place not unlike that of the National Football League in the world of football. That is to say, it is indispensable, but sometimes finds itself at odds with the players. In football, disputes arise from time to time when players refuse to wear the gear provided by the league's official sponsors; the NFL threatened to eject Marshawn Lynch, star running back, from the 2015 NFC title game, not because he'd done anything reprehensible, like getting arraigned on domestic violence charges, but because he threatened to commit the awful sin of wearing the wrong cleats.

In cubing, there is the elaborate game of cat and mouse involving the manufacturers and distributors of speedcubes and Seven Towns, which is backed by the customs authorities. Not long after the advent of speedcubes in the mid-2000s, Seven Towns started a yearly tradition of putting out press releases condemning counterfeit puzzles and urging consumers to guard against them. "Badly made imitations can never work as well as the Professor's ingenious original," one of the press releases from 2007 read. "Our picture illustrates what a crushing blow this was to the companies involved," the same press release stated. It included a picture of a tractor rolling over a shipment of what was said to be one hundred thousand non-Rubik's-brand twisty puzzles confiscated by customs agents in Long Beach, California.

This is hardly a new issue. One of the theories regarding the Cube's collapse in the 1980s has to do with the fact that so many counterfeit Cubes flooded the market, sapping demand for the real thing and making everyone sick of the puzzle. These were poorly made, it is said, making Rubik's Cube seem harder than it already was, either by exploding or simply getting stuck. (Waugh, the doctor who coined the term *cuber's thumb*, blamed his condition on having purchased a cheap Taiwanese knockoff, which he found difficult to turn.)

When I first came into contact with Seven Towns at the 2013 World Championship, I was surprised that the firm didn't seem overly concerned with the prospect of supporting a competitive endeavor that uses knockoffs to promote its most famous product. "Not really," said Christine "Chrisi" Trussell, one of the senior executives, when I asked her if speedcubes were a sticking point. The puzzles were out there, she said, sounding more or less resigned to the fact.

In 2011, the *Wall Street Journal* published an article on the controversy. "We really spend a lot of time on this," said David Hedley Jones, a Seven Towns executive, who has since retired. According to the article, the company spent half a million dollars a year to keep unlicensed Cubes from reaching the market. The journal also reported that Rubik was designing a speedcube of its own. "We've been working on it for five years," Kovács said.

In late 2013, the Cube finally came out. "Now, I'm not expecting these Cubes to be any better than, like, the DaYan ZhanChi," said memyselfandPi, a popular cuber on YouTube. "But I do think it's really cool to see that the Rubik's company is actually taking steps to get a better Cube in stores."

The puzzle was designed like a speedcube. That is to say, the inside was rounded. It was adjustable. It even came with a syringe of lubricant. "It's pretty decent," said memyselfandPi. Considering the standards to which cubers hold their puzzles, this was hardly faint praise. "Seems to turn smoothly and the corner cutting feels *nice* . . . For a store-bought cube, you know, I like it. This is something that will be great for first-time beginners that will be able to get into the speedcubing community." The video, which memyselfandPi posted to YouTube shortly before Christmas, has since been watched upward of half a million times.

The fact remains that, for Seven Towns, and all its licensees, cubing is publicity of the highest order: viral and cheap. In order to sponsor the World Championship, as it does every two years, Seven Towns donates a fair sum, and in return gets to see Rubik's Cube splashed in headlines all across the globe. It doesn't matter that some of the puzzles in question are DaYan Zhanchis or MoYu Weilongs; Rubik's Cube is Rubik's Cube, the same way, to most people, a baseball is a baseball.

However, it's not so clear-cut. In early 2015, the forums cubers frequent online exploded with the news that Seven Towns had forced eBay to remove all listings for non-Rubik's-brand puzzles. The same thing had happened several years prior, when the theory circulated that, if you just ordered one of the puzzles disassembled, it couldn't be stopped at customs. But the dispute obscured, and continues to obscure, the fact that, without Seven Towns, neither cubers nor anyone else would ever have heard of Rubik's Cube in the first place.

When I visited the Seven Towns offices in London a few days after leaving Budapest, I was met by Chrisi Trussell in the main lobby. She led the way up to the second story, where the main administrative outpost appeared to be located: there were folders lying around, with titles like *Inventor Submissions, May 2014,* and three clocks on the wall, one for Hong Kong, New York, and London. There was also a framed photograph of the Rubik's Cube prepared by Diamond Cutters International, a white-gold confection lined with rubies, sapphires, emeralds, and other precious stones, bearing the legend *World's Most Expensive Toy.* The photograph was signed by Rubik himself, who had dated his signature 11.10.95.

The office was charming, in the way that so many British things seem to be. There was a cheery yellow armchair by the window, adjacent to a black coffee table with a booklet about a tablet computer for kids on it. On the wall, above the chair, was a painting of the Thames, Big Ben, and the London Eye outlined against the orange-hued dusk. Trussell, who had gone to the pantry to prepare two mugs of tea, returned and sat down with me to chat.

There was a workshop on the first floor, she said, and the administrative side of things occupied the other two stories of the building. Trussell, who has bright blue eyes and a keen sense of fashion, wore a light gray sweater and blue Hermès bracelet. She told me she has worked for Seven Towns "since the beginning," as she puts it, which is to say the late 1970s, not long after the firm was founded and stumbled upon Rubik's Cube.

Of course, like any business, Seven Towns didn't just spring into being. Someone founded it. His portrait stared down at us from the wall, looking on while his employees discussed things like inventor invoices, licensees, advances: Tom Kremer, the Hungarian émigré who negotiated Rubik's Cube's leapfrogging of the Iron Curtain. Kremer, who is in his mideighties, rarely comes into the office, but I happened to be lucky and catch him on a day when he was in.

At the appropriate time, Trussell escorted me down the staircase, a modern, zigzagging thoroughfare in wood and glass, to a conference room on the first floor. She took a seat at the table, a large oval that could easily have fit a dozen people, and turned her attention to the man sitting across from her, instantly recognizable from the photograph in the office upstairs. Kremer introduced himself with a soft voice and firm handshake and had on a heavy gray cardigan, pinstriped slacks, and a white shirt open at the collar. In the corner of the room, I noticed, was a stack of giant Rubik's Cubes, presumably made of cardboard or some other promotional material, facing the cobblestones of Lambton Place.

Kremer does not shy away from publicity to the degree that Rubik does. But he doesn't boast of his accomplishments either, which is all the more surprising, since he has accomplished more in one lifetime than most people would have given several.

He was born in Transylvania. His family was Jewish. In 1944, when he was thirteen years old, Kremer and his family were rounded up and sent to Bergen-Belsen. In those days, Bergen-Belsen had not yet become a slaughterhouse; it was designed to hold Jewish prisoners to be exchanged with German prisoners abroad. In a miraculous twist of fate, Kremer participated in one of these exchanges—one of only 2,260 or so Jews ever to be let go from Bergen-Belsen—and was delivered to Switzerland.

Two years later, having become an ardent Zionist, Kremer went to Palestine to live on a kibbutz. When he realized farming wasn't for him, he returned to school. But his studies were interrupted in 1948, when Israel declared independence and war broke out.

By this time, Kremer's family—or what survived of it—had dispersed across the globe. In 1950, he visited his parents in Rhodesia and decided to move to South Africa, where he studied at Witwatersrand University in Johannesburg. He dabbled in everything from mathematics to philosophy, but decided that his passion was literature: he wanted to write.

In 1953, Kremer immigrated to Scotland, where he enrolled at the University of Edinburgh, reading for a degree in philosophy. There, he met his wife, who happened to be a peer of the realm: Lady Alison Balfour, a relation of Arthur Balfour, who served as the prime minister of the United Kingdom in the early 1900s under King Edward VII.

In the early 1960s, living in West London's Holland Park, Kremer started working two jobs: one as a football coach, the other as a teacher of special-needs children. It was by combining these two pursuits, attempting to make educational games, that Kremer lucked upon the idea of entering the toy business.

The invention of puzzles is not a modern phenomenon, but only in modern times has it become a business. Even three hundred years ago, there was not enough leisure time to make puzzles a viable consumer product—in those days, there were hardly any consumer products. The Industrial Revolution, and all that came with it, was just getting under way.

The first modern puzzle craze took place in the early nineteenth century when the tangram, which involves rearranging a square cut into seven pieces into different shapes, came over from China and swept across the West. According to Jerry Slocum, a retired executive at Howard Hughes Aircraft who has amassed one of the largest puzzle collections in the world, everyone from Edgar Allan Poe, the famous mystery writer, to Lewis Carroll, the mathematician and author of *Alice in Wonderland*, to Napoleon Bonaparte, the French emperor, to Hans Christian Andersen, the fairy-tale writer, to John Quincy Adams, the sixth president of the United States of America, enjoyed playing with the tangram.

"Every hundred years, you get a popular puzzle," observed George Miller, the puzzle collector and designer, when I visited him in San Francisco. After the tangram faded away, it was the 15-puzzle's turn to shine. This puzzle, which consisted of fifteen squares that had to be arranged in numerical order, rose to such heights that, like Rubik's Cube, it even appeared in political cartoons of the day. (In one memorable example, the squares of the puzzle stood in for the Republican primary candidates of 1880, who were giving the party leaders a headache and proving that not only puzzles repeat themselves.)

To Western audiences, anyway, the tangram and 15-puzzle were radical breaks with the puzzles that had come before. Indeed, some thought the 15-puzzle could never be solved. (In fact, half the random arrangements of the puzzle *were* impossible to solve.) Still, like many industries, the world of toys and games is notoriously conservative—why risk money on something that differs radically from what you've done before?

This made what Kremer saw, midway through the 1978 Nuremberg Toy Fair, the industry's largest gathering, all the more surprising. "I saw somebody doing funny things," Kremer recalled, with a chuckle. "I mean, doing something with a cube, like this"—he rotated his hands one way and then the other—"and like this." Kremer has a garrulous laugh, which he now unleashed, echoing around the room. "And I say, That's not possible. You can't do it one way and, at the same time, do it the other way. That's not the way things work!"

Just as during the Industrial Revolution the same things were invented by different people at more or less the same time, Rubik is not the only person to have come up with the notion of a twisty, rotating cube. In the late 1960s, a Boston-based scientist named Larry Nichols filed a patent for a cube that was similar in some respects—it was designed to be scrambled and rearranged—but different in others. (It was held together by magnets, and could easily come apart, rendering the challenge essentially moot.)

But only certain inventions make it. We had the DVD, not the laser disc. Alternating current, not direct current. VHS instead of Betamax. In 1975, Rubik filed for a patent in Hungary that took two years to get approved. In the meantime, someone else had come up with a similar invention—a Japanese ironworks owner named Terutoshi Ishige. But the magic of the market-place, that coming together of the right buyer and the right seller with explosive results for all to see, touched only one of these inventions. In other words, there's a reason you've never heard of Ishige's Cube.

It was Kremer's last day at the Nuremberg Toy Fair. Normally, he only stayed a couple of days anyway. By the end, he told me, it was just toy fanatics trading trinkets with each other. There was no business to be made. In the process of saying good-bye to friends, at the booth run by a large German toy conglomerate, Kremer found himself arrested by the sight of this Cube, impossibly turning one way and then the other.

He asked one of his friends about the people with the Cube. Just some Hungarians, the friend said. They had some rubbish that wasn't worth a second glance.

All the same, Kremer said, he wanted to speak to the man holding the Cube. When the man arrived at Kremer's booth, about fifty yards away, he introduced himself as Dr. Dr. Laczi.* (The *c* was silent, so it was pronounced like "Yahtzee.") This, of course, was none other than Tibor Laczi, the enterprising Hungarian businessman featured in Tierney's article.

In those days, if you were Hungarian and wanted to sell something outside Hungary, you needed permission from the state, as you did for just about everything. The body to approach was Konsumex, a giant state-owned trading company. "They laughed at me," Laczi said. "They had ordered ten thousand from the manufacturer and then canceled half the order." Part of the problem, he told Tierney, was that no one could properly demonstrate how to use the Cube—it just sat on a shelf, unsolved. No one was even sure if it had been taken out of the box.

As with any invention story, this one differs in the telling. It is agreed upon that Kremer and Laczi first met in 1978, on the floor of the Nuremberg Toy Fair. It is also agreed that they made an arrangement to try to sell Rubik's Cube to the rest of the world. But, as Tierney tells it in his magazine article, the interaction was virtually frictionless.

According to Tierney, Laczi handed Kremer one of his Cubes and sealed the deal then and there. "We are now holding in our hands a wonder of the world" is how Laczi recalled Kremer's reaction. "Later that year," Tierney wrote, "Kremer helped arrange the breakthrough," a massive order of one million Cubes from the Ideal Toy Company.

Only, as Kremer recalls it, that meeting was significantly more dicey—and the Cube substantially less assured of success than Tierney makes it out to be. "I said to him, 'Well, show me what you're doing with it—what is that thing?'" Kremer remembers asking Laczi.

Kremer started laughing. "So he then explained it to me. But he couldn't solve it. I mean, he couldn't." Kremer had to pause to

---

* According to Kremer, Laczi had two doctorates.

catch his breath. "It wasn't showing me how to do it! It was just demonstrating that you *could* do it, if you see what I mean, and you could do one side easily!

"But I thought to myself that was something interesting," he continued. "And I said to him. 'Right, very simple. We'll shake hands now.'" Kremer mimed shaking hands. "And I said, 'Write up an agreement. I'll take it to the world. You deal with Hungary.' Simple."

"Not so simple!" Trussell said. She'd been following along with a smile, occasionally tucking her hair behind her ears, and now she and Kremer looked at each other and burst out laughing. "I went around the world as usual," Kremer said. "Twice. And I showed the Cube to about forty leading companies in the toy world."

You might expect Rubik's Cube to have been easy to sell. It wasn't. It didn't talk, light up, require batteries, appear in a movie, or any of the other things toys normally did. It was also extraordinarily hard to solve. "I think they gave me five reasons why," Kremer said, when the companies declined to pick up Rubik's Cube. "All of them good reasons."

For one, it was too expensive. The ideal price point back then was two dollars, or maybe a dollar and a half. The projected cost of Rubik's Cube was five dollars. "I mean," Kremer recalls being told, "this is lunacy."

What's more, puzzles were not exactly popular. They amounted to less than 1 percent of the global toy market, Kremer was told. Why would anyone bother with something so insignificant?

Finally, it was just too hard. "Look, maybe it's interesting," the toy companies said, in Kremer's summation, "but how many professors at Harvard are there?"

His wife asked him, "Why do you go with your Cube? No one is interested, it can't be interesting."

"But I am very, very peculiar," Kremer told me, "in the sense that once I tackle something, I find it very difficult to give it up."

Kremer carried the Cube with him everywhere he went. He brought it out at dinner parties. The guests were universally intrigued. They wanted to play with it. "I couldn't get it back!" Kremer laughed. He realized that, whereas the toy companies were 100 percent uninterested in the puzzle, the reverse was true of the general public. "One of them is right and one of them is wrong," he recalls thinking. "They cannot both be right."

In September of that year, he got a phone call from the Ideal Toy Company. "Ideal at that time was one of the major companies," Kremer told me. Indeed, in the early twentieth century, Morris and Rose Michtom, a young couple in Brooklyn, New York, who ran a penny candy store, started putting dolls for sale in the windows to make extra money. Inspired by a cartoon in the *Washington Post*, which showed Teddy Roosevelt refusing to shoot a bear while hunting—since it had been tied up and beaten, he considered it unsportsmanlike, although he was happy to let others kill it later, to put it out of its misery—they conceived of a stuffed bear with button eyes, which they named after Roosevelt: Teddy's Bear.

And Ideal was going bankrupt. "It was one of the majors," Kremer said, "but tough times. They were ready to go. And they said to themselves, 'What if you go bust, whether with the Cube or without the Cube? It makes no difference.'"

By this time, Kremer had already become something of a success. He had branched out into real estate, buying and selling properties in London. He was the father of three and almost forty years old, which is nearly three times as long as he might have expected to live. Anne Frank and her older sister, Margot, who arrived at Bergen-Belsen around the time Kremer's release was negotiated, both died there a few months later.

The steely resolve with which Kremer went about achieving all of this might explain what happened next. When Ideal sent a representative to London, he met Kremer while changing planes at Heathrow Airport, heading to Budapest. The two of them sat next to each other on the flight. "Look," Kremer recalls the man telling him, "don't think that we are going to buy the Cube. I mean," the man went on, "the chances of it are not great."

The man in question was the son of one of the executives of Ideal. Kremer had dealt with his father, an amateur magician to whom he'd sold a number of other toys. The son was in marketing—he'd never been involved in the acquisition of new toys until now. "The idea was that he negotiates," Kremer said. "And, in the middle of negotiations, twice a day, he called his father in New York, to tell him what there was and what there wasn't and so on."

While the negotiations took place, Kremer sat in the middle, so to speak, literally and figuratively. "I sat in the middle of the conversation," he says, "which always only one half understood." Since neither the Hungarians nor the Americans spoke the others' language, Kremer translated. "That was lucky," he told me. "Because I realized that, unless I twist things, very quickly it would come, more or less, to a full stop."

In those days, of course, Hungary was Communist, in the orbit of the Soviet Union. It was not a country particularly skilled with commerce. "They didn't know how to begin anything," Kremer said, but the Cube wouldn't sell itself. They decided, according to Kremer, that the worldwide price for Rubik's Cube should be three dollars. They also decided that the Americans must guarantee a shipment of one million Cubes.

To Kremer, these demands were absurd—who were the Hungarians to make a show of negotiating, when they didn't know how to sell Rubik's Cube abroad? But it was what he had to work with. The negotiations went on for a week, by which time Kremer had got the head of Ideal's European branch on the phone. Kremer proposed setting two prices: one for the United States and one for Europe. If the two prices added up to three dollars, all parties would be satisfied. According to Kremer, this is precisely what happened—the price in the United States would be two dollars and fifty cents, and in Europe, fifty cents.

They were ready to sign the agreement, but ran into another problem. It was Friday, and in Communist Hungary, hardly anyone worked on Fridays. They had to hunt around Budapest for a notary, but eventually the documents were signed.

By this point, I'd heard many answers as to why Rubik's Cube has been so successful, when so many puzzles have not. "That is an interesting question," said Kremer, when I brought up the subject. "If it was a simple answer," he added, after a long pause, "I wouldn't have had a problem with putting it onto the market."

The answers ranged from its size to its coloration. "If it's too small, it's bad," George Miller, the puzzle designer, told me. "If it's too large, it's bad." He added that the ideal size for a puzzle was about three by three by three inches, which is almost exactly the dimensions of Rubik's Cube. "You want something that fits in your hand," he said.

"It's got colors," noted Marc Waterman, the Dutch cuber, "and that attracts babies." What he meant was that Rubik's Cube has a pull, visually speaking, that reaches out and touches something embryonic.

For his part, Kremer thought all of these ideas had merit. It was the right size. The colors were certainly attractive. But, for him, the answer went further than that. "There is something there that hit the human mind in a certain sort of way," he said.

In 1978, at the University of Toronto, a little-known philosopher, Bernard Suits, published a treatise called *The Grasshopper*, a meditation on the nature of games. Suits contended, in the face of Ludwig Wittgenstein, who said that games could not be precisely defined, that games—which Suits defined, more or less, as the overcoming of unnecessary obstacles—were the only suitable activity in life.

The book took the form of a dialogue, full of ribald humor and full-page illustrations. (This may be why it received so little attention in the academic press—it was too fun to read.) It took place in the world of Aesop's fables, specifically the tale about the improvident grasshopper and the industrious ant. The fable, of course, is a metaphor for the burdens of life—if you put off your responsibilities, you may wind up like the grasshopper. (The grasshopper fails to store food for the winter while the prudent ant refuses to help.)

The moral of the story is that we should emulate the ant, not the grasshopper. This may seem eminently practicable—who wants to starve in winter? Or not be able to pay the electricity bill? But Suits, as a philosopher, was not entirely concerned with practicalities. "I have the oddest notion," says his Grasshopper, "that everyone alive is really a Grasshopper." He meant that, from a philosophical point of view, it might be a worthier aim to do nothing but play games, even if it meant starving to death.

"That my way of life may eventually be vindicated in practice is beside the point," his Grasshopper says. "Rather, it is the *logic* of my position which is at issue."

Suits based his argument on the simple fact—well, simple, at any rate, as far as he spells it out—that in a utopia, the only possible activity, and thus the highest form of activity, would be to play games.

Rubik's Cube was released in Hungary well before it hit the international market. As early as 1977, there were people in Budapest attempting to solve the Cube. One day, around that time, Rubik took his daughter to the park. There, he saw two Rubik's Cubes.

"The first belonged (I am sure only temporarily)," he later wrote, in his unpublished autobiography, as quoted by Tierney, "to an eight-year-old street urchin, barefooted, shirt torn, covered in bruises, broken and chewed nails, badly in need of a good wash—a small Oliver Twisting.

"The second," he continued, "emerged from the elegant handbag of a still youthful mother in her thirties who must have just emerged from the beauty salon. She was sitting on a bench and cast only an occasional glance at her baby in the pram, so thoroughly was she immersed in the Cube.

"It was astounding to catch on the faces of these diametrically opposite people—the very same expression."

This was only the beginning. When Kremer began to show Rubik's Cube at trade shows in the United States, Rubik, whom he'd brought along to demonstrate the puzzle, could hardly budge for people wanting to see him solve it. At the time, Rubik was the only person in the world who could solve Rubik's Cube. According to Kremer, the American who'd come along to Hungary to represent Ideal in the negotiations refused to sign any documents until he'd seen proof that the puzzle could be solved. (It did not persuade him that since the puzzle started out solved, it must be possible to solve it.)

At the trade shows, there was a booth into which distributors would walk to see Rubik solve his Cube, as if he were some kind of sideshow, an organ grinder's monkey. "He didn't speak English, but he could do this," Kremer said. "They let him out from time to time, but otherwise he was in prison there."

This, Kremer thinks, is the ultimate appeal of Rubik's Cube. "The combination of the simplicity and complexity," he said, was "extremely rare to find, and very astonishing. It gives it a magical quality, if you see what I mean." Of course, Rubik's Cube wasn't actually magical, but that didn't make any difference. "It *seemed* like magic," he said.

The marketers certainly thought so. When Rubik's Cube was introduced, it was with a campaign designed to play up its complexity. "Billions of combinations," went the tag line. "Only one solution." (In fact, this drastically understated the number of possible arrangements, but the marketers figured not enough people knew what a quintillion was.)

The public went nuts. It took several months to get the Cube into stores—the manufacturing wasn't up to par; for a while, the Hungarian firm that had insisted on producing the puzzle kept making shoddy cubes that fell apart—but until the fad died, two and a half years later, it was impossible to keep them in stock.

"They established manufacturing in Brazil, manufacturing in Puerto Rico," Kremer said. "All the places in China. So they geared up. But the gearing up was behind the demand, always, for two and a half years." In that time, upward of one hundred million Cubes are reported to have been sold—a number that doubtless increases if you include all the counterfeits.*

The puzzle had a halo effect, boosting book sales and becoming a buzzword in everything from fashion to politics. In the fall of 1981, Patrick Bossert, a thirteen-year-old, made it onto the *New York Times* bestseller list—one of the youngest to ever do so— with his paperback guide, *You Can Do the Cube*, which ran to 112 pages. "I'm honestly surprised that the book has done so well," the boy told the *Times*. It sold over one million copies. Starting in the summer of 1981, books explaining how to solve Rubik's Cube topped the bestseller list for forty consecutive weeks. When Prince Charles married Lady Diana, St. James's Palace was opened to the public to display some of the five thousand odd gifts they had received: a Rubik's Cube, of course, was sent to them by, of all people, an American.

The success of Rubik's Cube spawned imitators so quickly that Ideal found itself playing a game of legal Whac-A-Mole. The company filed a complaint with the government asserting that no fewer than ninety-six different companies had infringed on its

---

* Today, cumulative estimates range from 350 million to upward of one billion.

rights to produce and sell Rubik's Cube—most of them in Taiwan, but about a dozen in the United States. "We could never have enough," Kremer said. "They were always 20 percent, 25 percent of what they ordered." In a sense, the piracy was just filling the lack of supply, and feeding the overwhelming demand. "There was a huge outstanding order," Kremer said.

The fever peaked when Ideal was bought by CBS, the entertainment conglomerate, for $58 million in April of 1982. That summer, Rubik's Cube starred at the World's Fair, in Knoxville, Tennessee, where the largest Rubik's Cube in the world was put on display. Minh Thai, Jessica Fridrich, Guus Razoux Schultz, and the world's other top cubers convened in Budapest around the same time for the inaugural World Championship.

"And so there came a day," Kremer said, "two and a half years after meeting the Cube," when something momentous happened. Kremer sounded like Grandpa Joe in *Charlie and the Chocolate Factory*, telling his grandson about the day Willy Wonka closed the factory because of spies. "And what happened then," Kremer went on, "nobody could sell a single Cube.

"And imagine, *imagine*, from the beginning, the materials, the factories, the shipping going to wholesalers, all over the world, wholesalers to retailers, imagine all this *volume* going on, one night to the other, stop. Stop completely." It was like a light switch flicking off.

Virtually overnight, everything that had gone so well for Rubik's Cube turned around. Practically every home in America had one and the charm of not being able to solve it had worn off. Just before Christmas, in 1982, Eddie Murphy hosted *Saturday Night Live*, which aired the following skit.

> **Narrator:** First, there was Rubik's Cube—baffling.
> Then there was Rubik's Snake—ingenious.

Next there was Rubik's Revenge—mind-bending.

[Dramatic music]

Now comes the ultimate challenge—Rubik's Grenade.

[Image of a multicolored hand grenade]

The thrill of a lifetime in the palm of your hand. Just scramble the colors, pull the pin, and then begin. You've got exactly ten seconds to put those colors back in order.

[Hands try frantically to unscramble the puzzle]

Rubik's Grenade.

[Text splashed across screen]

Maybe the last puzzle you'll never solve.

[Screen explodes]

Worse perhaps than the cultural shift away from the Cube, shortly after CBS spent millions to purchase Ideal, it was hit with a $60 million lawsuit. Larry Nichols, the Boston-based scientist who had invented a similar puzzle, years earlier, was now saying his copyright had been infringed. The suit dragged on for years, as CBS lost and appealed, lost and appealed, lost and appealed. (It eventually was found to have infringed on Nichols's design when it came to the 2x2, or Pocket Cube.)

Just two years later, with the market for the Cube completely dried up, Kremer approached CBS. He knew they had something like 150 various patents and protections in place, and those had to be renewed every year or couple of years. He offered to rid them of the trouble. "I say, 'Well, what do you want?'" Kremer recalled.

Like any good businessman, Kremer knew a distressed asset when he saw one. When CBS declined to give him the rights, instead asking him to buy them, he asked how much the firm wanted. "You tell us," was the response. "So," Kremer said, "for twenty-five thousand dollars, we permanently acquired the Cube, with all its extensions, all its protections, everything."

The first floor of 7 Lambton Place is the kind of place you imagine Pixar Studios being like, only writ smaller, since they're making toys, not movies. You can find nearly anything there—a 3-D printer, a lathe, sophisticated rendering software—that you might need to help turn the idea for a toy into reality.

The second floor houses the administrative offices, where I met Trussell on the way in. The main office has shelves of products with which Seven Towns has been involved, from Thomas the Tank Engine–branded board games to Spider-Man action figures.

The third floor is devoted to—well, if you can't guess from the mannequin wearing a sweat-wicking cycling jersey dotted with large, colorful squares, you have only to cast your eyes to the mannequin's lower half. It sports matching underwear, a pair of boxer briefs speckled with Rubik's Cubes. Right over the mannequin's, ahem, *member*—it approximates the male figure—is a particular Cube that seems designed to draw attention. It is scrambled, inviting you to solve it, while the rest are already resolved.

In recent years, the Rubik's brand has sold everything from mini-refrigerators—$149.99 at thisiswhyimbroke.com—to flashlights—a bargain at $6.99, sold directly on the Rubik's website. There is still the original puzzle, of course, which the company has taken to updating. Most recently, it replaced the stickers with tiles. "There were long years of absolutely no sales of the Cube," Kremer told me. "First of all, you couldn't sell it because people had it. They were full of it. On the loft, in the basement, whatever. But gradually, you know, it wore away." In the early 2000s, Joe Sequino of Winning Moves, one of the brand's American distributors, told the *New York Times* the puzzle "was in the closeout bin." Sales finally began to tick upward following *The Pursuit of Happyness*, reaching fifteen million units globally in 2008.

They have since leveled off—in 2011, the *Wall Street Journal* reported that ten million Cubes were sold worldwide—but Rubik's Cube has reached the place Kremer thought it would. It's an integral part of the world's culture. "It's one of the great classical toys," he said. "It's guaranteed, like Monopoly, like Scrabble, it's going to survive."

I'M SO SORRY FOR YOU

I felt electric. It was the afternoon of July 17, 2015—one hour before my heat in the first round of the eighth World Rubik's Cube Championship took the stage. Would all my hard work—I'd spent two years practicing, effectively cutting my average in half—pay off? Or would I be left sitting on stage, wondering what I could have done differently? The charge I felt was partly nerves—it was the World Championship, after all—but partly from the thrill of what I had just accomplished. I was sitting on the edge of the bed in my hotel room, overlooking Paulista Avenue, one of the main thoroughfares in São Paulo, Brazil.

I came into the competition having finally averaged sub-20 at home. On June 29, around 7:30 in the evening, I used my phone to record five solves. 22.42 seconds. 17.88 seconds. 21.92 seconds. At this point, the average could have gone either way—another solve above twenty seconds, and I'd have no chance. 19.08 seconds. I held my breath.

I'd come close to a sub-20 average plenty of times before, before I injured my thumb. More recently, when I got a 20.13-second average—a new personal best—in practice. It was like trying to reach the speed of light—the faster I went, the harder it got to get there.

18.55 seconds. Heart pounding, I clicked to the screen that showed my average. 19.85 seconds. I jumped out of my seat, threw my hat on the ground and stomped on it, ran in circles, banging my hand on the wall. It was almost ten years to the day since Toby had written that missive in orange marker in my CTY yearbook: "Hit sub-20." I started to cry.

Now, in my hotel room, warming up for the competition, I'd hit sub-20 again. What's more, I'd done it with a +2, a penalty for not starting the timer soon enough. (Yes, even the programs for timing yourself dish out penalties.) It would have been a 19.25-second average without the added time, but 19.92 seconds was perfectly acceptable. Or, at least, it would be, assuming I could do it in an hour, onstage, with the rest of the cubing world looking on.

From the closet, I pulled out a red, white, and blue Windbreaker, a replica of those worn by American athletes at the Beijing Olympics. It had USA written in bold red letters on the back, and the American flag stitched on the left shoulder.

I'm hardly one for jingoistic displays, but it seemed only appropriate. The Japanese arrived in matching tracksuits of black, red, and gold. It was like the Olympics, writ small: you had to represent your country, even if, at the end of the day, you became friends with your competitors. In the elevator, on the way down, I took a selfie. The combined effect of the Windbreaker, my red pants, and the competitor badge hanging around my neck was to suggest that I was about to run the marathon. I'd never seen my face wear such a grim expression.

The day I arrived in Brazil, I bumped into Ron van Bruchem, Hanneke Rijks, and Mats Valk in the hotel lobby. They had just arrived from Peru, where Valk had participated in a tune-up for the World Championship, along with Feliks Zemdegs and a number of other top cubers. We were all checking in. Van Bruchem had just been told by the concierge that anyone who could solve the ratty old Rubik's Cube behind the desk, which was hard to turn—it had presumably never been lubed—and whose stickers were starting to peel off, would be awarded complimentary tokens to the breakfast buffet.

"This is a bad idea," van Bruchem said.

After solving the Cube, much to the astonishment of the concierge, who seemed unaware of who had booked the hotel, van Bruchem handed the Cube to me. I solved it, received my tokens, and passed the Cube to Rijks, who solved it in turn. At this point, the concierge wore a sour expression, although he couldn't hide his own amazement. After handing the puzzle to Valk, who solved it, Rijks offered her Cube, which was much easier to turn, to the management, and suggested they get rid of the offending older Cube.

The following day, I deposited my tokens and entered the buffet. In Brazil, breakfast is a sweet and savory affair: there were breads—milk breads, yeasty breads, little fried balls of dough— alongside slices of ham and cheese, wedges of papaya, and fresh guava juice. I could hear the rest of the cubers in the room before I saw them; the pop music playing over the loudspeakers was drowned out by the sound of cubers cubing, that incessant *click-clack, click-clack*.

Natán Riggenbach, the Peruvian cuber, who had served as one of my judges at the prior World Championship, and his two daughters, Jael and Rachel, were sitting at a long table. They were accompanied by a number of cubers I didn't recognize, and to whom I was shortly introduced: Juan Camilo Vargas, from Colombia; Oscar Alberto Ceballos Contreras, from Venezuela, and Ernesto and Eduardo Gutiérrez Cuba, twin brothers from Peru.

We're very proud, Riggenbach said. There were more Peruvians here, he told me, than competitors from any other country in South America besides Brazil, despite the fact that Peru was one of the poorest countries on the continent. To fund their travel, the brothers Cuba, among others, had spent the better part of a year busking in the most extreme manner possible. When the light turned red at intersections, they would jump in front of cars, scramble *and* solve their Rubik's Cubes, and collect what money the drivers threw out the windows.

In fact, it was really good practice, Riggenbach said. For a while, one of his daughters joined them. At first, it was pretty nerve-racking for her to step in front of a car, but that's what made it such good practice. In competition, if you screwed up, you just had a bad solve. In this situation, if you were too slow, you risked getting run over.

The venue for the competition was ETAPA, a private school located on the Rua Vergueiro, a bustling boulevard of artistic graffiti, restaurants, and high-rise developments, with a few barely-held-together buildings thrown in.

The entrance, which was flanked by security guards and set behind a white fence, announced the competition with a pair of cardboard Rubik's Cube cutouts suspended, like Christmas ornaments, above the double doors. If you got close enough and the traffic died down, you could actually hear the cubing going on inside, the sound trickling outward like the voices of Rumor in Ovid's *Metamorphoses*, emanating from the thousand apertures of her house, a sanctuary atop a mountain, made of faintly reverberating bronze.

One of the first people I ran into waiting to register was Rita, Feliks Zemdegs's mother. She didn't have an identifying badge, and the orderlies—that's how I thought of them anyway, since the employees of the school wore pale green scrubs, as if they were welcoming us for an extended stay in a sanitarium—were conferring among themselves, trying to figure out whether or not they should admit her. I'm Feliks's mother, she said, pointedly.

Inside the venue—the orderlies relented—Rita told me that Feliks was much less nervous than the previous time around, in 2013. If he didn't win then, she said, he never would have. But now that he was the defending champion, he didn't have anything to prove.

Much the same way the Oscar for Best Supporting Actress is awarded early in the night to give the audience something to chew on, there was a final held the first day. It was an event that normally draws little attention: solving with the feet. The final followed immediately on the heels, so to speak, of the preliminary round. Qualifying first was Jakub Kipa, a Polish teenager with the build of a fullback, with an average of thirty-three seconds, followed by a lithe Brazilian, Gabriel Pereira Campanha, with a 37.75-second average, and Yuhei Takagi, a Japanese who sat on the floor to complete his solves, with an average of 39.13 seconds.

The first time I saw "Rubik's Cube: With Feet," as the WCA officially designates the event, was at the first competition I attended, the 2012 U.S. National Championship, in Las Vegas. There, I witnessed Tim Sun, my erstwhile college classmate, set the American records for both a single solve and average of three solves—solving with the feet is computed differently than with the hands, presumably because it takes so much longer—in 48.12 and 55.13 seconds, respectively.

At the time, Sun told me that solving with the feet got no respect. It was literally quite dirty, he admitted, which might account for why it took place off to the side. There was also a general prejudice against the event since the media so often held it up as an example of how weird cubing was.

Only now, in Brazil, the event was taking place in the main auditorium. All eyes were on Kipa, who had recently set the world record for a single solve, at 20.57 seconds—or nearly half a second faster than I'd yet solved Rubik's Cube in competition with my hands—and Campanha, who owned the world record for an average of three solves, at 29.92 seconds.

Watching Kipa, who had removed his socks and shoes before entering the stage, and was wearing a blue sweater emblazoned with a large orange (presumably) lucky seven on it, inspect his Cube, with all the dexterity of a chimpanzee opening a door with its feet, I began to understand why the auditorium was packed. In the last two years, lots of records had fallen—I had just witnessed the most famous record, for a single solve with both hands, drop while in Hungary—but few events had progressed as rapidly as solving with the feet.

While some cubers turned the Cube over on the floor, using one foot at a time to examine it, Kipa picked the whole thing up between the arches of his feet, and twisted it first one way and then the other. While Campanha solved, Kipa did practice solve after practice solve, resting the Cube on the floor this time, his feet moving as rapidly as if he were playing the pedals on a piano, sometimes twisting it, at others flipping it from one side to the other.

Despite a fast start—cheers of "Bravo! Bravo!" met Kipa's first solve, a 29.86—he faded fast, hamstrung by his second attempt, a lackadaisical 48.29, when he couldn't seem to do anything right. The audience treated the affair as less the vanquishing of the foreigner by the hometown favorite than the clash of two titans, whom it was a privilege to witness do battle. When the round finished, and Kipa doffed his noise-canceling earmuffs and sheepishly nodded his head, the crowd rose to give him and his rival a standing ovation.

"If you look at the World Championship, you know, the level of the organization of the competition hasn't changed since, like, Germany, in 2009, I guess," Michał Pleskowicz, the Polish cuber, told me. (In 2011, Pleskowicz, in a stunning upset, beat Feliks

Zemdegs in the main event.) "It still looks the same. Like, the prizes are the same. It hasn't moved forward."

In Poland, he said, things were developing along the lines cubing might have to head toward if it is to survive. There was a legally incorporated federation to represent the interests of Polish cubers, and to organize competitions and liaise with sponsors— the first of its kind, as far as Pleskowicz knew.

Indeed, in speaking with cubers at the World Championship in Brazil, I got the sense that cubing was heading for a kind of tipping point. "I can say we are in sort of a peak of speedcubing today," said the moderator of a panel. "Records are being broken every time, every month. Speedcubers are getting faster and faster and faster." But it remained to be seen how that speed would translate into success.

The very fact of cubing's popularity was making it hard to maintain quality control. "We have lots of problems with poorly run competitions around the world," said Riggenbach, the Peruvian cuber, who had by then served two years on the World Cube Association's board, alongside van Bruchem, Perge, and the Korean organizer Ilkyoo Choi.

Case in point: at a recent competition in Australia, Zemdegs broke the world record for a single solve of Rubik's Cube one-handed. (He lowered it from 8.27 to 6.88 seconds, a drop so steep that his solve now qualifies as one of the fastest of all time, one- or two-handed.) Only, later, reviewing the footage, the organizers determined that the Cube had been misscrambled—that is, Zemdegs started from a different point than anybody else.

Riggenbach, who appears more or less ageless, his dark hair and olive skin belying the fact that he is a father of three, rubbed his head with his hands. He cited another competition, in Mexico a few years back, that went so badly they had to fire the delegate in charge. Thanks to some really egregious cheating—the cuber in question plugged the scramble into a computer and memorized the optimal solution—the world record was "broken," lowered to 4.41 seconds, by a cuber whose previous best solve was 15.72 seconds.

If the WCA had significant funds, Riggenbach said, these sorts of problems could be avoided. The World Championship alone required a staff of eighty people, not to mention the fifty employees of ETAPA helping out. If they had money, then they wouldn't have to rely on delegates who weren't as well trained as they might have been. "I think we're eventually going to end up having maybe big sponsorship," he said. "That's going to change cubing a lot."

When I asked what kind of sponsors—Seven Towns?—he replied they were looking to bigger fish, like Coca-Cola. If they couldn't land sponsorships, he added, they might start asking cubers to pay to fund the WCA, perhaps just a dollar for each competition, which would add up to quite a lot of money, considering how many tourneys now took place.

At the end of the World Championship, Riggenbach said, he'd be retiring—from cubing, at least—returning home to Peru to work at his zip-lining business, organizing the occasional competition but setting aside the responsibilities of being a board member. "I'm happy to leave it in their hands," he said, referring to the other board members, who had been joined by Pedro Santos Guimarães, a Brazilian student.

When I remarked that it was amazing the WCA has grown as much as it had—it encompassed every continent but Antarctica, sponsoring more competitions than there were days in the year—especially since no money was involved, Riggenbach said, "We like it that way. When money gets involved . . ." He shook his head.

Of course, at the end of the day, solving Rubik's Cube is solving Rubik's Cube. No matter how much money is (or isn't) being made from it, it's still just as difficult.

On the first day of competition, I managed to secure an audience with Zemdegs. This was just about as hard as it sounds: the entire competition, the Aussie was mobbed by fans—even his mother, Rita, at points was surrounded by well-wishers and hangers-on. Zemdegs and I found ourselves in the cafeteria, shortly after he broke the world record in the 7x7, the largest Cube recognized by the WCA, in the preliminary round of that event.

I asked him if he wouldn't mind watching me solve. It's like watching a slower version of a ten-second solve, he said. I wasn't sure if this was praise or criticism. So I wasn't doing anything wrong? Well, Zemdegs said, the solve was okay. There weren't any egregious mistakes. But I wasn't executing as fast as I needed to if I wanted to go sub-20.

At this point, I was starting to get a little confused. Some cubers said I was going too fast, as hectic with my movements as someone trying to collect all the twenties in one of those closets on game shows with fans that blow stacks of cash into the air. This was the opinion, more or less, of Makisumi, for one, who advocated going slower. But now Zemdegs—and, likewise, Perge—had told me I needed to speed up.

Zemdegs recommended an exercise I'd heard of before: try to solve two pairs without looking. "If you've done two pairs," he said, scrambling my Cube, which I'd handed him, "you should always be able to do the last two." In a flurry of movement, so fast the clicking of my Cube sounded like a pair of shoes tap-dancing in a marble room, Zemdegs solved the cross and the first two pairs. He handed me the Cube, and had me try to solve the final two pairs at once. "That's a hard case," Zemdegs said, gently, after I failed to resolve them.

When Zemdegs left to get lunch, I turned to Andrea Javier, an Australian cuber. I couldn't help feeling a little down on myself after my lesson with Zemdegs, I said. "This is why I don't—like, I'll cube with him," she said, with a sympathetic expression, "but

I just don't ask him stuff, 'cause he'll explain things and I'll just feel sad and stop."

"Quick, breathe on his neck," said Jeremy Fleischman. I was sitting in the audience, waiting to go onstage. Fleischman, the former president of the Berkeley Rubik's Cube Club, along with Tim Reynolds, a former WCA board member, and Fangyuan Chang, a delegate from China, was trying to help quell my nerves. He wasn't helping. I was messing up PLLs and OLLs I'd had down cold only hours before.

"I'm just going to do a lot of slow solves," I said to Fleischman, now in his late twenties, but still with the same ginger hair, square glasses, and scruffy beard.

"That's the ticket," he said.

The first round of the main event was taking place in ETAPA's gymnasium, which had been converted to a stage for the occasion. The basketball hoops had been retracted toward the ceiling and a platform erected, before which sat rows and rows of folding chairs. In the middle of the room, the nexus for all the activity, was a giant Rubik's Cube, the size of a small boulder, at which the emcee—Riggenbach, holding a microphone—called out the names of the competitors.

They were to deposit their Cubes atop the large Cube and then proceed to the stage for further instruction. Only, like most of the audience, those about to compete couldn't wait to see the fastest cubers solve. They started to gather in the aisles, obstructing foot traffic to the point that Riggenbach had to make an announcement. "I can't help but notice there a lot of chairs here," he said, even his magnified voice struggling to be heard above the din. It was utter pandemonium, made even worse when Valk and Zemdegs took the stage.

With his penultimate solve, Zemdegs stopped the clock in 5.59 seconds. The roaring was enormous, but unfortunately, the attempt was penalized—Zemdegs received a +2 for not align-ing the Cube properly. Only, with his next solve, he clocked a 5.60-second effort, virtually replicating the penalized result. "What a maniac!" Fleischman yelled, waving his arms, along with the rest of the crowd.

When my name was called, I deposited my Cube at the scram-bling table—that is, the giant Rubik's Cube in the middle of the room—and found myself sitting on a bench at the back of the stage. The youngest cuber in the world—Hong Yan Chan, a three-year-old girl from Curitiba, Brazil, whose older brother, Chan Hong Lik, had already solved Rubik's Cube under ten seconds at the age of seven—happened to be in my heat; the staff lifted her onto the stage and set about stacking enough chairs for her to be able to reach the table.

My judge for the first solve was Pedro Henrique da Silva Roque, the cubing equivalent of Cristiano Ronaldo. Suave and athletic, with artfully manicured stubble, Roque is the fastest cuber in South America. (He hails from Brazil.) When I told him that I hoped to go sub-20, he gave me a faint smile, the sort of pitying look Ronaldo would give to someone trying to score his first goal.

24.53 seconds. My fourth fastest solve ever, behind the twen-ty-two and twenty-three I'd clocked in Hungary, and that one, improbable twenty-second solve at Yale. But I'd have to do bet-ter than that. Fortunately, I still had four more solves. At least one of them would be thrown out, since the fastest and slowest solves don't count toward your average. The next solve was more promising—20.98 seconds, nearly a personal best. If I managed to clock a few solves under twenty seconds, I'd still have a shot at averaging sub-20.

24.98. The journey was over. *Up in smoke*, I thought to myself. *Might as well try for a sub-20 single.* At least I could try to walk away with proof that I'd get there someday, that I could break twenty seconds, as I'd done only an hour before in my hotel room.

Before the fourth solve, I took a deep breath. 21.94 seconds—faster than Minh Thai, the first world champion, had ever solved in competition. But still over twenty. The last attempt, 23.50, was pedestrian, entirely unremarkable, undeserving of pity or plaudits.

I left the stage in a daze, trying to figure out what had gone so badly wrong. I'd practiced for months, done all the exercises my masters—the equivalents, for me, of Minh Thai's sage in the mountainside cave—had taught me. And still I'd come up short.

My sulking was interrupted when I heard a cry. One of the judges, a young woman studying law in Brazil, was lying on the ground, tears streaming from her face. She'd fallen off the stage and seriously injured her leg. It was a good reminder that all that had been wounded was my pride. After offering to help, I returned to my seat. That's not the first broken leg at a cubing competition, I heard someone remark.

Later that night, I returned to the gymnasium. There, I found, as I had at the prior World Championship, scores of competitors on the stage, even though no one was timing them and the audience was nonexistent. They were cubing for themselves. And so was I.

I was determined to get a sub-20 solve before I left Brazil. Even if it didn't count, even if it would never be official. I sat there for a good long while, attempting solve after solve after solve. The red numerals of the timing display resolutely refused to begin with a one: I kept making small mistakes, like accidentally twisting a corner, resulting in a DNF, or screwing up an algorithm that I'd just learned.

"Guys, it's over!" shouted Juan Camilo Vargas, the Colombian cuber. "You can go home now, it's over!" Just then, I finally got a 19.33-second solve.

When I returned to the hotel, I stumbled into van Bruchem at the elevator. He was wearing a canary-yellow T-shirt, a gift from the South Korean cubers, and an expression so grief-stricken that I actually asked him if someone had died. "I'm so sorry for you," he said.

Before I could say anything, he wrapped me in a bear hug. When he was entering score sheets earlier in the WCA database, he had come across mine. *Ah, shit*, he thought, when he saw my times. "It's not a bad average," he said, "but it's not sub-20." When I reminded him that I had the video and could do the postmortem later, he raised his eyebrows.

"Now who's saying that no one died?"

Did Feliks ever get nervous? That's what the final questioner at a panel on Sunday, the last day of the competition, wanted to know. We'd packed the auditorium where the foot solving had taken place. There, Gabriel Dechichi Barbar, a Brazilian cuber with a boyish face, was animatedly relaying our questions to the panel, on behalf of his sponsor, Hobbz, a clearinghouse for all kinds of hobbies in Brazil, from cubing to throwing boomerangs.

"I think everyone gets nervous in competition," said Zemdegs. "Except Mats," he added, to general laughter. "Mats doesn't really get nervous at all. At least, that's what he tells me."

Attention turned to Kevin Hays, the burly American cuber and Big Cube specialist, who picked up his microphone. "I do worse at competition, pretty much, 98 percent of the time," he said. "Worlds is always going to be nerve-racking. It's different than any other competition. Especially here, the nerves really set in."

About two weeks before the competition began, Zemdegs wrote a blog post about his preparations for the World Championship. It sounded as if he were practicing for the Olympics. One night, he decided to run through every solve he would attempt during the competition: a mock Worlds, if you will.

It took him longer than expected—about two and a half hours—and he started at 11 p.m., with the result that he finished the last of his 117 solves in the wee hours of the morning. Still, he pointed out, he wanted to simulate the experience of competition as closely as possible. Being tired—after flying halfway around the world—would be part of the bargain.

He also played videos of previous competitions, to get the timing down right—there's a pause between each solve, while the Cube is scrambled—and to pipe in the right amount of crowd noise, like the New England Patriots preparing for the Super Bowl by blasting loud music on the sidelines during practice. "Tallied five world records," Zemdegs wrote. "If only it were that easy!"

In the end, it *did* seem that easy. "*Segundo lugar*," announced Rafael Cinoto, one of the lead Brazilian organizers of the competition, "*média sete com sete quatro*, Mats Valk!" It was the last event of the last day—the finals of the 3x3, and the finalists were being welcomed to the stage. Pedro Santos Guimarães, the WCA board member, translated: qualifying second, with an average of 7.74 seconds, was Mats Valk. The cheers were enormous.

But it escaped no one that, even with one of the best averages of all time—his fourth fastest to date, and among the fastest in history—Valk hadn't qualified first. "*Em primeiro lugar*," Cinoto continued, "*seis ponto nove sete*—" He paused, while excited murmurs ran through the crowd. "Feliks Zemdegs!" The tumult brought down the roof; it was so loud you almost couldn't hear Guimarães translate the announcement into English: Feliks Zemdegs had qualified first, with a 6.97-second average.

The only person who had ever solved faster than Feliks Zemdegs was Feliks Zemdegs. In the semifinals, apparently, which hardly anyone had watched, since we'd been preoccupied with the other finals—events like the 2x2 and 4x4, which took place in different rooms—Zemdegs had recorded his fastest solve yet, 5.39 seconds, at the time the second fastest in history, leapfrogging past Valk to stand only behind the 5.25-second effort the American teenager Collin Burns had laid down in April. (Burns, who was spending the summer in Japan, was unable to make it to the World Championship.)

The finals themselves were almost anticlimactic. The only people who solved faster than they had in the semifinals were Jakub Kipa, the Polish foot wizard, who improved by two one-hundredths of a second, from 8.65 to 8.63, and Seyyed Hossein Fatemi, of Iran, who likewise dropped from 9.02 to 9 seconds flat. Everyone else, as is typically the case, slowed down, beset by nerves.

Valk solved well—his 8.56-second average was hardly bad, given the circumstances, even if it was his slowest average of the competition. But Zemdegs was something else. With his second solve, he recorded a 5.69, marking the fastest time ever recorded in the finals of the World Championship. The crowd lost its mind, but he tried to stay impassive, tapping his fingers on the table while the judge initialed his score sheet. Despite using the same routine he had in Vegas—after a practice solve, Valk took his earbuds out, then prepared for inspection—he couldn't seem to match Zemdegs.

On the fourth solve, Zemdegs mouthed, "Oh, fuck," just after completing the H-permutation to solve the last layer. The audience started to clap, but the judge, Guimarães, raised his hand for silence. One face of the Cube was twisted, well beyond forty-five degrees. The shoe was on the other foot: Zemdegs was penalized two seconds, just as Valk had been two years before. The timer read 6.94 seconds, but the official result was an 8.94-second solve.

A few minutes later, after his final solve, which even Valk, having finished his attempts, turned around in his seat to watch, Zemdegs wiped his face with his hands, as if waking from a frightful dream. "Did I win?" he asked Guimarães, who didn't seem to hear him at first. "Did I win?" When Guimarães said, "Yes," curtly and without fanfare, Zemdegs pounded his Cube into the table.

Later that evening, before the prizes were awarded, Riggenbach played a short video. "Hello," the video began, in English, with Portuguese subtitles, "I am Natán Riggenbach, and this is the story of the Peruvian cubing dream. Sort of. It is a story of things seemingly impossible happening, and things undreamed of coming to pass, much like cubing itself."

Riggenbach explained how, in the late 2000s, he and a friend, Marvin Castañeda, were the only cubers active in Peru. They would chat online, dreaming of raising enough money to travel to Chile to compete. There were no delegates in Peru, so they could not hold competitions of their own. When he finally got in touch with Tyson Mao, Riggenbach said, in 2011, his life changed so much that his head was still spinning.

"As you can see," he continued, to widespread laughter, when the screen changed to show the map from *The Hobbit*, zooming in on the Lonely Mountain, "much like in Bilbo's case, once you embark on the road of cubing, there is no knowing where you might be swept off to."

But since the end of the road—where cubing might end up—could not be foreseen, he wanted to focus on the journey. It was better to be kind than to be fast, he said, showing footage of Zemdegs, slowly turning his puzzle, teaching a youngster an algorithm. It was all of us together against a common, relentless enemy: that is to say, time itself. "We are all here because of that unexplainable thing," he said. "That thing that cubing has that drives people to achieve what was unthinkable."

The video was Riggenbach's swan song. "What this really is," he concluded, "is an attempt to say thank you to cubing for all the wonderful things it has put on our road."

*   *   *

Several nights earlier, while cubing in the hotel lobby, I heard a number of Brazilians discussing the breakfast deal at the hotel. Apparently, it no longer existed. We'd exhausted our share of free breakfasts. Someone in the management realized they were losing too much money on it and decided to put the Rubik's Cube away.

On my final day in Brazil, before I checked out of the hotel, I went to the front desk. The same concierge was there as when I arrived. Did they still have their Rubik's Cube? Oh, yes, the concierge said, with a pained smile. He pulled it out from a drawer in the desk. Would I still be offered complimentary tokens for breakfast if I solved it?

He said he had to check with his manager. When he returned, several minutes later, he placed the Cube on the desk between us. Yes, he said, I think you're going to get the free breakfast.

MAXIMAL ORANGE

The judge lifted the covering before I was ready. To focus my mind, I had closed my eyes and bowed my head. My inspection time was five seconds in before I realized it had even begun.

The time I recorded is better left unsaid, which is all to the good, since I was so flummoxed I failed to turn on my camera and record it. It had been three months since the World Championship. I had performed thousands of solves at home. And, despite getting faster than ever, I was still banging my head against the wall in competition.

By the second solve, I'd remembered to turn on the camera. Whatever followed—success or failure—would now be recorded not only for posterity but also for analysis.

Sitting next to me was Eric Zhao, whom I'd met months earlier, at the tournament at Yale. Back then, he was a round-faced high school senior from Queens, a kind of East Coast analogue to Cameron Brown, the enterprising teenager from California. Zhao was a college freshman now. His boutique, the Cube Depot, had set up shop and was doing a brisk business. The competition itself was taking place in Lexington, Massachusetts, in the local Elks lodge. The night before, I'd gone for Chinese with a group of friends in Somerville. When I opened my fortune cookie, it didn't have a fortune inside. "Good luck," Zhao said.

I didn't have any, as the fortune cookie foretold. 24.13 seconds. At this point, I had no chance of making the second round, let alone going sub-20. "That was so bad," I said to the judge, shaking my head. My fingers had turned to lead.

In the audience, only minutes before, I'd recorded an 18.88-second average of five solves. My worst solve—21.44 seconds—was still faster than I'd yet managed onstage.

"Let's turn this average around," I muttered, more to myself than to the judge for my third solve, a student at Lexington High School. Without much trouble, I made the cross, solved the first two layers, and oriented the last layer. Only, when I went to permute the last layer, I misapprehended the case. It was the G-permutation, but not the variant I had in mind. As a result, the algorithm didn't solve the case. It just transformed it. I had to permute it all over again.

26.22 seconds.

I was getting slower by the solve.

The next attempt proceeded smoothly, almost without interruption, from the very first twists to the orientation of the last layer. Even though I had to perform three algorithms to orient the last layer—one of those "three-look OLLs" that Olivér Perge, the Hungarian cuber, had so disdained—it ended up costing only a few seconds. The final result: 18.81 seconds.

"So close to sub-20," I heard a shrill-voiced kid announce during my next solve. He was referring to his own efforts, but I could imagine saying the same thing to myself. The 18.81 was just my second sub-20 solve in competition, the first since I'd clocked a 17.97-second solve at another competition in August. "Nice turning," the judge said, when I finished my last solve.

"Sorry?" I replied.

I was trying to calculate my average in my head—it would probably wind up in the low twenties, better than I had done in Brazil, but worse than I'd done in August, when I recorded a 20.91-second average. In Brazil, Jeremy Fleischman, the former president of the Berkeley Rubik's Cube Club, had noted proudly that I'd still maintained what he called "maximal orange": even though I didn't go sub-20, I'd managed to get a personal best. The WCA database highlights your PBs in orange, so the column of my averages remained completely in that color. No longer: 22.48 seconds.

"I like your turning," the judge repeated. "It's, like, very smooth."

"Well, that's something."

It wasn't the first time I'd heard that my solves looked nice. Weeks before, at the competition in August—the 2015 edition of Nisei Week—the judge nodded appreciatively after my fourth solve. "That's a really nice slow-turning style you have there," he said. I thanked him, but wasn't sure there wasn't a hint of something snide buried within the compliment. If that was slow turning, then what did that make me, especially since I wasn't trying to turn slowly?

It was probably the side effect of hewing so closely to Makisumi's advice. I'd been solving as smoothly as possible, with the goal of being able to go sub-20 not by spamming moves—that is, performing sequences in bursts of frenetic activity—but by methodically ticking off each step of the solve. Not only did my solves look nice—smooth, controlled—but when I didn't pause, I stood a good chance of going sub-20. At home, I'd once averaged 17.9 seconds.

After the round ended, Zhao went back to selling puzzles. I took a seat at the table next to him. "You know what they say, like, 'Turn slow and look ahead'?" he asked. "If you're turning slow and *still* pausing, you might as well just turn fast." He was accompanied by Vishantak Srikrishna, a wiry high school freshman from New Jersey with a faint mustache. "Yeah, turn fast," he said. Srikrishna had a bitter edge to his voice—he'd just missed his own goal, which was to go sub-10. "I'm pissed," he said. "I need to stop caring!" He'd averaged 10.94 seconds.

Zhao, who has the round and gentle aspect of a Taoist monk, had just gotten a personal best average—11.45 seconds. "I could do really bad next round," he said. "I'll be okay in my life."

Paradoxically, both Zhao and Srikrishna urged me to stop timing myself in practice. Rushing my inspection, they both said, was hamstringing my ability to plan the cross, the first step of every solve. "Take an hour to plan your cross," Srikrishna said. "I don't care how long it takes. Find it out, have it in muscle memory. Get it down." He paused. "I hope I don't sound pushy."

"No, that's okay," I said. "I need pushy."

"It should be automatic," Srikrishna told me. I replied that I knew it should be, but it just wasn't—at least not yet. They both pointed out that, when I took a long time to transition from the cross to the first two layers—known as cross-to-F2L transition, in cubing parlance—I wasted time that I could have used to keep solving the puzzle.

"That's a pretty decent solution," Srikrishna said, after I solved the cross for him, "but say you get a scramble, you should see your four pieces, and it shouldn't be, like, 'Oh, I have to do this move, this move, this move.' As soon as you see them, you should immediately know the best solution.

"It's about not getting rushed during the solve," Srikrishna said. "Just slow down and see your pairs." Even turning at my speed, he demonstrated, it was possible to solve Rubik's Cube in twelve to fourteen seconds: he did so, without ever pausing, leaving me to shake my head. "That's faster than I've ever gone," I said.

* * *

Meanwhile, a small eruption seemed to take place in the audience. Most of Zhao's customers ran toward the stage. Apparently, Drew Brads, one of the fastest cubers in attendance, had just broken the world record for a single solve of the Pyraminx—a twisty pyramid invented by Uwe Mèffert, a German puzzle maker, in the 1970s—lowering the record from 1.36 to 1.32 seconds.

A few minutes later, when the crowd exploded again, cameras up and hands clapping, Srikrishina surmised that Brads had broken the world record for an average of five solves. Indeed, he had, lowering the mark from 2.56 to 2.52 seconds.

Zhao had been competing, too. He returned to the table, shaking his head. "I was just, like, 'Write it down!'" he said, recalling what he told the judge, after he'd recorded a thirty-second solve. "He started *and* finished during my solve," Zhao said, referring to Brads, who'd recorded a 2.53-second solve while sitting next to him. "That's awful," Srikrishna said.

At least Zhao had advanced to the second round of the main event. I'd placed sixtieth, out of eighty-four competitors, even though my average, 22.48 seconds, was my second best yet.

My next competition wasn't for another month. It would take place at Manhasset High School, on Long Island. The week before the competition, I got an e-mail from Oscar Ceballos, the cuber from Venezuela I'd met at breakfast in Brazil on the first day of the World Championship. He was coming to New York and planned to compete in Manhasset. Ceballos, who is in his late twenties, lives in Mérida, a city high in the mountains of Venezuela, and works as a computer programmer for a company based in Los Angeles.

"*Siento que el solve fue rápido,*" he said, midway through the first round, "*pero en realidad fue lento!*" There was a look of anguish about his face. I knew just what he meant: he felt that he was solving faster than he actually was. It was the morning of the competition at Manhasset High School, and neither of us was doing well—at least by the standards we'd set ourselves.

Ceballos's goal, which was lofty but hardly out of reach, was to break the Venezuelan national record for an average of five solves, which then stood at 11.56 seconds. Beforehand, the two of us practicing side by side, Ceballos had no problem breaking the record. Likewise, I easily went sub-20, even racking up two eighteen-second averages. Before going onstage, we dapped. It seemed a foregone conclusion that Ceballos would get the record, and I would finally go sub-20.

But the best-laid plans of mice and men, not to mention those of cubers, have a habit of going awry onstage. My first two solves were decent—a 20.90, followed by a 20.17—but I was too conservative. With my third solve, I got a twenty-five, followed by a twenty-two; I knew my chances of breaking twenty seconds, even were I to achieve a personal best with the last attempt, were nil. Ultimately, I averaged 21.56 seconds. More black, no orange.

"10.19!" Ceballos exclaimed, after his last solve. "I thought it was sub-10," he said, "because I *feel* really fast solve, and it wasn't." Still, Ceballos would get to give the record another crack. He'd advanced to the second round. And I got a compliment from a pint-sized kid with straw-colored hair. "Nice try," he said. "That would be better than I did. I always get, like, a minute."

"That's Collin's shtick, right? Anyone can do it."

It was a few hours later, and I was speaking to Ron Burns, a grizzled man who'd been sitting in the corner of the cafeteria, watching YouTube guitar videos and checking the latest news about ISIS on CNN's website. "Ron Burns" was how he had introduced himself. "Father of Collin Burns, paternity test pending on *Maury Povich* next Thursday at eight." Collin Burns, of course, being the teenager who broke the world record for a single solve, lowering it to 5.25 seconds.

Burns—Ron, that is—displayed pride in his son's accomplishments, but also regretted that his son hadn't done more to use the platform he'd been given. "He's self-deprecating to a fault," Ron, who works in software, said. "I've been a small-business owner, and I've had to promote myself to live. And for him to reach this *level*, and not have the *desire* to promote himself, 'cause he feels it's kind of dirty to promote himself? That's the disconnect, right?"

Ron continued: "He broke the record, just now, and he was the *first* one to say, 'Eh, it's probably a misscramble.'" Earlier, during the second round of the main event, Burns broke the record again—or, at least, he appeared to—stopping the clock in 5.21 seconds.

"I would have been, at his age, 'I broke the record! I broke the record!'" Ron said. "So that humility is inspiring to me, right? Because I know that's the right way to be, but I'm not like that, you know?" His father's objections notwithstanding, Collin was right to question the solve. "It was a really egregious misscramble," he told me. He looked frustrated, pained even.

"Sadly, today, as I talk to you," Ron said later, "it looks like my son's world record has been broken." In fact, it had been broken twice, at the same competition.* "The friendship in this," Ron added, "that's why it's not a sport. It's not competitive. They compete with themselves. They don't compete with each other." He added, "It's a great thing to watch. It really is."

By this point, I was starting to get a little frustrated. I'd gone sub-20 more times than I could count at home. I'd even done it in the audience, waiting to go onstage. "That's the way for me, too," Collin Burns said, when I told him what had befallen me. He

---

* A pair of teenagers at a competition in Maryland recorded two world-record-breaking solves, one a 5.09, the other a 4.90. (Only the faster one counted as the record; it also marked the first official solve under five seconds.)

added that he'd gotten better at controlling his nerves, but even *he* slowed down in competition.

What was I to do? At this point, I'd gotten lots of advice from lots of cubers, and none of it seemed to add up. Some said I needed to turn faster. Others that I didn't need to turn fast. Some said I needed to learn more algorithms. Others that I did not. Some said I needed to do more solves. Others that I just had to pay more attention to the solves I did. Weirdly, it wasn't until I spoke to Collin's father that I heard something that finally made sense. "[Collin] doesn't really know as many algorithms as other people," Ron said. "And I'm not sure he has the best dexterity. He has the best *look-ahead*. And I think that's where this moves from science to art."

This is what I'd been looking for, what I'd originally been trying so hard to find out, the question that captivated not just me, but everyone who'd ever seen a YouTube video of cubing, the question of what makes the seemingly impossible happen. I'm not a math person—that is, I can do math quite well, but it's not my native instinct. And I'd been told by plenty of cubers that math has nothing to do with it, but if algorithms aren't mathematical, what are they? "If you look at his world record in slow motion," Ron said, "there's a tiny pause. People have slowed it down. There's a tiny pause in the middle that seems like it lasts forever. And you can just see him calculate and look ahead. And it's not a thought.

"I don't think it's the mind," he added. "I think it's unconscious, emotional intelligence, to look ahead in time, just a little bit, it's only a few moves ahead—that's the key to this. And I don't think that's math. I think it's something spiritual about this, man."

IT'S NOT A CRIME

Starting in the 1970s, Mihály Csikszentmihályi, a psychologist of Hungarian descent, began sending out surveys to people around the world. He sent them to factory workers, to professional dancers, to doctors, and to artists, among many other professions. He wanted to understand what made these people happy.

Their answers surprised him. It wasn't that they all found happiness in the same things. On the contrary, surgeons enjoyed performing surgery, dancers enjoyed dancing; lots of people enjoyed simply reading a good book. What surprised him, and the researchers with whom he worked at the University of Chicago, was that all of these people described happiness in similar terms.

"Apparently the way a long-distance swimmer felt when crossing the English Channel was almost identical to the way a chess player felt during a tournament or a rock climber progressing up a difficult rock face," wrote Csikszentmihályi, in *Flow: The Psychology of Optimal Experience*, the 1990 book that introduced his work to a general audience.

The kind of happiness these people experienced, he wrote, was of a very particular sort. It wasn't pleasure per se, the kind of feeling you get when you have a need quenched, like drinking a cool glass of water on a hot day. It was something more profound.

Csikszentmihályi heard the same word, again and again, from the various respondents: it felt like they were carried along in a flow. "The purpose of the flow is to keep on flowing," said a rock climber and poet, "not looking for a peak or utopia but staying in the flow. It is not a moving up but a continuous flowing; you have to move to keep the flow going."

Being in the flow, some of the respondents said, was an ecstatic, almost religious experience. "When we realize that we become one flesh, it's supreme," said a Japanese motorcycle enthusiast, who participated in runs involving hundreds of motorcycles streaming down the streets of Kyoto. Others compared it to taking drugs.

Oddly, for the respondents, this feeling didn't come easily—it wasn't something you could turn off and on, the way you could satisfy your hunger by eating an apple. Rather, it was the result of intense concentration—paradoxically, flow took a lot of practice to achieve. "It's exhilarating to come closer and close to self-discipline" was how one prominent rock climber put it.

Csikszentmihályi was led by his subjects to believe that flow was intensely pleasurable not in spite of the challenges involved, but because of them. "Happiness is not something that happens," he wrote. The best moments, he explained, typically occurred when his subjects were taken to the limit, either mentally or physically, like the sailor who traveled unaided across the ocean, or the chess player who said he wouldn't have noticed if the roof fell in.

All of these subjects—and by the time the book was written, Csikszentmihályi claimed to have collected more than a hundred thousand responses—seemed to indicate that happiness was not the passive accumulation of wealth, or even of pleasurable feelings, but the active pursuit of some goal. "The experience itself," he wrote, "is so enjoyable that people will do it at great cost, for the sheer sake of doing it."

Sometimes, the state of flow was powerful to the point of altering time itself. Csikszentmihályi heard from dancers who described turns that, in reality, took seconds, but lasted longer in their minds. It sounded, when I first read the passage, not unlike what happens with cubing, which is hardly an accident. Rubik himself seems to be the kind of person who pursues these activities with the utmost vigor. "I am an active person," he wrote, in *Rubik's Cubic Compendium*, an out-of-print anthology that contains the only autobiographical essay Rubik appears to have published. "Activity is my element."

Like flow, cubing can also be dangerously addictive. Csikszentmihályi cites Bobby Fischer, the famous American chess player, who became so enamored of the state of mind chess gave him that he essentially failed to live a normal life. "The problems of puzzles are very near the problems of life," Rubik once said. "Our whole life is solving puzzles. If you are hungry, you have to find something to eat. But everyday problems are very mixed—they're not clear.

"A good puzzle, it's a fair thing. Nobody is lying. It's very clear, and the problem depends just on you. You can solve it independently. But to find happiness in life, you're not independent. That's the big difference."

"I don't really know how to explain my process of thinking," said Eva Kato, a teenager from New Jersey wearing leggings and a gray long-sleeved top, "but you can see, like, this corner will be affected, but only by a U move, so it will end up here"—she pointed to the far side of her Cube—"when you're solving a cross."

We had scrambled our puzzles in identical patterns. The goal was to compare solutions. That way, I'd learn how she solved. And, hopefully, she'd learn something aside from the fact that I was still trying to go sub-20.

Kato had been cubing for three years. In that time, she'd gotten down to numbers that few cubers have ever reached. She then held the female world record—an unofficial distinction—for a single solve, at 7.55 seconds. In addition to cubing, she is an avid soccer player.

Rubik himself told me, in his reply to my e-mail, that he hopes to see more female cubers, perhaps even female-only competitions. There's certainly a dearth of girls and women in cubing: the percentage of new cubers who identify as female peaked in 2005, at 13 percent. Margaret Wertheim, a journalist and educator who consulted on *Beyond Rubik's Cube*, the exhibit at the Liberty Science Center, attributes this to the larger cultural bias that characterizes math and science as masculine subjects. "Obviously, some countries are able to erase a lot of this bias," said Jessica Fridrich, in her taped interview at the exhibit. "I'm not sure how they are doing it, but I know it's possible."

"Honestly, it doesn't bother me that much," Kato says. "There are a lot more guys than girls, but it doesn't really—if there were more girls, I don't think it would affect my cubing." Perhaps because she had yet to enter the working world—she was only thirteen—the gender bias in cubing hadn't yet rooted itself in her consciousness as a problem to be weeded out. Her biggest concern was having a good time. (And, of course, getting faster.) "I probably wouldn't have a better time at competitions if there were more girls," she said.

In this, she's hardly alone. Riggenbach's daughters, Jael and Rachel, told me, one night in Brazil, that the lack of female cubers didn't bother them. "We have an expression in Peru," said Natán, who was translating, while his daughters giggled. "We call very shallow girls *flores*, like flowers. We have turned this into a verb, so *florcia* is to be very shallow." His daughters, he said, attributed the disparity to the propensity of girls their age—that is, on the cusp of puberty—"to *florcia* a lot."

Wertheim, the journalist, says this is backed up by empirical research. "Girls and boys," she told me, "do equally well at math and science until about puberty. In fact, girls tend to do slightly better now. But when puberty comes, girls suddenly start drop-ping in the rankings." This isn't because girls have suddenly lost their intelligence. What the research suggests, Wertheim says, is that girls, as Natán put it, learn they're supposed to be flowers. "It's just perceived as being unsexy," she told me, "to be compet-itive with boys in something that is so culturally affiliated with boyness."

Alese Devin, another female cuber, learned this the hard way. "He was like, 'Oh, a girl can't solve a Rubik's Cube,'" she recalled of a boy in middle school. She went on YouTube to learn to solve it, just so she could prove him wrong. (She has since solved Rubik's Cube in 10.03 seconds.)

"You don't see many girls who do it," Devin said. "If you were to see somebody solve a Rubik's Cube, it's more than likely a guy. So then they're, like, 'Oh, it's something that guys only do.'"

Still, there are some advantages—as Sesi Cadmus, one of the best blindfold solvers in the world, who studies at the University of Virginia, told me, "People are going to remember you. 'Oh, you're not that random white or Asian guy I saw.'"

Kato practices about two hours a day, which has afforded her the ability to look ahead during inspection and plan not just her cross but part of her F2L. "It might be something that you want to work on," she told me as we held our Cubes side by side. "Your cross-to-F2L transition will be a lot smoother."

Kato and I were waiting for the first round of the main event to begin. It was mid-December, and the two of us had arrived, along with about a hundred and twenty other cubers, for a competition at the Liberty Science Center in Liberty State Park, the sliver of land just across the Hudson from the Statue of Liberty.

If the gender disparity didn't bother her, it certainly both-ered me. By now, I'd attended nearly a dozen competitions. The crowds kept getting larger and younger, but the number of female competitors wasn't increasing. In fact, it was going down. There wasn't any reason for this—that is, there wasn't any reason there shouldn't be as many female as male competitors.

Still, if there were to be any change, it would probably be slow, just like the battles women were fighting—and still, slowly, winning—in the world at large. When I started cubing, a female cuber had yet to set a world record. It finally happened at the 2014 Asian Championship. Yu Da-Hyun, a twelve-year-old girl from South Korea, smashed the single and average records for the Megaminx, a twistable dodecahedron, lowering the single from 39.57 to 37.83 seconds, and the average from 45.77 to 42.89 seconds. In 2015, she lowered the record for a single solve again.

Kato asked me, in the way of the young taking the old to task, what my weaknesses were. It was a good question, and I had no shortage of answers—my cross-to-F2L transition could be a lot better, and I still had yet to learn all of the OLL algorithms. I also sometimes made dumb mistakes, simply because of old habits, going for inefficient but familiar maneuvers.

We'd already done a couple of solves together, leading each other through what we'd do—no surprise, Kato was more efficient, but I managed to comport myself decently. Then she asked me to do a solve in real time. "Wait, what?" I said, close to the end. I had come across the N-permutation, one of the most complicated PLLs, which I'd finally learned, but here mangled, sending my Cube into a tailspin.

"Yeah," said Kato, when I remarked that I had messed up. Her tone was matter-of-fact, like that of a passenger in your car who knows you're taking the wrong exit but decides not to say anything. Only, rather than getting back on track, I wound up at another unfamiliar juncture: OLL 55, a line of yellow squares also known as the Highway. (This was the same OLL that Burns had used to such great effect, leaving Bernát scratching his head.)

"This is the one OLL I'm always having trouble with," I told Kato. "R', F . . ." I started spelling out the moves as I performed them, but had to pull out the sheet on which I'd written them down. Kato raised her eyebrows. "I just have a quick question," she said. "Um . . . do you apply OLLs that you're just learning, when you're up there, like, competing?"

"Well, I've been told that I shouldn't," I said. Indeed, Cornelius Dieckmann, the German cuber, once told me that two weeks before a competition, you should stop trying to learn new algorithms.

"Yeah," Kato said, with a chortle, "you should not!"

The competition had been organized by Bob Burton, the same burly, bearded cuber who threw the party in his room at the 2012 U.S. National Championship. His girlfriend, Jaclyn Sawler, whom I had met at that competition during the staff round of the 4x4, was now Jaclyn Burton. Staying true to his roots as a math teacher, Bob had arranged a wedding on March 14, 2015, at 9:26:53 a.m.—Pi Day. Jaclyn was now expecting, but still helping out, entering scores. They weren't the only familiar faces: I recognized Vishantak Srikrishna, whom I'd met at Lexington. But there were a lot of new faces, too.

When I remarked to Justin Mallari, a veteran one-handed specialist whom I'd met several times, that I felt like Rip Van Winkle, he said he knew what that was like. "Over the past, like, five years," he said, "I've seen so many people come and go." Cubing, as a whole, seemed to be getting younger and younger.

Mallari shook his head. "And all of them are fast," he said.

In the warm-up area, about twenty minutes later, Kato asked me how it was going. I wasn't sure, I said. That's what I was hoping to find out myself. I was calculating what I needed to get with my last solve. One more solve under twenty seconds, I figured.

The first solve had been a dream. Like getting in a sports car and just gunning it down the highway, with the stereo blasting and no care in the world, breaking the speed limit on the way to your destination. It felt like it lasted forever, but it only took 17.77 seconds, a new personal best.

The next solve was hardly as good, but still managed to get under the barrier. 18.96 seconds. I arrived at the OLL, which I didn't know—or, rather, I had recently learned—and took Kato's advice, transforming it into a familiar case. This added what must have been a second or two. But, when I stopped the timer, my goal was still within sight.

The third solve was an unmitigated disaster. Aside from a slight hesitation during F2L, it started smoothly, with no interruption. Recognizing the OLL, I jumped at the chance to use a new algorithm. I'd been practicing it for days, as if I were trying to memorize a musical scale for an audition. Only this time, for some reason, the algorithm didn't work as planned. If I'd been actually playing an instrument, the strings would have popped, or an errant squeak escaped the mouthpiece. It had taken fewer than ten seconds to solve the first two layers. By rights, I should have been on my way to another sub-20 solve, perhaps even another personal best.

Evidently, I'd taken a wrong turn. Too flummoxed to recall the proper algorithm for dispatching the case, I accidentally transformed it into another, the wheel, a case that's as easy, for most cubers, as turning one. You pull a pair out of the first layer, remove the adjacent pair, and then reinsert them, by rotating the upper layer, as if you were yanking the steering wheel of a car first one way and then the other.

I reached the PLL after twenty seconds had already elapsed. It didn't matter that I dispatched it quickly. When I finally stopped it, the clock read 23.49. If I didn't mess up again, I'd still have a shot at going sub-20, but what were the odds of that happening? I finished my fourth solve in 20.16 seconds.

"Just one more decent solve," I said to Billy Burier, my last judge, whom I recognized from Manhasset, a twentysomething student living in New York City. "Not too much to ask, right?"

"All right," said Burier, all business. "Ready?"

The Cube was covered with a white box. "Ready," I said. When the Cube was exposed, I picked it up and studied it. What I was thinking I can't recall. Those moments are literally blank for me. Looking at the video, I can pick out the pieces of the cross, some of them, anyway, the blue-white edge hiding out in the back like a marble glittering in the bottom of a jar.

Before eight seconds had elapsed, I was off and running. My first move was to rotate the entire Cube, during inspection— which is entirely legal—so that the white face was on the bottom side, and the yellow face staring up at me. Then I built the cross, relaying one edge around the puzzle, from front to back, like a point guard whipping a pass crosscourt.

I had to rotate—twice—to find my first pair, a move for which I knew every cuber I'd studied with would (rightfully) chastise me. Those wasted seconds might come back to haunt me.

The first pair, though, was easy to execute. I just had to break it up—it was already in the top layer—and insert it. The second wasn't much harder—although I did waste precious seconds, again, finding it. It, too, was located in the top layer, ready for insertion. Two pairs down, two pairs to go.

The third was a little harder—I had to break the corner and edge apart using an empty slot, since they were jammed together—although I managed to convert it into a simple trigger.

The fourth and final pair was easy—I had an algorithm for just this occasion. The corner and edge were incorrectly paired in the top layer. The next thing I saw was an orientation case I knew, but didn't trust myself to execute correctly. Instead of tackling it, I sidestepped the problem, using another algorithm to convert it into something different.

What greeted me was the first case I learned at CTY. Back then, I only knew it as the Jesus Fish, since that's how Toby described it: a cross with one quadrant filled in. Now I knew its proper name, the anti-Sune, a square block with two lines extending from it, or, as Toby might have put it, the tail to the fish's head.

The algorithm for resolving the anti-Sune is simple. You remove a pair from the first two layers, and put it back differently. R U R' U R U2 R'. In my hands, the puzzle transformed from a churning mass of colors to—solved?

"What?" said Burier as I threw the puzzle down and stopped the timer, which read 17.62 seconds. "Do you have any idea how lucky that is?" I'd been the beneficiary of a PLL skip, one of the rarest occurrences in cubing. Every time you orient the last layer, there's a one-in-seventy-two chance that you'll solve it entirely. This is what happened to Erik Akkersdijk, the Dutch cuber, when he set his world record of 7.08 seconds in 2008.

"It's not a crime to be lucky!" I said, borrowing Akkersdijk's line.*

Afterward, in the waiting area, I ran into Vishantak Srikrishna. He was still on his quest for a sub-10 average. The weekend before, he'd attended a competition at the Massachusetts Institute of Technology and averaged ten seconds flat. With Srikrishna standing by, I calculated my average. I had made it, with room to spare: 18.96 seconds.

---

* Without the PLL skip, I still probably would have gone sub-20. To get a 19.99-second average, I would have needed a 20.87 on my last solve.

Before long, my phone started buzzing. Ceballos, all the way in Venezuela, had been tracking the competition online, and wanted to extend his congratulations. "Mission accomplished," I texted van Bruchem. Srikrishina was curious if I'd still be competing, now that I'd achieved my goal. Sure, I said. But I wasn't sure I'd be going sub-10 anytime soon.

Srikrishna sighed. "Same," he said. "Same."

Srikrishna returned to the stage, where he logged an 11.33-second average, exactly the same result as his final round at MIT, while I returned to the audience. During my last solve, I noticed the boy next to me raise his arms in celebration of his first sub-20 solve. Now I found him sitting near me, and we struck up a conversation.

His name was Jasper Waldman. He was wearing a blue track jacket with ITALIA embroidered on the front and a funky, electric-blue hat. In other words, he was from Brooklyn. "This is my third competition ever," he said. Waldman, who was accompanied by his mother, a professional dancer, had started cubing in the fourth grade. That was five years ago. "I've been practicing a lot," he said, "and I'm basically sub-20." At this competition, he'd nabbed the single—the average still eluded him.

When I asked him what it meant to go sub-20, he sounded thirteen going on thirty-five. "It's a real big accomplishment, in my opinion," he said. "Because I've been doing this for a long time, and I've finally, like, reached that summit."

EPILOGUE

The Cube is back. It's not the 1980s, but it's not just nostalgia. At this point, I've lost count of the number of times I've seen Rubik's Cube in TV commercials and movies. It's just everywhere. In the celebrated Pixar film *WALL•E*, the puzzle even outlives us. The hero, a waste-disposal robot, finds one, nearly a millennium from now, picking through the trash humans have left behind after abandoning the planet. (He doesn't know how to solve it either.)

My mother is a schoolteacher. Lately, and with increasing frequency, I've been hearing from her about kids solving Rubik's Cubes, which is something I never remember seeing. One high schooler, she told me, left class one day with a rapturous look. "I just love it," he said. She'd asked him about the puzzle, which he couldn't stop solving. (Having put up with me doing the same, on my visits home, she understood where his fascination came from.)

If you chart the growth of cubing, it looks like a tree recovering from a lightning strike. The growth in the number of people in the WCA database would make any CEO's eyes pop. Between 2003 and 2013, the annualized rate of growth—a proxy for the number of cubers—was about 75 percent.

Whether this growth can be sustained remains to be seen. "I hope it will not be a commercial organization," Ron van Bruchem told me when I first met him, at the 2013 World Championship. He pointed out that, once a sport became professional, the organization that ran it *became* the sport. "We will have something similar like that in cubing, as well, I think," he added. "But we have to make the right decisions there."

But Rubik's Cube is not going anywhere. This may be more important than most people realize. I wrote earlier that Rubik's Cube has become a symbol of the world today. It's hard to solve. It doesn't submit to easy answers. And once you solve it, you have to start all over again.

If Rubik's Cube really is back, I hope that means the next generation will have a different approach to problem solving. The old way, of applying a single, powerful solution, to a single, defining problem, is over. There are simply too many problems, with too many disparate potential solutions, that have to be juggled. Take agriculture. We have to simultaneously figure out how to feed an additional two billion people, without any more arable land, all the while expecting that crop productivity will decrease as the climate heats up. This is to say nothing of climate change itself, or stateless terrorism, or, in the United States, campaign finance reform.

If we actually manage to tackle these problems—and that's a big if—Rubik's Cube may have played an important role in opening people's minds.

"We turn the Cube and it twists us," Rubik once said. Hopefully, he's right.

ACKNOWLEDGMENTS

Writing a book is kind of like solving a puzzle. You have to figure out how to approach it, apply yourself, take the wrong direction a couple of times. When you finally get to the end, it's with a sense of the pieces falling into place: so this is what's supposed to happen.

I couldn't have solved this puzzle, that is to say, written this book, without the guidance of nearly as many people as helped me to go sub-20. My agent, Irene Skolnick, was not only steadfast in her support, but an invaluable guide through the stages of writing a book, from the proposal to the final draft. The same goes for Kent Wolf, who provided crucial support and feedback. Many thanks as well to Irene's assistants, Sally Chabert, Brita Lundberg, Lexi Wangler, and Elizabeth Horner, not to mention Clare Mao, at Lippincott, Massie, McQuilken.

The wisdom of my editor, Matthew Benjamin, has been invaluable. As I learned, a book is both large in scope and small in execution. You have to write it one chapter at a time, and yet keep an idea of the whole in your head. This is even harder than it sounds. Yet Matthew, time and again, made sure I was on the right track, or suggested interesting detours that always proved worth my while. He made sure the manuscript was not only well told, but well made, tightening up chapters, paragraphs, and even individual sentences, like the best of cosmetic surgeons: when his work is done, you hardly even know it took place. I'd also like to thank Lara Blackman, Matthew's assistant, for her perspicacious edits.

A book is only a book if other people read it. Fortunately, this book had the assistance of a lot of people helping make sure it will be read. I'd like to thank Susan Moldow, the publisher of Touchstone; David Falk, the associate publisher; Tara Parsons, the editor-in-chief; Brian Belfiglio, director of publicity; Courtney Brach, publicist; Meredith Vilarello, senior marketing manager; Kelsey Manning, marketing manager; and Elaine Wilson. Many thanks to Cherlynne Li, for designing the cover; Marty Karlow, for copyediting the manuscript; Kyle Kabel, for designing the interior; and Linda Sawicki, for handling the production editing.

This book is the culmination of many years of effort and instruction. I was fortunate enough to have teachers in elementary, middle, and high school who nurtured my interest in writing, including Rosie Berson, Chrysta Powell-Bikoff, Denise Hansen-Booker, Sarah Braff, Janice La Duke, Cory Holding, Pete Barraza, John Harris, Leslie Plesko, and Berkeley Blatz.

The first step toward writing, of course, is reading. I never lacked for books, for which I'd like to thank my parents, grandparents, extended family, and all the librarians at the Santa Monica Public Library who checked out book after book after book. In particular, I'd like to thank Sylvia Anderle, who made sure that avid readers like me always had a place to discuss books—for which, I'd like to note, she was recognized by the *New York Times*.

Nothing prepared me better for writing than music. I studied clarinet from the fourth grade until the end of high school. It was easily one of the most meaningful experiences of my life. It's where I learned discipline. For their contributions to my sense of what it means to live a creative life, I'd like to thank Allen Lloyd, Angela Woo, Victor Aguilar, Cecile Blanchard, Terry Sakow, Abel Ramirez, and especially Joni Swenson, and above all, Amanda Walker.

I had the good fortune of attending Columbia University, which has nurtured those with literary ambitions since the days when it was Kings College and Alexander Hamilton was a student. Thanks to Dan Futterman for his encouragement, and for suggesting I study with Kathy Eden and Ann Douglas. Jason Kim also has my gratitude for his steadfast support and sage counsel.

Michael Rosenthal, Kathy Eden, James Shapiro, Andrew Delbanco, Ann Douglas—to anyone who didn't study with them, these are just names on the page, but for me, they are less teachers than guides. In their hands, a book isn't just a book, it's a way through life. I'd like to particularly thank Professor Shapiro, for his unerring guidance in the professional world.

My gratitude to Ann Douglas, not only for introducing me to the literature of the Beat Generation, but also to Joyce Johnson, a fine writer, without whom I would never have met Irene Skolnick.

I'd like to thank Sam Lipsyte, for showing me that writing isn't always glamorous, and my cohort at Writers House, which believed that it was worth being serious about writing.

I also had the good fortune—no, who am I kidding?—the *unbelievable* fortune, to intern at the *New Yorker* not once, but three times in college. I can't thank Amelia Lester enough for her mentorship; she took my hopes and dreams seriously, and encouraged me to write, even though I was just an intern. Many thanks to Bob Mankoff and Marc Philippe Eskenazi, for keeping things light; to

Silvia Killingsworth, for pulling me on board and showing me the ropes; to Ben McGrath, for answering my questions; to Burkhard Bilger, for his advice; to Daniel Zalewski, for his shrewd counsel; to Andrew Marantz, for being awesome; to Whitney Johnson and Elisabeth Biondi for providing my entrée in the photo department; to Jessie Wender and Maria Lokke, for their support; to Stanley Ledbetter, for the great conversation; to Susan Morrison, for letting me try my hand; to Richard Brody, for his provocative arguments; to Andrea K. Scott, for the stimulating discussions; to Bruce Diones, for his wry humor; and to David Remnick, for making the *New Yorker* what it is.

I'd like to single out Alex Koppelman, who, when I met him, was in the Web pen. Before I left, he'd graduated to his own office, with a fancy coat and leather briefcase to match. Alex is a peerless editor. It was one of the great gifts of my internship that I didn't just leave it with contacts, but an editor to build a relationship with.

Thanks, too, to Hilton Als, for reading my senior thesis, and providing feedback on it. It was incredibly encouraging to hear from someone I so admire that I wasn't completely wasting my time.

And, finally, thanks to Reeves Wiedeman, for his sterling example as a writer and employee, who went above and beyond the call of duty to check facts, and, more than he probably knows, to inspire this writer to follow in his footsteps.

This book is dedicated to my parents, Abby and Stephen, with good reason. They're the rare parents who understand the creative process, being artists themselves. I couldn't have done this without them. I'd also like to thank my aunt Sarah; great-uncle Phil and great-aunt Linda; great-aunt Marian, whose bequest supported me during my first internship at the *New Yorker*; my late grandparents, Robert Fels, Mili Fels, and Bernie Scheffler;

and my late godmother, Jacqueline Pierre, for their support and encouragement. Thanks, too, to Sari Yoshioka-Wexler and Aili Klein.

In addition, I'd like to thank Peter Butterfield and Laurie Levin. Thanks to Peter, I became familiar with Bernard Suits, the philosopher. He also introduced me to Bill Morgan, at USC, who provided further insight on Suits and his work. As always, I appreciated Laurie's encouragement; it meant a great deal to have such an accomplished writer cheering me on.

And now, the cubers. Toby Mao, Tyson Mao, Ron van Bruchem, Shotaro "Macky" Makisumi, Jessica Fridrich, Feliks Zemdegs, Mats Valk, Jeremy Fleischman, Olivér Perge, Niki Placskó, Andy Smith, Collin Burns, Balázs Bernát, Bence Barát, Vishantak Srikrishna, Eric Zhao, Oscar Ceballos, Cornelius Dieckmann, Stefan Huber, Natán Riggenbach, Michał Pleskowicz, Michał Halczuk, Marcin Zalewski, Jakub Kipa, Rafael Cinoto, Pedro Santos Guimarães, Jael Riggenbach, Rachel Riggenbach, Andrew Ricci, Tim Reynolds, Nurym Kudaibergen, Chia-Wei Lu, Lars Petrus, Anthony Brooks, Vincent Sheu, Sarah Strong, Timothy Sun, Philipp Weyer, Sebastian Weyer, Dan Knights, Ton Dennenbroek, Clark Xu, Stefan Pochmann, Shelley Chang, Kenneth Lu, Jasmine Lee, Peter Still, Alese Devin, Samantha Raskind, Shemara van Kuijck, Hanneke Rijks, Sesi Cadmus, Cameron Brown, Lynn Brown, Layne Brown, Barton Anderson, Channae Anderson, Clark Cheng, Alexander Phan, Dan Dzoan, Ravi Fernando, Clément Gallet, John George, Miroslav Goljan, Dan Gosbee, Rowe Hessler, Mike Hughey, Troy Koochin, Chris Krueger, Fangyuan Chang, Bobby Krupa, Kyle Kulickowski, Ty Law, Aaron Lester, Chester Lian, Daniel Lo, Jayden McHargue, DeOnte Mullins, Mark Polinkovsky, Guus Razoux Schultz, Anneke Treep,

Marc Waterman, Ambie Valdés, Adam Zamora, Ernie Pulchny, Justin Mallari, Antoine Cantin, Claude Cantin, Rita Zemdegs, Kevin Hays, Rob Stuart, Joey Stahl, Ric Donati, Joseph Dzaluk, Hector Trujillo, Isabela Maria de Aguiar Milani, David Adams, Arthur Adams, Simon Westlund, Colin Boyd, Alexander Hall, Donna Hays, François Courtès, Breandan Vallance, Kirstine Buus Aagard, Kit Clement, Seyyed Hossein Mohammed Fatemi, Omid Fatemi, Chris Hardwick, Katie Hardwick, Karen Brooks, Hunor Bózsing, István Kockza, Weston Mizumoto, Andrea Javier, Joey Gouly, Robert Yau, Lilianna Kohann, Jasper Waldman, Julianna Bennet, Arlo Sims, Jonah Crosby, Drew Brads, Saransh Grover, Jabari Nuruddin, Ricardo Lutchman, Aryan Kejriwal, Juan Camilo Vargas, Eduardo Gutiérrez Cuba, Ernesto Gutiérrez Cuba, Pedro Henrique da Silva Roque, Edward Lin, Tim Wong, Gabriel Dechichi Barbar, Samuel Chiu, James Hamory, Phil Hamory, Kabyanil Talukdar, Bhargav Narasimhan, Dana Yi, Anna Leidner, Eva Kato, Billy Burier, Deven Nadudvari, Patricia Li, Dániel Varga, Oscar Roth Anderson, Zoé de Moffarts, Nóra Szepes, Michael Young, Ian Bourn, Phil Yu, Kian Daniel, Bob Burton, Jaclyn Burton, David Gomes, and anyone else not mentioned here—thank you for more than you can know.

When I started this project, I expected to get involved, but I never imagined my involvement would continue beyond the end of the project. In cubing, I found a fantastic story, but also a community, one I expect to belong to for the rest of my life.

Thanks in particular to those who extended me hospitality on my travels, from Alex Kaplan, Lizzy Foydel, Tyson Mao, Joyce Huynh, Toby Mao, Daniel Vallela, Weston Mizumoto, Shotaro Makisumi and George Miller in the San Francisco Bay Area; to Ron van Bruchem, Hanneke Rijks, Mats Valk, Natalia Valk, Guus Razoux Schultz, Anneke Treep, Marc Waterman, Oskar van Deventer and his wife, José, in the Netherlands; to János Kovács,

Olivér Perge, Niki Placskó, Balázs Bernát, Viktor Böhm, and particularly Ernő Rubik, in Hungary; to Chrisi Trussell, Andrew Singer, David Singmaster, and Tom Kremer, in London; to Caio Alves in Brazil; Henry Gruber in Boston; Annelisa Leinbach in New Haven; and Werner, Beatrice, and Luca Rien in Germany.

I'd also like to thank the staff of the Columbia University Library System, including Zak Rouse and Richie Walters, of Avery Library, where much of this book was written.

Without Seven Towns, of course, Rubik's Cube would not exist. Thank you for bringing a fantastic toy—and, more than that, an icon—to the world. I appreciate the access granted me by Chrisi Trussell and Holly Riehl. Thank you to Viktor Böhm, for gamely answering my questions, and to Tom Kremer and Ernő Rubik, for sitting for the rare interview.

Thank you to Gary Cartmell, for sharing the wonderful stories of his father, Brian, who masterminded PR efforts for Ideal Toys in the early days of Rubik's Cube.

I appreciate the efforts of Professor Michael Klass, at UC Berkeley, in introducing me to group theory, and to Jessica Fridrich, for explaining the history of her method in such detail to me. My gratitude goes out to Paul Hoffman, the president and CEO of the Liberty Science Center, for organizing such a fine exhibition, and answering my questions, as well as the wonderful folks at Google, for making what I think is the best doodle of all time.

Last, but not least, I'd like to specially thank Ernő Rubik, without whom the world would be a much less colorful place.

APPENDIX

"You don't have to be a mathematician to solve the Cube," its inventor, Ernő Rubik, once said. "If a five-year-old can do it, it's obvious you don't have to be a genius."

It's beyond the scope of this appendix to teach you to solve Rubik's Cube. Entire books have been devoted to the subject, some of them over one hundred pages long. There are thousands of YouTube tutorials.

If you want to solve Rubik's Cube, the next couple pages will give you a good idea of how to go about it. If you want to get fast, you'll want to try all the steps. If you simply want to learn to solve the puzzle, you can just stop after the first step.

I

Every Rubik's Cube nowadays comes with instructions. This didn't use to be the case, but I guess Seven Towns figured out that people wouldn't keep buying Rubik's Cubes if they couldn't solve them. The guide used to have virtually the same method Toby taught me.

If you just want to learn to solve the puzzle, there's no harm in buying a Rubik's Cube and following the guide inside. Seven Towns also has a number of video tutorials online, at rubiks.com.

Using this method, you should be able to solve the puzzle without any trouble. If you practice regularly, and manage to memorize the handful of necessary algorithms, you may be able to solve Rubik's Cube in as little as a minute.

II

If you want to get faster, it's a good idea to dip your toe into the online cubing community. There are plenty of cubers on speed-solving.com, the most popular English-language forum for cubers, who have never attended a competition; beginners are more than welcome. So long as you read the forum's rules about posting, which can feel byzantine to those, like me, who didn't grow up on the Internet, you shouldn't have a problem finding assistance. There's also a wiki attached to the forum, which helpfully lists lots of different algorithms.

III

Now, if you want to get really fast, you'll have to go to competitions. I say "have to," but it's really a privilege. You don't have to go to competitions. You *get* to go to competitions.

Cubing competitions are some of the strangest, most fun events I've ever attended. They happen in high school cafeterias, in world-renowned museums, in fancy hotels, in convention centers. They take place virtually every weekend of the year. They are held all around the world, from Malaysia to Ukraine.

If you sign up for a competition, you'll find that even the most accomplished cubers are usually willing to help newcomers. They were newbies themselves; no one forgets what it's like to have a world record holder show you a trick, or critique a solve. It's an experience that keeps on giving. If you go to enough competitions, soon enough, people will be asking you for advice!*

I've also included a brief list of the best resources for learning to solve Rubik's Cube. It's not complete, by any means, but using only these resources you shouldn't have a problem achieving your goals, whether that's solving the Cube in your closet or going sub-20.

YouTube

Dan Brown's "How to Solve a Rubik's Cube"

This is the *Gilgamesh* of YouTube tutorials. It's old—it dates to 2007, when YouTube was in its infancy—but no less effective. This is still not a bad option for beginners. Brown is clear, although he speaks a bit fast. There aren't many algorithms required. However, if you plan on getting faster, you may want to try the following tutorial.

BadMephisto "How to Solve a Rubik's Cube"

BadMephisto (not his real name) has a whole site devoted to Rubik's Cube. It's great for beginners and for slightly more advanced solvers, basically anyone who wants to get faster. You can find YouTube videos, algorithm sheets, and a handy guide to becoming a speed-solver. You can access it for free at badmephisto.com.

---

* To sign up for a competition, just go to worldcubeassociation.org. If you live in the United States, you may also want to join Cubing USA. It's at cubingusa. com. Cubing USA will send you notifications about competitions in your area. Once you've attended a competition, congratulations! You are now a member of the World Cube Association.

DVD

You Can Do It! with Tyson Mao

For a time, Rubik's Cubes were bundled with this DVD, which you can still find online. It features Tyson Mao, using the method his brother, Toby, taught me. The DVD lasts about an hour, and includes very explicit, easy-to-follow instructions. The DVD also includes several algorithm sheets, which you can access via computer.

Books

The Cube: The Ultimate Guide to the World's Bestselling Puzzle—Secrets, Stories, Solutions, by Jerry Slocum, David Singmaster, Wei-Hwa Huang, Dieter Gebhardt, and Geert Hellings, with an introduction by Ernő Rubik

This book is fairly comprehensive. It includes animated essays about the history of the Cube and previous puzzle crazes, and entertaining photographs of ancient amusements, like the tangram puzzle. The solution included is a bit odd, in that it's Corners-First—a throwback to the 1980s, when Minh Thai used a similar solution to capture the first world title.

INDEX

Ian Scheffler is a writer living in New York. He has written for *The New Yorker*, *The Guardian*, the *Los Angeles Times*, and the *Los Angeles Review of Books*. This is his first book.